WITHDRA

DATE DUE

JAN 03 2012

West Frankfort Public Library
402 East Poplar Street
West Frankfort, IL 62896

The Life and Times of a Fly Caught Up in a Spider's Web

In 1929 the last class graduated from the Chamness Elementary School. Art Hanseman, Carbondale, Illinois, studied the building's structure. As he walks away from the schoolhouse, he waves at some friends who happen to be passing by.

The Life and Times of a Fly Caught Up in a Spider's Web

This Is the Way It Was

Charles D. Neal, Ph.D.

VANTAGE PRESS
New York

Photo Credits

Model T Ford—Courtesy of the Ford Motor Company.
The Erin Huffman photos and the one-room log schoolhouse were taken by Professor K. Gordon Butts and printed by the author.
The remaining photos were taken and printed by the author.

FIRST EDITION

All rights reserved, including the right of
reproduction in whole or in part in any form.

Copyright © 1995 by Charles D. Neal, Ph.D.

Published by Vantage Press, Inc.
516 West 34th Street, New York, New York 10001

Manufactured in the United States of America
ISBN: 0-533-11062-9

Library of Congress Catalog Card No.: 94-90077

0 9 8 7 6 5 4 3 2 1

To the memory of my late wife, Fairy Berneice (Bacon) Neal, the best of women, who gave her love and devotion to me with no strings attached

Contents

Acknowledgments   ix
A Message to the Reader   xi

PART ONE: THE PUPIL
1. The First Day — 3
2. Rules and Regulations — 14
3. The Daily Schedule — 27
4. Hickory Tea — 36
5. Individual Differences — 47
6. An Atypical Day — 55
7. Visitors — 63
8. Teacher Gives More Invitations — 70
9. Education beyond the Classroom — 79
10. My Final Month as a Pupil — 91

PART TWO: THE TEACHER
11. From Flunky to Teacher — 111
12. Teacher Finds a Vacancy — 122
13. Teacher's First Day — 134
14. Tom "Skunk" Costello — 144
15. Suicide or Murder? — 155
16. Mary Lou Hawkins — 164
17. Never a Dull Moment — 173
18. Teacher Learns a Thing or Two — 191
19. Surprise and More Surprises — 203

20. Christmas	216
21. Tobacco Invades the School Premises	227
22. Motivation	237
23. Community Service	249
24. Finis	258
Epilogue	271
List of Selected Publications	275

Acknowledgments

Some typists are careless. Other typists are middle-of-the-roaders. A few typist are perfectionists.

I was fortunate in hiring Miss Nancy Peck to type the manuscript for this book. I don't understand how she took my scribbled chapters with numerous addendums, inserts, and deletions, and turned them into a highly professional typed manuscript. But then again, this should not have surprised me, for she is a perfectionist.

I extend my heartfelt gratitude to the people in both the Crawford School District and the Dutch Hill School District for my having had the pleasure of associating with them. However, at the time both they and I were unaware of the important role they were playing. Without them this book would have been nothing more than a number of blank pages between two covers.

I am grateful to everyone who served as models.

Special thanks go to Prof. Gordon K. Butts, my longtime friend and colleague, for his professional advice and his assistance in shooting the three pictures of model Erin Huffman and the Chamness one-room log schoolhouse with model Art Hansman.

Last but not least, I salute the elementary teachers of my day who, like myself, deplore using cruel and inhuman punishments on their pupils. Furthermore, we believed the paddle was to be used only as the last resort.

A Message to the Reader

Send the boy and the girl to a school with good teachers, rather than send the man and the woman to a prison with armed guards.
—Author

When I was twenty-one years old my interest in country schools came during one of my visits with my Uncle Bill Neal.

Following lunch I spotted one of his books, *History of Education*. The title intrigued me, especially the section on country schools. Reading the following account I think had much to do with my desire to teach, especially later when Uncle Bill suggested I take the teacher's examination to qualify me for teaching in the country schools.

The period of 1825–60 was the formative period for the elementary schools, both urban and rural. By the early part of the twentieth century, every state in the union was dotted with rural schools, most of which consisted of one room. Here all eight grades were taught by one teacher. Sometimes music and art were a part of the curriculum, provided the teacher felt qualified to teach them.

Rural schools were located in such a way that children would not be required to walk great distances to obtain an elementary school education. Enrollment varied within the different school districts from a few pupils to as many as sixty. Although only one teacher for sixty pupils was unrealistic, it was surprising how much some of the youngsters were able to learn.

Generally the school year of only seven or eight months was adapted to crops being raised on the farms. Even with a short school year, many of the pupils had to miss days at a time because they were needed to help with farmwork. This arrangement, going to school and doing farmwork, was as fair to the girls as well as to the boys, since parents found plenty of work for both, especially during the crop-growing season. Frequently, pupils attended school only long enough to learn how to read, write, and figure. "Readin', writin', and 'rithmetic" were all that were needed to make a "livin'," believed many farm families.

Some of the schoolhouses had much to be desired. Roofs leaked. Outhouses were unsanitary. Few school supplies were furnished, unless the teacher supplied them. A common water dipper was used by all, including the teacher. Building and ground maintenance were almost nonexistent in many instances. However, some of the rural residents took pride in their one-room schools, keeping them A-1 in all respects.

With the advent of improved roads coupled with school buses, the one-room rural school is fast becoming a part of American history, much like the horse and buggy. Currently, there are only 650 one-room rural schools in existence, and these are located where it is impractical to use buses or boats to transport the pupils to urban schoolhouses.

While writing the manuscript for this book, I let a number of avid readers give me their opinion on certain sections of it. These readers were all under forty years of age. Many of them had no knowledge at all regarding a one-room country school. The majority of them agreed that some background material, such as a short history of the one-room school in America, would do much to enhance my personal memoir and should be included in the early part of the book.

The following is my true story of my experiences during my first year as a pupil in a one-room country school; sixteen years later, I spent my first year as a teacher in a similar institution. During each experience, I soon had the feeling I was a fly caught up in a spider's web.

The two schools were in the same general area, approximately thirty miles apart. It is my story. However, it parallels the kinds of experiences found in most one-room schools of that era. I do not pretend that this is an objective book about public school education in general during the first third of the twentieth century. In fact, it is a highly subjective book. What happened to me in those fifteen months, first as a pupil and later as a teacher, made it possible for my having the highest respect and regard for all elementary teachers.

Part One and Two are accounts of my experiences. Fortunately, I kept a diary, as I still do, beginning on my first day in school. I could read and write a little by age five. However, I have taken the liberty of transcribing my childish phrases and sentences in Part One into adult language. Also, my father, before he passed away, filled in the voids of my diary and told me of related incidents that I didn't know about or had failed to understand at the time. For his help I'll be ever grateful.

The identity of actual people and locations of cities, towns, villages, and streams where this drama unfolded is not important. What is important is the fact that it really happened. To protect the guilty as well as the innocent, I have changed the names of all persons, except those of my father, my mother, my wife, myself, and the people identified in the pictures. The names are changed to protect the privacy of those without whose experiences this book would not have been possible. Any similarity between these people and people living or dead is purely coincidental. Beyond that I have done my best in writing this book to honor a promise I once made to my father when he said, "Tell it like it was."

The Life and Times of a Fly Caught Up in a Spider's Web

PART ONE

THE PUPIL

The author, in 1914, feeding his farm project, "Buttons" the calf.

Chapter 1
The First Day

I'll never forget September 8, 1914. That was the beginning of my formal education, spanning a period of nineteen years. Neither will I forget it because that was also the beginning of many memories, some good and some bad, during my one and only year attending a one-room country school.

"Sunny Boy, Sunny Boy, rise and shine! Remember what Grandpa always says, 'The early bird gets the worm.' It is a cliché, but it is worth remembering."

"Oh, shucks! Who wants the worm anyway!" I replied, half-asleep.

"You don't want to be late on your first day of school," ordered my mother, as she jerked the covers off my bed.

"OK, Mom. I'll be up and dressed in a jiffy," I said, still somewhat sleepy.

On the previous day I had made a vow that I would leave no stone unturned to get the approval of my parents and teacher when it came to getting a good education.

We had no running water or electricity, the same as everyone else in our rural community. Going from the bedroom to the washstand in the kitchen, I was well aware that today was Tuesday, the first day after Labor Day, 1914. Also, it was my sixth birthday, something I was very proud of.

I washed my face and hands and combed my hair. Then I paid particular attention to the cleanliness of my hands because they had to be shown for inspection before sitting down at the breakfast table. Mother never failed to tell me, "Cleanliness is the next thing to godliness."

Breakfast that morning consisted of oatmeal, buttered toast, and sweet milk. While I was eating, Mother prepared my lunch bucket.

In it she put an apple, a hard-boiled egg, a piece of angel food cake, and a small jar of orange juice.

The time was 7 A.M. by the clock on the mantel as I walked out the front door of our four-room frame house. To get to the one-room country school meant walking over clay country roads for a mile and a quarter. In those days there was no such thing as a school bus in my school district.

I trudged up the twin hill. The Main Country Road (as we called it) was dry, so I was making good time. Midway down the second hill, the road passed through the middle of Orthodox Cemetery. Its outer dimensions, lined with tall, whispering pine trees, accompanied by the cooing of mourning doves, made for an eerie feeling for all who passed through it. Ever since I was a little tyke, I'd heard frightening stories about ghosts moving among the tombstones, even in daylight hours.

As the cemetery came into full view, I stopped dead still. I didn't want to be late on my first day at school, but I couldn't decide whether to return home or to run like mad through it. The very thought of ghost stories ran chills up and down my spine.

As I stood there, scared stiff, my encounter with Dave Childers came to mind, and I began to let my mind wander. Dave hunted "coons" (raccoons) by night. Frequently, his hunts took him through the cemetery.

"Dave," I had once asked him, "is it true that Herbert 'Skinflint' Jones prowls the cemetery?"

"You had better believe it, boy. He comes out of his grave every night in the form of a perfect replica of himself. Furthermore, I've had conversations with him. One of them went like this:

" 'Dave, why don't you pay your monthly grocery bills?'

" 'I don't owe you any money; never did in fact.'

" 'Yes, you do! You're just like all my other creditors. You're all a bunch of cheapskates.'

"That said, Herbert vanished in a cloud of vapor."

Standing still, knees shaking more than ever, I recalled a conversation I had once had with John Browning when he was teaching me to play horseshoes.

"John," I inquired, "did you ever see Skinflint's ghost?"

"You had better believe I have, Charles. Just the other night, as I neared the cemetery, I became aware of a very loud noise. Then I saw Skinflint's ghost. He even introduced himself. Otherwise, I would not have recognized him. It was nothing like I'd ever seen before, just a large foglike mass."

"What did it sound like, John?"

"Not so much like a boom, more like a clap of thunder repeated at odd intervals."

"Did it vary in pitch or intensity?"

"No."

"What happened next?"

"Sudden like, everything was quiet. Then the foglike mass vanished without saying another word."

"Did this experience happen only once?"

"No. As you know, I pass through the cemetery on my way to the village. Sometimes nothing happens. At other times Skinflint's ghost reappears, making that awful, shattering, loud, booming noise before he disappears."

As I stood there, the ghost stories seemed more real than ever. Now my knees were shaking like crazy as I wondered what would happen if I went on. There was only one way to find out if I didn't want to be late for school—run at top speed. So I did just that. To my surprise and gratification nothing happened, with the exception of the wind gently blowing through the pine tree branches.

When the cemetery was far to my rear, I began reminiscing about yesterday's visit to Granny Hawkins's house.

Most of the adults in my neighborhood couldn't have cared less about the opening of the new school term. Important to them was the fear that America might become involved in another war, especially if the Europeans didn't stop bickering.

The war began as a local conflict between Austria, Hungary, and Serbia on July 28, 1914. At that time none of our neighbors gave a second thought about it. After all, I had heard Eric Jones say, "Those Europeans do nothing but fight anyway, so why the fuss? Let's keep our nose out of it. Let them fight it out."

When Germany declared war against Russia on August 1, 1914, it was a different ball game. A few people became worried; others became frightened. Would America become involved? No one knew the answer, so a delegation (I slipped along uninvited) was formed to call on Granny Hawkins. She was the seventh daughter of the seventh daughter in the Hawkins family. This birthright was supposed to give her supernatural powers, so most people believed. As I trudged along with the delegation, I couldn't have cared less about tomorrow being the first day of school.

I heard Hiram Brown say, "Didn't she predict the corn failure of 1911?"

Then Marvin Piper quipped, "What about her predictions of the coal mine explosion, the election of Pres. Woodrow Wilson, and the death of Old Man Meyers. She said they will come to pass and they did."

As the delegation approached the small, three-room, unpainted cottage, eighty-two-year-old Granny, in her old gingham dress, wearing her old faded straw hat, and smoking a corncob pipe, was sitting on her back porch.

"Howdy, gentlemen. I just come in from diggin' taters. Sit a spell and I'll get you all some of my homemade coffee cake and coffee."

After all had had a second serving, Granny said, "I know you all didn't come here to offer me a beauty prize, so what can I do for you all?"

"Well," replied Sam Jones, leader of the delegation, "do you think America will get involved in the European war?"

"It's not a question, boy, of *will* we get into it. The question is *when* will we get on the firin' line? I predict America will be fightin' well nigh two years from now."

Granny was a little quick on the trigger, but on April 6, 1917, America declared war on Germany. Before the war's end, thirty-two nations became involved. So Granny added another score to her predictions.

My daydreaming ended as I suddenly realized I'd never get to the schoolhouse if I didn't come back to reality.

Soon I arrived at a place everyone referred to as the *T*. This was a location where the schoolhouse lane joined the Main Country Road. A few minutes after I turned onto the lane, I thought I must be dreaming. Surely, those were not tents and covered wagons I saw through the white oak timber and tall saplings south of the lane. *It must be a mirage*, I thought.

As I drew nearer, everything came into focus. Not only were the tents and wagons real, but there were two Gypsy women cooking something in a large iron kettle suspended over an open fire.

Knowing nothing about Gypsies except what I had seen in the

movies, I decided to give their camp a wide berth by circling north of the lane.

Walking no more than thirty steps, I saw a Gypsy man coming out of a tent carrying a violin. What was he going to do, I wondered. As I peered from behind a large white oak tree, my thoughts went no further. He placed the violin under his chin, followed by positioning the bow. Then he played several arpeggios. Next he played the most beautiful melody I had ever heard. As if this were not enough, he made the violin literally sing as he launched into several variations of the melody, each one more difficult than the previous one.

I played some clarinet myself, and I heard the Benton Civic Orchestra play numerous concerts, but nowhere had I heard music played that compared to this Gypsy violinist.

Looking at my dollar watch, I took off on a run, for it was only fifteen minutes 'til books.

It wasn't long before the white-painted one-room schoolhouse with its unpainted coal shed, two outdoor privies (one for the girls and one for the boys), and the well with its common water dipper came into view.

Entering the schoolhouse, I went directly to the teacher, Mr. Johnston, to register. Later in the term, the pupils nicknamed him "Egghead." Of course, this was never said in his presence. Not only was his head egg-shaped, it was as bald as a billiard ball. He was at least six feet, six inches tall, and he had the longest feet I had ever seen. His faded, worn blue suit was at least two sizes too large, giving him the appearance of a scarecrow.

When Mr. Johnston looked up from a book he was reading, he said, "Good morning, youngun. What do you want?"

I quickly replied, "Sir, I am six years old, and I want to register for the first grade."

"OK, give me your name. Then take the first small seat and desk over on the south side of the room. Put your tablet and other things in the desk. Registering pupils and giving them their books and tomorrow's assignment is all we do on the first day of school, but see that you are here by 8:30 in the morning. Classes begin promptly at nine o'clock sharp."

My lunch wouldn't go to waste, since I would arrive home just about noon.

Jacob Boner and I started toward home together. We knew each other from Sunday school.

"Jacob," I said, "I heard the most beautiful music this morning pl——"

"Played by the Gypsy violinist," Jacob butted in.

"I didn't know we had Gypsies camped around here. Aren't you afraid of them?"

Jacob laughed so loud I thought his sides would split. "What's so darn funny?"

"You're ignorant, you know that, Charles? They've been camped there all summer. Now that it is September they plan to travel south to warmer weather."

"How do you know so much about them?"

Jacob told me that he and his parents passed the camp every time they went to the village. In fact, his father frequently stopped and talked to the head man. Jacob said the Gypsy women told fortunes to people in the neighborhood who wanted to know about their future. In addition to telling fortunes, the women asked for cast-off clothing, but they never applied pressure to give.

The head man used one of the wagons for his blacksmith tools. In it were a forge, an anvil, and a metal vise fastened onto a metal workbench. Jacob went on to tell me that the head man had shod three of Mr. Boner's horses. No money exchanged hands. He paid the charges with chickens and eggs. Jacob also said no one reported any stealing in the neighborhood.

By now we had reached what was the camp. Nothing remained except trampled grass. The Gypsies had packed up lock, stock, and barrel since I had heard that beautiful violin solo on my way to school.

Jacob and I made small talk until we reached the T. Then he went south, and I went north on our separate ways home.

As I walked over the ridge of the twin hill, who should I see coming to greet me but no one other than Sport, a short-haired, black-and-tan, three-year-old hound dog.

His tongue stuck straight out, his long ears flopped up and down, and he was running at top speed. He was two inches taller than I was when he stood on his back legs, and he was as clumsy as a bear wearing boxing gloves. But I dearly loved him.

He was the kindest and most affectionate dog I ever knew, and it was almost impossible to avoid his kisses. He outweighed me by fifteen pounds, and many a time he knocked me down with his good intentions of welcoming me home. This time was no exception. As I arose from the dusty dirt road, I knew I had to see Old Man Dobbin. He knew all about animals. Maybe, just maybe he could help me break Sport of his one bad habit.

John "Dobbin" Sawyer lived catercorner across the road from our house. Today we would say that his house looked like something out of *Tobacco Road*. It hadn't had a coat of paint in years. One of the porch posts was broken in two, leaving the northeast corner of the roof sagging. An old relic of a Model T Ford automobile adorned the front lawn. Dobbin and his forty-eight-year-old wife lived there alone. Their two boys, now twenty-two and twenty-four years of age, lived in San Francisco.

"Hello, Sunny Boy," Dobbin said, greeting me as if I were a long lost child coming home after years of staying away. "I jest seed what ole Sport did to you. Want to break him of that?"

"Sure do, Dobbin. Can you tell me how?"

"Sure can, Sunny Boy. It's as easy as fallin' off a log in a fast runnin' stream."

"Gee, how do you do it?"

"I don't do it. You do it."

"How, how?" I asked eagerly.

"Call him. When he jumps on you, nudge him in the lungs with your knee, all the while sayin', 'Down, boy, down!' Keep doin' it several times a day. In three or four days he'll get the message." (It worked. By the middle of the following week, Sport was completely broken of his habit.)

"Thank you, Dobbin. How much do I owe you?"

"Not a thing, Sunny Boy. Let's call it a favor. Now you know no one charges for a favor. One of these days me or the ole woman will ask you for a favor. That's the way we men folks 'round here pay each other."

"Gee, I can't thank you enough," I said as I started home.

"Hold on a minute, Sunny. I'm goin' down to Squire Wiggins's house to check on some sick chickens. Want to come along?"

"Sure thing. I'll check with Mother. I'm sure I may go."

"The old car won't run. Think it has played its last tune. I'll hitch up the horse and buggy. Then I'll pick you up right after dinner [lunch]."

When we arrived at Squire Wiggins's house, he looked as if he had lost his best friend. He really seemed down in the dumps. The squire looked every bit the country gentleman. He wore a clean, pressed navy blue suit, a black derby hat, and his highly polished shoes would have passed any army sergeant's inspection.

"Dobbin, before I tell you my troubles, let me ask you a question: Why do you always wear that old, beat up, blue felt hat winter and summer?"

"Well, Squire, it's like this. My father wore a hat like this winter and summer. His father wore a hat like this winter and summer, and his father before him wore a hat like this winter and summer. Why should I break tradition?"

Dobbin always answered a question he didn't like with a question. To my knowledge no one had ever caught on to his little trick.

"Now, Squire, let's get on with it. Where are those five sick chickens you told me about yesterday in the village grocery store?"

"Back here in the pen. They are starving to death, and there isn't a thing you can do about that."

"Starvin' you say! How do you know that?"

"Well, if you must know, my Aunt Susie examined them day before yesterday. She said, 'They are starving to death, and there is no way to cure them.' Has something to do with the nature of the moon, she explained."

"Then, man, why did you have me come all this way for nothin'?"

"I wouldn't have, but it's my wife's idea. She doesn't like my Aunt Susie, and she thinks you have some of God's gifts with animals. Course I didn't agree with her."

Dobbin walked into the pen, picked up a Rhode Island Red chicken, and opened its mouth for a look-see.

He shook his head, then said with an impish grin, "Hogwash. Starvin' to death? Yes, but not because it wants to. These chickens can't eat because of the 'pips.' "

"Pips?" mocked the squire. "Are you out of your mind?"

"Look for yourself. See this white patch on its tongue," replied Dobbin as he held the chicken, mouth wide open, right under the squire's nose. "I don't know the high-toned medical name for it, but I calls it the 'pips.'"

Dobbin lost no time. He opened his medical bag, taking out a razor sharp knife, a bottle of turpentine, and some cotton swabs.

"Good heavens, man! Do you know what you are doing?" inquired the squire, all the time shaking his head, not believing what he was seeing.

While the squire was jabbering, Dobbin, quick as a flash, peeled the white patch from the chicken's tongue with his knife. Then he swabbed the tongue with turpentine.

While he was treating the remaining four chickens, Squire was wringing his hands and shouting, "Man, you're killing my chickens! You're killing my chickens!"

I glanced at my watch. It took Dobbin only twenty-five minutes to treat the five chickens. All the while he ignored Squire's raving and ranting.

"Your chickens will start eatin' shortly. In less than a week, they'll begin puttin' on weight."

"They had better get well, or I'll sue you," threatened Squire. "How much do I owe you."

"Squire, you know I am not a licensed veterinarian, so I can't charge a fee."

"Well, I don't take charity," said Squire, all the time pulling on his left earlobe. "I know for a fact that some people pay you the price of a schoolteacher's daily wage of two dollars, a dime or two more or less. Other people think your treatments are not worth a penny more than fifty cents. Still other people don't pay you anything. I'm a man of the middle of the road. So here is fifty cents," as he begrudgingly handed Dobbin a new fifty-cent piece.

I stood there feeling the frustration build inside me. Of all the gall, handing Dobbin a measly fifty-cent piece for a job any veterinarian would have been proud of and would have charged four times as much for.

"Come on, Charles. Don't stand here all day. Let's be on our way, or your ma will think I've kidnapped you," Dobbin said as he waved a good-bye to Squire.

Squire turned on his heel, went toward his house, not even acknowledging Dobbin's good-bye.

As we entered the car, we both watched the beautiful scene high in the western sky.

"It's a great day, eh Charles?"

I never answered him, I was so full of anger and frustration. I couldn't get Squire's stinginess out of my mind. I had heard that he was tighter than bark on a tree. Now I knew it was a fact.

Dobbin pulled up to our house. I got out and started up his driveway.

"Hey!" I shouted. He looked straight at me. "You're right!" I shouted. "It's a great day."

My primary education was not limited to the one-room country school. My father was an avid hunter, not for sport but for survival. Times were hard.

His job in the coal mine was limited to three or four days a week during the winter, and he was lucky if he got one day a week during the summer. Also, the pay was poor, not like it is today.

We varied our diet among stewed rabbit, fried rabbit, baked coon (raccoon), baked possum and sweet potatoes, fried squirrel, and fried quail. Coupled with vegetables we grew in the garden, milk from old Bossy the cow, and eggs provided by our chickens, we ate well-balanced meals. I learned to like that diet and follow it to this day.

My father presented me with a .22-caliber Stevens rifle for my sixth birthday. My eyes almost popped out of my head when I saw it. I'll never forget that blue steel barrel with its walnut stock as long as I live. It really was a beauty, especially to my young eyes.

As I rushed toward my father to take the gun, he said, "Hold it! Hold it! Sit down a minute. I have pointers to say before I turn this gun over to you for inspection.

"One: Never, and I mean, never look down the barrel. Always think a gun is loaded even if you know it isn't.

"Two: Always carry the gun with the barrel pointing down toward the ground. Then if it goes off accidentally the bullet will strike the ground, not some person or animal. Always remember a bullet from this rifle travels at least one-half mile on the level.

"Three: Never point this gun unless you intend to fire it. A gun is not a plaything and should not be treated as such.

"Four: When crossing a barbwire or rail fence, place the gun, barrel first, through the fence. Then move down the fence line three or four feet before climbing over it.

"Five: When returning home, store your gun in a safe place, being absolutely sure that the gun is not loaded.

"Six: Never take this gun on your own without your Uncle Bill or me being with you.

"I know you can't remember all these points on hearing them only once. I have written them on this large piece of cardboard. I know you can read some, so tonight after supper I'll help you until you can read them and understand them. Then every night after homework, we'll have a little more education. You will not only memorize these points, but you will demonstrate each point until it becomes a habit.

"Now examine your present. What is the first thing you are going to do?"

"See if the gun is loaded," I replied.

"Good boy," he said.

My father was a kind and gentle man, but he was a man of his word. I knew better than to violate any of his points unless I wanted a trip to the woodshed. I had that once, and I vowed to never have that experience again.

Recently, I told my early school days story to one of my young neighbors, Marvin Browing. He didn't say a thing for a few moments. He just stared at me as if he didn't believe a word I was saying.

"You sure were as dumb as an ox."

"What are you driving at?" I said painfully.

"You should have taken the school bus. I'd never walk to school," he said arrogantly.

Marvin could not believe that school buses were practically nonexistent in 1914.

"Yes, Marvin, we knew about a few schools in America that had horse-driven buses," I said. "However, in our school district, if one went to school, rain or shine, walking was the way to get there."

Chapter 2
Rules and Regulations

Rain had poured down most the night, turning the clay road facing me into a sea of mud. After walking the mile and a quarter to school, my shoes were a mess—mud from soles to tops.

Although walking was difficult, I made good time. My Sears, Roebuck and Company watch showed twenty-five minutes after eight as I started up the schoolhouse steps where I was met by the teacher, Mr. Harris Johnston.

"Don't you dare come in here with those muddy shoes! Didn't your mother teach you anything? Get back down those steps and clean your shoes, and I mean clean them good if you don't want a good dose of hickory tea!"

I'd never heard of hickory tea and had no idea how it tasted, but I would find out soon enough.

With shoes wiped clean, I walked into the schoolroom, received an okay from Mr. Johnston, placed my bottle of paste, new tablet, and pencil inside my desk, and put my lunch pail on the floor under my seat.

All of the thirty-six seats and desks in the room were alike. However, they were in three sizes: small, medium, and large. Both seats and desks were screwed to the floor. The backs were hinged at the rear so they could be raised or lowered, making it easy for stout children to get in and get out of them easily.

A long seat was located directly in front of the teacher's desk. It was here that classes recited their lessons and received assignments for the following day. It was called the recitation seat.

Since it was twenty-two minutes until books (start of classes), I sauntered out onto the playground.

Fourteen boys and sixteen girls were gathered in two separate groups. Although some of the older boys dated some of the girls after school hours, you would never know it during the day. Any boy showing interest in girls during school hours was considered a sissy.

The girls ranged in ages from six to fourteen. All of them wore pigtails down their backs tied with beautiful ribbons. Each wore a clean gingham dress. They were playing jacks and making girl talk to pass away the time. Some of the little girls brought their dolls to play with.

Education for most of the girls ceased when they graduated from the eighth grade.

The boys ranged in ages from six to sixteen. Those fifteen and sixteen years old were not necessarily going to school because they failed a grade or two. The county high school was six miles away in Benton. Very few boys had the tenacity to walk that distance through rain, snow, or sun, so they repeated the seventh and eighth grade twice. This was not such a bad idea. More than likely they would come under more than one teacher during the four years. Hopefully, at least one would be a good teacher.

It was the custom in our school, as in many country schools at that time, to fire the teacher at the end of the term whether he was a good, bad, or indifferent teacher. Few teachers lasted more than two years in any given rural school. Somehow school directors gloated over the fact that they hired and fired teachers as they pleased. When the teacher tenure law was passed many years later, a number of school directors either resigned or would not run for another term. Jason Atwater said it for many when he refused a friend's suggestion that he run for another term: "No way. If I can't fire a teacher at will, there's no fun being a school director."

Opposed to views like those of Jason Atwater was County Superintendent, Dennis Newhouse. He believed strongly in higher education and in a teacher tenure law so that qualified teachers couldn't be fired at the drop of a hat.

He gave the main address at a recent National Grange meeting, commonly called "the Grange." All the way through it, he stressed the value of education beyond the eighth grade.

Robert Boner, Jacob's father, a farmer from down in the lowlands, didn't like any part of the address. In fact, he hated it. He said it all for most fathers in the district when he wrote the following letter to Superintendent Newhouse.

dere supertendint
    more education then 8 grad haint no good nohow readin written & spelen is good enuf fer eny youngun geometer geogfry & histry haint gona do eny youngun no good to mak a livin no how sciense it be a waste of tim Stedy the bible it will larn you moore then eny ol sciense booke

                                        sinserly yurs
                                        Robert Boner

    Long before books Boner's son, Jacob, told the boys that his father was going to fix old County Superintendent Newhouse's wagon good by writing him a nasty letter, which Jacob was going to mail the next day.

    Since I was keeping a diary (I learned to read and write a little, long before coming to school), I just had to have a copy of that letter.

    "Jacob," I said, "let me make a copy of your father's letter!"

    "I don't mind, Charles," replied Jacob. "What will your father say?"

    "I don't think he'll do a thing about it. He didn't vote for Mr. Newhouse, and, as you well know, our fathers couldn't care less about each other."

    "Gee, I don't know."

    "Nothing to be afraid of."

    "Maybe not for you, but if my dad finds out he'll skin me alive," Jacob moaned.

    "Here's how we'll do it. Instead of mailing the letter tomorrow, bring it to school."

    "What will we do with it then?"

    "We'll steam the letter open by first boiling a little water in a tin can."

    "Can't anyone tell the letter was opened?"

    "Not a chance! I'll copy the letter, then reseal the envelope."

    "But Charles, what if it doesn't stick tight?"

    "No problem. I'll coat the flap with some paste, then reseal it."

    "Then what will we do with the letter?"

    "Simple! You drop it in the rural mailbox on your way home."

    When I finished explaining the plan to Jacob, he accepted it. Then I joined the other boys where I felt right in style with my overalls and blue shirt, for they were dressed the same way. Some wore caps; others were bareheaded, either by choice or because their folks didn't have the money to spare. The same went for shoes. Even though fall was just around the corner, six of the boys were barefoot.

Looking around I observed several marble games, called "big ring," in progress. To play the game, one of the boys used a short stick to mark a circle approximately four feet in diameter. Usually, two to five boys played in a game. They agreed on how many marbles each player was to put in the center of the ring. Next, straws were drawn to determine the order of shooting.

As each player's turn came, he knelt, placing his shooting knuckles on the line. Then using a marble or a "steely" (usually a large ball bearing) as a shooter, he tried to knock as many marbles out of the ring as possible. Marbles clearing the line were his to keep. Those stopping on the line were returned to the center of the ring.

No one thought of "big ring" as gambling. Even Egghead Johnston approved, and this was the surprise of the year. Generally, we were to find out later, he stood firmly against anything his pupils enjoyed.

Four games were going on simultaneously, and everyone was enjoying himself. However, as quick as a flash, all hell broke loose at the game farthest from the schoolhouse.

"Hiram," Tom shouted "quit your fudging! You're a cheat and everyone knows it!"

"I never cheat!" said Hiram emphatically.

"The heck you don't! I've seen you cheat before, and I just saw you cheat again!"

"Well, well, what do you intend to do about it?"

"That depends. Do it again and I'll show you!"

"You'll show me nothing!" snapped Hiram angrily.

"Shut your big mouth, Hiram."

"I'll play the way I want, and there isn't a damn thing you can do about it!"

Tom Pierson and Hiram Chasteen were evenly matched. Both were in the eighth grade, sixteen years of age and weighed approximately 180 pounds.

Both were now hot under the collar. I looked at my watch. It was exactly ten minutes 'til books.

"Hiram, I don't take your kind of talk from anyone! Apologize!"

"I don't apologize to anyone, especially the likes of you!"

That started the fireworks. Tom drew back, coming up with a haymaker to Hiram's chin. Hiram reeled around as if demented. His glassy eyes seemed to stare off into space.

Suddenly, Hiram was his old self again. He waded into Tom savagely, swinging hard with both fists.

The boys exchanged blows.

As I looked at my watch, my pride and joy, the fight was going into the third minute. Neither one was doing much damage to the other. Then Tom came up with a sharp left to the jaw and a right to the chin.

Hiram knew when he was licked. When he gained his senses, he reeled over to Tom, saying, "I apologize for everything I've said. You're the best man."

Tom accepted his apology just as Mr. Johnston pulled the bell rope hanging from the belfry. The bell's soft melodious tones sounded over the cornfields and meadows for miles, much more pleasing sounds than Tom and Hiram's fighting.

All of us trooping into the schoolhouse noticed one pleasantry: Tom and Hiram were coming in together.

"I'll bet they get it now," Jacob whispered as we neared our seats.

"What do you mean?" I said softly as if I didn't know.

"Why, a tanning they'll never forget," answered Jacob sotto voce.

When all were seated, Mr. Johnston gave some opening remarks. "Good morning, boys and girls. I have some announcements to make.

"First, raise your hand when you want to speak.

"Second, address me as Mr. Johnston. I'll call you by your first name."

"Is it okay if we call you 'Teach'?" asked Jimmy Sanders with raised hand.

"I'm new to southern Illinois, but I understand the name 'Teach' shows respect to the teacher. Yes, you may call me Teach."

"Third, extend one finger from your raised hand when you want permission to sharpen your pencil."

With extended hand Sadie inquired, "Mr. Johnston, how do we let you know when we want to leave the room?"

"Extend two fingers from your raised hand."

Then Mr. Johnston walked to the old beat-up walnut bookcase with two dirty glass doors. Taking a thin hickory switch about three feet long and a bundle of five switches, fastened securely at their butts with strong cord, from the top, he returned to the front of the room where he explained their use.

"This little switch is for the little boys and girls if they are bad. This bundle of switches is for the big boys and girls if they are bad."

Placing the switches on his desk, Mr. Johnston pointed to what was written on the blackboard. (In 1914 it was called a blackboard, not a chalkboard. Later when boards came in green as well as black, they were called chalkboards.) Then he carefully explained the following rules and the punishments if they were violated.

"Spare the rod and spoil the child."
—Benjamin Franklin

Violations	Punishment
1. Throwing paper wads	10 licks
2. Spitting on the floor	15 licks
3. Speaking without permission	10 licks
4. Sassing or talking back to the teacher	25 licks
5. Tardy	10 licks
6. Playing hooky	25 licks
7. Absence without parental excuse	25 licks
8. Failing to do homework	15 licks or the wearing of a dunce cap for one hour
9. Copying	20 licks
10. Tattling	10 licks
11. Lying	25 licks
12. Showing disrespect to the flag	50 licks
13. Destruction of school property	50 licks
14. Using tobacco	25 licks
15. Using profanity	50 licks
16. Fighting	50 licks
17. Miscellaneous (catchall rule when no rule applies)	Hold nose in ring placed high on the blackboard

"Take time to write the rules in your tablet. Learn them well, obey them, and we'll get along just fine."

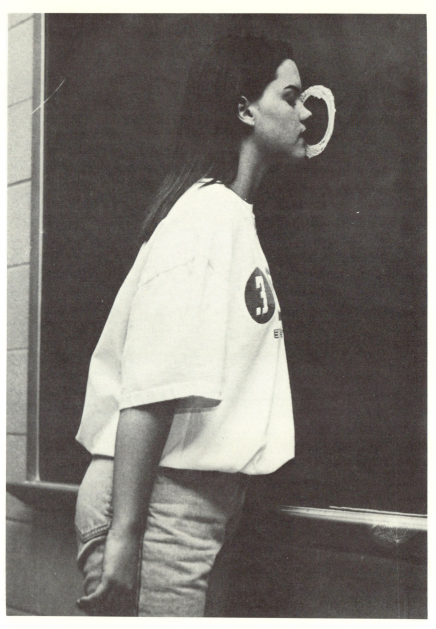

Erin Huffman demonstrates one kind of punishment boys and girls received for copying or the breaking of other rules dictated by the teacher.

Erin Huffman acts the part of a pupil wearing a dunce cap because she didn't know the lesson.

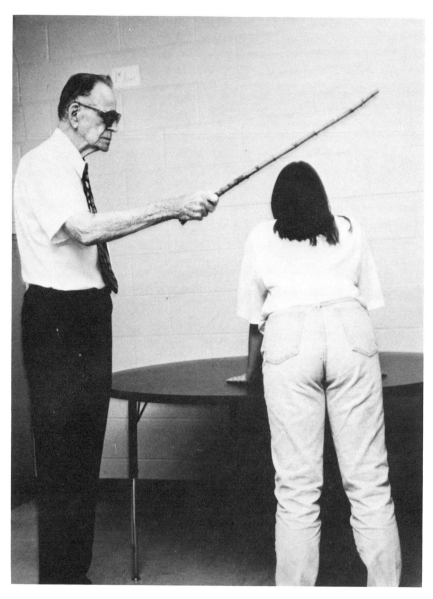
Erin Huffman plays the role of the mean little girl taking a dose of hickory tea.

"I can't write," moaned Jacob Boner after raising his hand. He and I were the only first grade pupils.

"All of you who can't write, raise your hands."

Three boys and one girl raised their hands. All were in the second grade. How did they ever get promoted, I wondered, almost saying it out loud.

Mr. Johnston pointed to four of the older pupils, ordering, "Each of you write a second set of rules. Then pass them to those four who can't write." Both first and second grade pupils were given the same assignment for the next day.

"I'll give you 'til recess to finish. Those of you who can't write practice your assignment for today. Who knows what it is?"

Four hands went up. "Why, Teach, it's write numbers from one to ten," they said in unison.

"Correct! Now write them twenty times so you will never forget them."

That said, Mr. Johnston began reading a book as he took a seat in the back of the room.

That we were surprised was putting it mildly, when Mr. Johnston, Egghead to most of us, didn't say a thing about the fight. Either he didn't see it or cared less. His pupils, including the girls, would never tell, since they were honor bound by a code of silence! Never squeal on a fellow pupil, they all agreed.

By the middle of the morning, 10:15 to be exact, Mr. Johnston arose from his seat in the back of the room and walked to the front. Then he tapped the plunger on the little bell perched on top of his desk. "It's time for recess," he said.

Without a moment to spare, thirty pupils bounced out of their seats.

"Hold it! Hold it!" ordered Teach angrily as his face lit up like the rising sun. "You're supposed to be a nice group of boys and girls attending school, not a bunch of animals running around in a barn.

"Yes, Mary. What is it?"

"Mr. Johnston, when recess came last year, we just jumped up out of our seats and ran out the door."

"This is not last year, Mary. Here's the way all of you will go out and come into the schoolhouse this year. When I tap the bell and say one, you sit up straight, place your folded hands on your desk. [Here Mr. Johnston gave a demonstration at his desk.] On two, turn sideways with your feet flat on the floor in the aisle. On three, stand erect; and on four, beginning with the last aisle to the left, march out the door to the playground.

"Before entering the schoolhouse, form a line. On my command to march, walk slowly up the steps. Then proceed to your assigned seats."

"All right," George Summers asked with extended hand, "what are you going to do about it if we refuse?"

"That will depend," Mr. Johnston replied.

"Depend on what?"

"Have you completed writing the rules and read them carefully?"

"Yes, sir."

"Then you can answer your own question!" said Mr. Johnston as he continued to ask questions. "Have all of you finished writing the rules?"

When Jimmy Shaw's right hand shot high in the air, Mr. Johnston acknowledged it by asking, "Yes?"

"I need about five minutes more."

"OK. Everyone not finished remain seated. Our schedule allows fifteen minutes for recess periods. However, I'm allowing thirty minutes this morning so that all of you will have time to relax."

"Most kind of the old goat," muttered Andy Detweiler softly with one hand over his mouth.

"What did you say?" whispered Mary Sloan.

"Shut up! Do you think I'm going to shout it to the world, then have the old goat have the pleasure of giving me a good strong dose of hickory tea?" whispered Andy in Mary's ear.

I was only six years old, but it began to dawn on me that hickory tea must be something you didn't drink.

"One . . . two . . . three . . . and four . . . " commanded Mr. Johnston as the pupils marched out of the schoolhouse onto the playground.

The boys gave up playing marbles, since the last games ended in a fight. Baseball was the game for the day.

The fight between Hiram and Tom was nothing out of the ordinary. The boys and men in our rural community were not mean or vicious. In fact, just the opposite was true. There wasn't a boy or man who would not give you the shirt off his back if you were without one. That is just the way it was.

The word *law* had a mean ring to it. No one trusted the lawyers or the judges who held court, so fighting was the way problems were settled. It was just a way of life. Our people looked upon fighting in about the same way they looked up eating breakfast, dinner, and supper. All four were functions of life. Even the local minister got into fights on occasion. One example will make my point.

It was early on a Friday evening. I was in the woodshed cutting kindling for starting a fire in the kitchen range the following morning.

Mother called me into the house. "Charles, go to the Red Store in Buckner and buy a loaf of bread. We'll need it for breakfast in the morning."

"Yes, Mother," I replied. I was eager to go because there was always something interesting going on in Buckner, especially on a Friday evening.

It was not only a Friday evening, but it was the coal miner's payday, and they were always ready for beer.

As I arrived at the grocery store, Rev. Jason McBride was entering the store. There were several coal miners sitting on a bench, known as "the liars' bench," outside the grocery chewing the fat.

I heard Big Nose Armato say, as he snickered, "What's new, Preacher? Goin' to save a few souls tonight?"

"Good evening, fellows," Reverend McBride replied, totally ignoring Big Nose's slurring remarks as he opened the door and entered the grocery store.

"Boys, did you get a load of that? That damn preacher ignored my friendly greeting. I'll learn the SOB a thing or two that he won't find in his Bible." With that he jumped up and entered the store followed by his cronies.

Reverend McBride was about to pick up his sack of groceries when he was approached by Big Nose.

"What is it, Preach? Too damn good to give a fellowman an answer to his friendly greeting?"

Reverend McBride, the gentleman that he was, said, "Sir, I resent being addressed like that."

"Oh, you do, do you? I'll learn you to have respect for your fellowman." That said, Big Nose took a swing at the minister.

Reverend McBride ducked the blow, backed away, took off his coat, and asked the grocery clerk to hold it. Just then Big Nose came at him a second time, swinging and missing again.

Reverend McBride could tell by Big Nose's stance and approach that he had never been in the ring. Unknown to everyone there, Reverend McBride had been on the boxing team for three years while in college.

Big Nose waded in swinging a third time. The reverend ducked or sidestepped each intended blow. This swinging and ducking went on for three or four minutes with Big Nose never making contact. He was getting angrier and angrier as evidenced by his face getting redder and redder.

Finally Reverend McBride had enough. He ducked the last intended blow, then he came up with a hard right to the jaw. Big Nose went out like a light, hitting the floor with a big thud that only a 190-pound man could make.

As Reverend McBride was putting on his coat, some of Big Nose's cronies shouted, "You've killed him! You've killed him!"

Reverend McBride answered very calmly, "No, he is far from being dead. In about fifteen minutes he'll come to. He'll be a bit addled for a few minutes. Other than a swollen jaw and hurt pride he'll be none the worse for his encounter."

As he picked up his sack of groceries, the clerk said, "Reverend, I'm sure glad you taught Big Nose a lesson. He's had this coming for a long, long time."

Reverend McBride left the store no worse from the fight, and I purchased a loaf of bread. Then I ran home as hard as my legs would carry me. I didn't want to be late for supper.

Chapter 3
The Daily Schedule

The next few days passed with tedious slowness. Anxious to get in plenty of playtime that Wednesday morning, I arrived at school five minutes after eight.

All the boys were there, ready for action.

As I came up to them I said, "Well, boys, what are you going to do? Play tiddlywinks?"

"Don't be a silly ass, Charles," said Sean Turner as he pulled his pitcher's mitt from his hip pocket. "As for you, Charles, keep your nose out of this. It's none of your business."

"I'll get my bat," said Curtis Talley as he sprinted to the coal shed where it was stored.

"Let's get started," said Jack Reeves as he flexed his muscles.

The umpire, captains, and team members were chosen at the first game for the entire school term.

Everyone agreed on Jack as the umpire because he played no favorites. Curtis and Loren Barker were chosen captains.

I watched as one of the captains flipped a coin. This gave the winner the right to choose the first player on his team. Loren won the toss. Then he chose his favorite player. From then on, the rule of the game was choosing back and forth by each captain until each side had nine players.

I, along with three other boys, was considered too small and inexperienced for either team. With us eliminated only six boys made up each team.

"We could still play the devil's advocate," I said. "What's wrong with having six players on each team instead of nine?"

"No way to play baseball!" said umpire Jack. "We must have nine on a team, or it's no longer baseball."

"What should we do, ump?" inquired Herman Smith.

"That's easy," I interrupted. "Have the captains choose six girls, three on each side."

"No way!" shouted the other boys in unison.

"That's a stupid suggestion if I ever heard one. As for you, Charles, keep your nose out of this if you know what's good for you!" shouted Marvin Lucas.

"If that's the way you want it, I refuse to umpire a piecemeal game! For your information, I umpired some games last summer with girls on the teams, and you want to know something? Some of the girls were better than some of the boys in both fielding and in hitting. Now with that said, you can take the girls or you can get yourselves another ump. Choose your poison!"

"Oh, OK. I'll choose three girls," said Captain Loren with hatred showing in his eyes.

"If that's the way it must be, I'll choose two girls, but the rest of the girls couldn't catch a ball in a washtub," slurringly remarked Captain Curtis.

That meant nine girls were eliminated. Playing jacks, just talking, or rooting for their favorite team was up for grabs. They chose the latter.

"Choose me! I can field balls and hit them as good as some of you can," piped little Henry Ainsworth, who had been turned down cold when the teams were chosen.

"You're the largest of the runts, so I'll take you, much to my sorrow. You can play right fielder, for there's little damage you can do there," replied Captain Curtis.

Later in the game, as I had predicted early in the game, Curtis would eat crow and plenty of it!

With teams selected and a flip of a coin, Captain Loren's team was first at bat.

The result of the first two innings was no hits and no errors. Just as the third inning began with a score of 0 to 0, Mr. Johnston came to the door ringing his small handbell, indicating it was time for books.

In we marched like little soldiers to our previously assigned seats.

When all were seated, Mr. Johnston explained our daily schedule.

"The school day is six hours in length in addition to one hour for lunch. During this time, twenty-six classes recite from the recitation seat where I hear your lessons and give your assignments for the following day. I check papers and assign grades during the evening hours about the time you are required to do your homework. In addition, I am responsible for the janitorial work; keeping the privies clean and sanitary; cleaning the yard of rubbish, tree limbs, and other trash; keeping fresh drinking water in the two-gallon bucket on the table in the rear of the room; and making the schoolroom as cheerful as possible. These duties are all stated in my contract.

"We'll need a new American flag, a set of up-to-date maps, a dictionary, and some supplementary books, especially in the areas of reading, geography, and history. [Social science was an unheard-of entity then.] I'll check with the school directors to see how much financial help they can provide. Later this year I'll met with your parents to discuss ways we can work together to raise additional money to improve our school.

"What is it, Mike?" Mr. Johnston inquired, responding to a raised hand.

"I have a large, new American flag. I'm sure my parents would be glad to donate it."

"Excellent. When do you think you might bring it to school?"

"First thing tomorrow morning."

"Do I have more volunteers?"

"I'll carry the coal for the potbellied stove," volunteered Susan Hunter. No job was too hard for her. She weighed 130 pounds, was five feet, six inches tall, had brown wavy hair, long skinny arms, and was said to be as strong as an ox.

I volunteered to bring in a fresh bucket of water from the well, morning and afternoon.

"I'll monitor the school yard, and anyone I catch throwing paper or trash will have to answer to me!" spoke up Jason DeWees loud and clear.

I began to think. Maybe Egghead wasn't so bad after all. Why would so many pupils volunteer their help if he were?

"It's now 11:40," announced Mr. Johnston as he looked at the wall clock. Then he tapped the bell on his desk.

"Since this is such a nice day, I'm going to dismiss you for a long lunch hour. By cutting class time this afternoon we'll get through all classes."

All of a sudden Joe Perkins jumped up, ready to run outside.

"Joe, sit down!" and Joe sat down pronto.

"Now is everyone ready for count one?"

No one made a move or said a word as they remained seated with clasped hands on their desktops.

"Two . . . three . . . and four," Mr. Johnston counted out loud.

On the way out, Joe remarked to me, "Old Egghead must have been a sergeant in the army."

"How's that?"

"Well, he barks orders just like my Uncle Howard, and he's a retired sergeant from the marines. Oh, heck, let's just forget old Egghead for the next hour and fifteen minutes, while we watch the ball game."

"Why, Joe, aren't you going to eat lunch first?" I wanted to know.

"Naw," replied Joe, "Ma put old hardtack and fat bacon in my lunch bucket. I'll bet an old hound dog wouldn't touch it!"

"What are you going to do with it?" I inquired.

"Why, throw it out on the side of the road on my way home!"

"Why not throw it down the privy?"

"That's not a good idea."

"Why not?"

"Well, if old-Egghead gets wind of it, he'll tell Ma and Pa at the Grange meeting tonight."

"So what will they do about it?" I inquired.

"Do about it? When they come home, Pa will beat the living hell out of me."

"Go with me over to that white oak tree on the other side of the school yard and I'll share my lunch with you."

"Would you do that?" Joe said, surprised.

"Sure thing. What are friends for?"

As the ballplayers finished lunch, they ambled over to the diamond, knocking flies or playing catch until all of the team members finished eating. Then they finished playing the third inning, where they had left off at the close of the morning recess.

The lunch hour ended at one o'clock when Teach rang his handbell, a signal to form a straight line in front of the schoolhouse.

On the command of "march" we quietly marched up three steps into the schoolhouse. Then we went to our assigned seats.

Nothing unusual happened during the afternoon. Recitations

came and went without a hitch and assignments were given for the following day. Even the ball game went well during the afternoon recess, ending in a score of 4 to 2 in favor of Captain Talley's team.

Teach looked at the wall clock. It was four o'clock.

With a resounding "one . . . two . . . three . . . and four," we happily marched out of the schoolhouse on our way home.

The first thing Jacob and I noticed was the lane. It was no longer muddy. The warm September day and the bright sun had dried the mud, making walking a breeze.

We headed east. In about twenty minutes we would reach the T. Here Jacob would turn left and I right, on our separate ways home.

As we continued to walk, I completely forgot that Jacob was with me. I began thinking about what our fathers did to make a living. Jacob's father was an illiterate farmer, while my father worked in an underground coal mine.

Other than the coal mine, there were no factories or other large industries in our county. Garages, grocery stores, and political jobs provided work for no more than twenty men. Women were left out of the workforce. Their place was in the home, keeping house and raising children, according to the menfolk.

The farmers raised corn, soybeans, clover, and timothy hay. In addition, a garden provided vegetables, plenty of milk came from a cow or two, a flock of chickens furnished fresh eggs, and a few hogs supplied the family with meat. Occasionally, a calf was butchered to vary the menu.

Father worked in the Number One Franklin County Mine. It was an underground mine, sometimes called a "deep mine." Here 605 men found employment.

The miners descended the main shaft in cages running vertically 598 feet down to the bottom, called "the pit." Two years ago while a cage was descending, the woven wire cable snapped, sending eight miners to their deaths. Since then, miners had a fear of an accident when they ascended and descended the main shaft. Some of the men met their fear by praying; others trusted to luck. Still others just didn't give a damn.

Entries, corresponding to long halls in a hotel, branched off from the main shaft. Then rooms were formed at right angles to the entries. The six-foot seam of bituminous coal was of excellent quality.

On top of the coal was a layer of rock. When the coal was broken loose with blasting powder, the rock served as a roof. Next, the coal was shoveled by hand into shuttle cars. When full, the cars were pulled by mules to the main shaft where the cars were hoisted, one by one, to the tipple seventy feet above the surface. Here, each car was automatically dumped into a shoot leading to an empty railroad coal car.

As the coal was removed, miners propped the rock ceiling with wooden cross members supported by wooden props. In spite of precautions taken for the miners' safety, occasionally the roof gave way, injuring or killing one or more of the miners. Such an accident happened my first year in school. Two miners, Harold Sims and Harvey "Buck" Jones, were placing posts under a cross member when a slab or rock about four feet square suddenly broke loose, crushing Harvey to death and breaking Harold's right shoulder and arm.

An air shaft was located about two hundred yards from the main shaft. Its purpose was to assist air circulation between the surface and the underground. Also, it served as an escape hatch if the two cages in the main shaft became inoperable. Since the air shaft was without cages, a ladder was built into one of the walls so miners could climb to the surface.

Each miner furnished his own carbide lamp. A miner lit it by twirling a small fixed wheel over a fixed flint mounted on the lamp's reflector. This created a spark, lighting the released gas.

I continued to reminisce as I walked. Actually, I completely forgot Jacob was even with me.

Sometimes the ventilating system failed to clear all of the dangerous gases. Then a violent explosion occurred if a miner's lamp flame or a lighted cigarette came in contact with it. Such an event happened on September 9, 1914.

It was a sad time for the families of four miners: Bobby Franklin, Oliver Bush, Cecil Armstrong, and Russell Martin. At 2 P.M. they were headed for a worked-out room to take a smoke. No sooner had they sat down when a *boom* sounded throughout the mine. All four died instantly without a struggle. One of the open flame carbide lamps touched off a pocket of gas seeping out from a pile of powdered coal, called "bug dust."

Today, power coal cutters and battery-operated lamps replace the pick, shovel, and carbide lamps. Safety-approved explosives replace the black powder used to blast the coal loose. Also, many modern mine and safety laws exist to help drastically reduce miners' injuries and deaths.

"Charles, what's the matter?" Jacob wanted to know. "Are you sick or something?"

"No."

"Then what is it? You're not talking, just staring off into space. You're acting like an idiot."

"Oh, there's nothing wrong with me, Jacob. I was just thinking."

"Thinking about what, for God's sake?"

"Nothing real important, just thinking."

"Well, then I'll tell you something that is important! Remember our little scheme for you to copy my father's letter to County Superintendent Newhouse?"

"Sure do, Jacob. How could I ever forget it? Did it work?"

"Like a charm. All of these days passed and no one is the wiser," Jacob said, laughing so loud his little stomach shook like jelly on a plate.

Just then a large raccoon crossed the road not more than a hundred feet ahead.

"Jacob," I said excitedly, "did you ever see such a large raccoon?" Both of us were surprised to see him during daylight hours, since raccoons are nocturnal animals.

"No, never, and I don't think anyone else has either. Boy, is he ever big."

The raccoon heard our voices. Then he raced about twenty yards into the woods, running behind a large white oak tree. Peeping from behind the tree, he watched us walk down the lane.

A funny thought came to mind. The raccoon's masked face reminded me of a masked gunman I had seen in a recent movie.

Jacob and I kept up a running conversation, while I admired the scenery. The lane ran through a forest of beautiful white oak trees with a few mulberry and hickory nut trees scattered here and there. Although it was not yet fall, some of the leaves were beginning to turn light yellow or red.

Finally, reaching the T, we promised each other to meet there in the morning at 8:15, then walk together to the schoolhouse. I started to leave.

"Hold up, Charles. Did you hear about Butch Buller?"

"No, Jacob, what about him?"

"Well, last Sunday he was walking over his farm, according to his wife, looking for stray hogs. Suddenly, the sky darkened and it began to rain. He must have thought it would be a short shower. Apparently, he took shelter under a large white oak tree that stood on top of a hill. Dad says the way he sees it, 'Lightning struck the tree putting an end to Butch Buller!' His folks are going to bury the old buzzard tomorrow."

"Jacob, Jacob, that's no way to talk. You should show respect for the dead. If you can't say something nice, then don't say anything. I'm surprised at you."

"Did you know, Charles, he never took a bath. Said, 'Animals never bathe and they are more healthy than man.' He believed that if you never took a bath a hard crust would form on your body. Then germs couldn't get through to make you sick."

"Jacob, that sounds like a lot of hogwash to me."

"Cross my heart and hope to die if it isn't the whole truth, so help me God."

"Funny thing, Jacob. I never did see Butch Buller at church."

"You didn't see him, Charles, because he went to a different church. A few years ago the congregation complained so much about Butch's foul odor that Deacon Gouforth brought a rocking chair with a nice soft cushion and placed it in the vestibule. On the following Sunday the deacon made one of his long-winded speeches, dedicating the chair to Butch for his perfect attendance at church. Butch never saw through the smoke screen. In fact, he told everybody he was honored by the church and he had a special chair to sit in when he attends church."

"Jacob, now I've heard everything," I said as I started walking toward home. I arrived home at five, did my chores, ate supper (no one in our neighborhood used the word *dinner* to announce the evening meal), and did my homework.

Close to eight o'clock Father, Mother, and I sat in the living room. With no radio or television to clutter our minds, we were free to talk, read, or play games. I had already mastered the "pointers" as they applied to my new rifle.

Father couldn't wait to ask me about school.

"How was school today, son?" Father smilingly inquired.

"OK."

"Didn't anything happen?"

I wondered if he heard about the fight on the playground. "Not that I can think of."

"Nothing?"

"No, nothing at all."

"See or hear any ghosts in the Orthodox Cemetery?"

"No, but I did discover the so-called ghost. A large limb protrudes from each of two pine trees; the limbs touch each other. When the wind blows they rub to and fro, creating a moaning sound. The stronger the wind, the louder the moaning. Something else: You know the pond just west of the cemetery?"

"Yes, of course! What about it?"

"Early in the morning when I go through the cemetery, a ghostlike mist arises from it, giving the illusion of ghosts or anything else one wants to imagine."

"Good for you, son. I'm really proud of you. Just wait for the boys at the poolroom to hear about it. They'll razz the ghost storytellers plenty. Now that the ghost story has been put to rest, what did you learn today that you didn't know yesterday?"

"Gee, I don't know. I never thought of it before."

"Keep this in mind, son: Every day when school closes, ask yourself exactly what you learned during the day that you didn't know the day before. This is the mark of a well-educated person. Don't ever forget it."

"I will do just that." To this day Dad's short speech still sticks in my memory.

Just then the mantel clock chimed nine.

"Time for you to hit the sack, son. Don't forget your prayers."

Chapter 4
Hickory Tea

Days dragged by with nothing exciting happening.

My third week at the Crawford School began as I walked up the twin hills and through the Orthodox Cemetery on my way to the *T* where Jacob and I would walk together up the lane to the schoolhouse.

While going through the cemetery, an exhilarating feeling came over me. The two limbs on the two big pine trees were moaning softly as the gentle breeze moved them to and fro against each other. I no longer feared ghosts. My heart didn't skip a beat, and I was as cool as a cucumber, as the old saying goes.

"My, what a wonderful feeling," I said as I met up with Jacob at the *T*.

"Charles, as we walk along the lane to the schoolhouse I want to tell you about one of the funniest things of the year. It happened during the ball game last Friday. Henry caught a high fly out in right field.

"The score was 6 to 3 in favor of Captain Talley's team; three were on bases, two boys and one girl. And it was the last of the ninth.

"Captain Loren came to bat. Everyone knew he was a place hitter. By his stance I could tell he was trying for right field. Remember Talley's remark about Henry being the biggest of the runts? 'I'll take you,' Talley said. 'You can play right field, for there's little damage you can do there.'

"Pitcher Sean Turner rubbed his pitching hand over a rabbit's foot he carried tied to a string around his neck. Then he wound up. Loren drew back his bat, ready for the pitch. A fast ball, waist high, was headed for the center of the plate, when *bam*! He made a perfect hit, high to right field. Everyone cheered. A home run for sure, everyone thought. Then a funny thing happened.

"Henry turned around quickly. Running like lightning for at least thirty feet, he whirled around. Then he jumped about three feet into the air to catch the ball one-handed.

"Loren was already on first, ready to run to second when the catch was made. 'I'll be damned and go to hell' is all that he said as he angrily walked toward the schoolhouse.

"Since it was the last of the ninth with two outs, the game was over. Loren was heard to say later that day, 'I'll get that runt if it's the last thing I ever do.'

"Charles, the reason I am telling you how the game went is because the old goat kept you in for a talk, and I wanted you to get the story straight. By the way, what did the old goat want with you?"

"Why don't you show more respect for Mr. Johnston? Why do you always call him an old goat?"

"That's simple. My older brother, Otho, calls him an old goat. Not to his face, of course. What's good enough for my brother is good enough for me."

"Back to your question, Jacob. Our talk went like this:

"Mr. Johnston, stroking his chin, said, 'Charles, I don't think you live in this school district. If this is true, you must attend the town school. What do you have to say about it?'

"Hanging my head I replied, 'Well, truthfully, I don't know much about such things.'

"Teach sat erect as a soldier as I went on trying to explain exactly where I lived. Finally, he gave me a sheet of blank paper and a pencil. Then he said, 'Draw the schoolhouse, the lane, the *T*, and the main clay road. When you finish, draw a square for your house, and show how far it is from the *T*. While you're doing it, I'll get a school district map.' He pitter-pattered over to a drawer in the bottom of the bookcase. Here he procured the map. Looking at it and comparing my drawing with it, he said, 'Charles, let's lay our cards on the table, shall we? You are telling me the truth, aren't you? I don't want a lie.'

" 'Mr. Johnston, I can't understand why you think for one minute that I'd lie to you.'

" 'Humbug, boy, pupils tell me more lies than truths, that's why. If you are lying, you know what the punishment is! If you're telling the truth, you live just one hundred yards inside the district. Now, go out and play for the time you have left.' "

"Well, Charles, what is it? Do you or do you not live inside the district?" Jacob was anxious to know.

"My father said to forget about Mr. Johnston's question. Furthermore, he said, 'I checked our location to find out which school you were to attend long before the school term began.'"

"Back the ball game, Jacob. Were you surprised that Henry is such a good ballplayer?"

"You bet I was, and so was everyone else that saw the play."

"Jacob, let me fill you in on the Ainsworth family. Joe, Henry's father, was playing baseball with a minor league team when he permanently injured his left knee. Not wanting to live in a big Michigan city any longer and unable to play ball in the big time, he was tickled pink when he heard that the boss of the Number One Franklin County Mine was looking for employees. After he was hired last month, he quickly bought the old Simpson place. As you know it is a godforsaken farm back in the boondocks. Shortly after the family moved in, he built a ball diamond so he could continue coaching Henry, a practice he began when his son was only four years old. Father says that the whole family literally lives baseball. And would you believe it? When Henry goes to bed, he uses a catcher's glove for a pillow."

Jacob and I reached the schoolhouse yard at 8:40. I thought of yesterday's assignment: "Learn your nines for tomorrow, Charles," said Mr. Johnston just before he called the fourth grade geography class to the recitation seat.

"Come on now, Charles. Don't look so worried. The old goat can't do any more than give us a taste of hickory tea," Jacob chided.

"That's easy for you to say, Jacob. Just because I could read a little and do simple numbers, Mr. Johnston assigned me hard multiplication problems. Your assignment of writing the numbers one to one thousand is a snap, so you don't have a thing to worry about."

The first grade recitation came second after the morning recess. *What will happen if I can't remember the answer to each of the nines?* I thought as I recalled the punishment rules.

"Charles and Jacob, go to the blackboard," Mr. Johnston growled as he stared off into space.

"Jacob, write the numbers one to one thousand. Charles, solve this problem: 987 times 479."

I shook my head and started to work, writing the numbers on the blackboard.

$$\begin{array}{r}987\\ \times 479\\ \hline 9774\\ 69090\\ 394800\\ \hline =472{,}664\end{array}$$

When I finished, Mr. Johnston said irritably, "Is that the correct answer?"

"Yes, Mr. Johnston, I think so."

"It isn't!" he said sarcastically, as he waved his hand in the air. "Do it over!"

"Yes, sir." *Bull*, I muttered to myself as I started to figure the problem again.

Teach interrupted my work, shouting, "What is nine times seven?"

"Fifty-four," I replied.

"You think so? Well, I'll teach you to do your homework." That said, he picked up the hickory switch. Then he pushed me face down onto his desk and laid on fifteen licks across my back. "Now, what is nine times seven?"

"Fifty-four," I said with tears streaming down my face.

"That's remarkable! I give you one simple assignment, and you can't do it. Sit down at your desk. Get out your arithmetic. Find out the answer to nine times seven. Then write it in your tablet a hundred times."

Stumbling back to my desk as I washed the tears from my eyes, I thought about my plight as a pupil.

Putting up with Mr. Johnston's rules and regulations, his stern demeanor, and his dosing me with hickory tea caused me to think of myself as a fly caught up in a spider's web. I thought of Teach as the spider, the schoolhouse and the school yard as the web, and, I, of course, as the fly.

Turning to Jacob, Mr. Johnston said, "What's your problem? Why didn't you finish your assignment?"

"So you're another laggard, are you?" Mr. Johnston said as he frowned facetiously. "Maybe I can refresh your memory. Come over here," he said as he picked up the hickory switch.

Just then an amazing thing happened. Otho, Jacob's older brother, jumped up, pointed his finger at Teach, then he shouted, "Don't you even think about hitting my little brother!"

Nothing was said for a few seconds. Then Teach broke out in a sweat as his face turned a crimson red. "I'm running this school. Your lazy brother didn't do his homework. For that he gets a whipping."

"Don't do it!" said Otho as he took three steps down the aisle.

Otho was in the eighth grade, weighed 175 pounds, had broad shoulders, and was strong as an ox. It was common knowledge that he could lift a two-hundred-pound weight with very little effort.

Teach started to push Jacob's face down on the big desk. Then Otho rushed forward. Facing Teach, he screamed, "Jacob didn't do anything wrong!"

Focusing his dark eyes on Otho, Mr. Johnston ordered, "You're expelled as of now! So you have nothing to say!"

"The hell I don't!" Otho shouted. "You hit my brother just once, and I'll mop up the floor with you."

Otho made a believer, so we thought, out of Teach. "Take your seat, Jacob. I'll tend to you later."

Otho and Jacob walked back to their seats. They sat down. Teach called the next class to the recitation seat. Classes continued for the remainder of the day just as if nothing had happened. If Teach ever did tend to Jacob later, I never knew a thing about it. Neither did Jacob nor Otho.

Last July Carol Epstein, his wife, and son, Michael, has come to Benton where Carl opened a store called Epstein's Dry Goods and Dress Shop. The family had lived in a subdivision near St. Louis.

The Epsteins bought a house an eighth of a mile down the country road from where I lived. It seemed that Mr. Epstein wanted to raise Michael in a rural setting where he wouldn't be subjected to the temptations of a large city. Gossip had it that Michael had had several run-ins with the police, and Mr. Epstein wanted to put a stop to that.

Dad (sometimes I used the word *father*. At other times, *dad*) promised to supply the Epstein family with fresh eggs. Since I was the delivery boy, I went in and out of their house occasionally. One Saturday when Mr. Epstein was at home, he invited me to sit down and talk. He explained much about the Jewish religion, things I had never heard before.

Late in the afternoon when I arrived home, Dad inquired, "What took you so long to deliver the eggs?"

"Well, Dad, Mr. Epstein invited me to visit a while. During our conversation he explained much about his religion. He told me the meaning of Yom Kippur, Passover, synagogue, rabbis, and some other things I don't remember."

"Very good, son. The next time I see Mr. Epstein I must tell him how much I appreciate his taking time to explain his religion to you. I'm sure you learned much more today than you do in a whole week of school." With that said, Father stood up to leave.

"There's one more thing."

"Yes, what is it?"

"Mr. Epstein was wearing a silly little cap without a bill."

"Hold it right there! Never, and I mean never, talk like that again. That cap you refer to is part of religious belief. We have no other Jews in this community, so you're excused this time. This country was founded on the premise that all people have a constitutional right to religious freedom."

"Gee, Dad, I didn't know that."

"Also, remember this: The goal of all churches is for the worshipers to go to heaven when they die."

Dad stood up and ambled off to the garden, while I went out to feed the livestock.

As I remember them, both Mr. and Mrs. Epstein were definitely assets to the community. Both were college graduates, and they blended in well with the locals, never putting on airs or acting superior to anyone. Their friendliness was infectious, putting everyone they met at ease. It's no wonder their store business grew by leaps and bounds.

Mr. Epstein was a short man, five feet, two inches tall. He always dressed in a plain blue or brown suit, white shirt and tie, felt hat, and a pair of black or brown low-cut dress shoes.

Mrs. Epstein was an elegant lady, five feet, one inch tall, and weighing around 125 pounds. She mixed well and was well accepted by the local women. The LSC (Ladies Sewing Circle) prided themselves in making beautiful quilts. None, however, could match her perfect stitches.

In the St. Louis suburb, children were often called "kids." The three Epsteins soon learned this was unacceptable in their new environment. Incidentally, anyone referring to children as kids was asking for trouble.

Kenneth Hanner spoke the feeling of the community when he told Hiram Wakefield, "I'll punch the bastard in the nose if someone calls my boy a kid. A kid is a small goat, and by damn no one is going to insult my child that way!"

Michael Epstein was a nice-looking boy, four feet, six inches tall, dark hair, and blue eyes. He had a mole under his left eye, near his nose, causing him to occasionally look cross-eyed.

Mike, as the children called Michael, was the exact opposite of his parents. He was obstinate, to say the least; referred to his peers as "a bunch of hillbillies," wouldn't join in any of the school games; and on several occasions came within inches of getting punched in the nose.

I was with Jack Reeves, Curtis Talley, Sean Turner, and Loren Barker when they put their heads together to decide what to do with Mike if he didn't change his ways.

"I know what we'll do! We'll give him the coal miners' initiation. That's what we'll do," spoke up Jack.

"Right you are," agreed Sean. "You lay the law down to him, Jack. Give him a chance to shape up. Then if he doesn't improve, we'll initiate him."

"OK," agreed Jack. "The noon period is almost over. I'll talk to him at recess."

As we marched out of the schoolhouse at exactly 2:15 P.M., I kept close to Jack as he caught up to Mike.

"Mike," Jack said, "I want to have a word with you. Let's get away from the other children for a little while."

"Jack, you're an old fart. What makes you think I care what you have to say?"

"Just listen a moment, or I'll rattle your head 'til your teeth fall out. Let's talk about the good things first.

"Mike, you are brilliant. You always have the correct answers in class, and for that we admire you."

"Jack, you're all a bunch of dumb hillbillies. You know that, don't you?"

"You just brought out your bad part. Not only are you rude to the boys, but you insult some of the older girls. Yesterday, after school, you asked Sean's sister to go with you to the cornfield to play. She knew what dirty thoughts you had in mind. That's why she ran away. So far you're a perfect shit ass."

Mike shrugged his shoulders as he said, "Aw, just forget it. I'll let the girls alone." Then he started to leave.

Jack jerked him back, scowling facetiously as he said, "Mike, this is your last warning. One more insult to the girls or bad mouthing to the boys, and we'll give you the coal miners' initiation."

"What's that?" he wanted to know, fear showing in his eyes.

"Keep up what you've been doing, and you'll find out soon enough. I guarantee you it won't be pleasant."

Jack reported his conversation with Mike to his three henchmen as they walked across the playground. Since I was with them, I heard the whole story.

Mike's attitude didn't improve. So on Tuesday of the fourth week of the term, Jack's committee began to lay plans for action.

"Curtis," Jack pointed out, "your uncle works in the coal mine machine shop. Have him give you a small can of black axle grease. You can hide it in the coal house until we need it on Friday."

At the beginning of the recess period on Friday afternoon, I was playing with Mike when Curtis caught up to us.

"Have you ever seen a Wampus cat?" Curtis inquired of Mike.

"No, never even heard of one."

"Well, there just happens to be one hiding behind the coal shed. Mike, you and Charles come with me, and we'll see if it's still there."

What Mike didn't know was that all of the older boys knew of Jack's committee's plans. They were all hidden behind the coal sheds, waiting for the action to take place.

As we reached the coal shed, Jack, Sean, Loren, and Curtis jumped Mike, dragged him behind the shed, and threw him to the ground. Sean came with the can of black axle grease.

Curtis laughed as he said, "Mike, you're the Wampus cat." Curtis and Loren each held a leg, while Jack pinned Mike's shoulders to the ground. Mike started to say something when Jack clamped one hand over his mouth.

"You can talk, but you can't shout so Teach can hear you. If you do, I'll gag you with my big red handkerchief."

"Well, what are you waiting for?" Jack said to Sean. "Unbuckle his belt and jerk down his britches and underpants!

"Now what's the problem?" Jack disgustedly asked Sean.

"He's wearing long johns. I can't pull them down."

"Then open the placket and pull them out, Sean.

"Holy cow! Look at that!" shouted Jack in disbelief as he pointed his finger at Mike's midsection.

"He's been hurt," said Joe Perkins pitifully.

"Naw," spoke up Marvin Lucas. "My dad's looks like that all the time, and he's never been hurt."

When I had my talk on Jewish religion with Mr. Epstein, he explained that all Jewish male babies were circumcised. However, Mike was the first boy I ever saw that way.

"Well, Sean, what are you waiting for?" inquired Jack.

Sean reached inside the bucket, pulled out a large handful of black grease, and proceeded to massage Mike's privates.

"Sean, use more grease! You've missed several places," Jack pointed out.

Finally, Curtis asked, "Jack, shall we turn him loose?"

"Not yet," Jack replied.

"Mike, let this be a lesson to you. If you continue to be a sore ass, you'll get another coal miners' initiation. Otherwise, we'll accept you as one of the boys."

"Now let him up," Jack instructed.

Mike jumped up, pulled up his britches, and buckled his belt. Then he ran like a jackrabbit, chased by the hounds, straight for home.

All the while the initiation was in progress, Mike never shouted out. He did, however, threaten the initiation team. He was going to tell Mr. Johnston, his mother and father, and anyone else who would listen to him.

As I walked toward the schoolhouse, Sylvia Slavins asked me, "What was wrong with Mike?"

"I don't know," I replied.

"Well, something was wrong. He came running through the playground as hard as his legs could carry him, and he headed for home. Was he sick?"

"I don't know. I guess he was sick." I wondered how a six-year-old boy would go about explaining to a fourteen-year-old girl exactly what happened. So I just walked away.

On the following Monday morning, we heard a knock at the schoolhouse door just as we finished singing "The Star-Spangled Banner." The time was 9:10 when Mr. Johnston opened the door as he pleasantly said, "Good morning, Mr. and Mrs. Epstein. What can I do for you?"

"Please come out in the yard, Mr. Johnston. We want a word with you," said Mr. Epstein.

The door was only closed half-way, and we could hear enough of the conversation to realize the Epsteins were hot under the collar about Mike's initiation.

As the Epsteins were getting into their Model T Ford to drive back to the store, Mr. Epstein shouted angrily, "Mr. Teacher, if this ever happens again to our Michael, I'll sue the three school directors, the boys involved in the torture, and you! Good-bye!"

When Mr. Johnston took over the next class, he was white as a ghost. He said nothing about the Epsteins' visit.

Just before Teach counted one, two, three, and four for recess dismissal, he asked the four boys of the initiation team to remain in their seats when the rest of us filed outside.

All of us on the playground crowded around the windows. Looking inside we wondered what was going to take place.

"Are you the four boys who did this dastardly act to Michael?"

"Yes, we are," answered Jack.

"Was Charles involved?"

"No, sir," said Sean.

Teach picked up a large hickory switch as he said, "You will all get fifty licks, and we'll start with you, Jack."

The boys were laughing, not loud enough for Teach to hear, when they trooped out of the building. All of us followed them out behind the coal shed. How could they be so happy after their lickings, we wondered.

"All of you girls get going. And I mean now!" Jack ordered. "We're going to strip naked."

"You're all laughing like you just came from a picnic. Didn't it hurt?" I inquired.

45

"What do you think?" chuckled Sean. "Hang around a few minutes and you'll find out why it didn't hurt."

It didn't hurt because the four boys came to school prepared. First, they removed their overalls and shirts. Next, they removed a heavy pair of trousers and a heavy wool shirt. Disrobing was followed by removing several layers of newspapers covering their bodies from neck to ankles. With their protection paraphernalia removed, they put on their overalls and shirts. Then they ran toward the ball diamond for a little play before books.

Sean, leading the way, shouted, "Last one there is a monkey's uncle."

Chapter 5
Individual Differences

During the humdrum days that followed, things began to liven up a bit.

We were all looking forward to Saturday that Friday morning when George Summers came into the limelight.

All of us pupils knew that George was a slow learner. Some thought he was an idiot. Others said he was just a step above a moron. Still others said he was a simpleton because his mother saw a shooting star only a few minutes before he was born.

Only last week I heard Jack Reeves say he didn't want to be in the same marble game with George. He went on to say that a trained monkey could do everything that George could do and even do it better.

It was a morning, in October, that Mr. Johnston made a startling announcement.

"How old are you, George Summers?" Mr. Johnston inquired.

"Fifteen, and I'll be sixteen day after tomorrow. Mom is going to bake me a big banana cake with candles on it and everything. Oh, boy, oh boy——"

Mr. Johnston interrupted him. "George, you've been punished much too long. I'm promoting you to the fifth grade as of right now. What do you think of that?"

"Gee, Teach, I don't know what to say. Thank you, and I know my mother and father will thank you."

"Good enough. From now on sit with the fifth graders on the recitation seat."

I saw George as a good, kind, and gentle boy. His red hair, freckled face, and pale blue eyes didn't distract from his pleasing personality in the least. He just couldn't dig schoolwork. Intellectually, he was as different as day is to night when compared to Michael

Epstein. Mike could learn his lesson after one reading. George could never quite understand his lesson, no matter how many times he read it. As a result, Mike always made 100, while George was lucky if he made 70. As a child I couldn't understand why God made such a difference between two boys of approximately the same age. But were they so different after all? George was a failure playing marbles, but he was an excellent baseball player. The local men's team drafted him to play second base because he could hit and field as well as any man on the team. One day, I heard Henry Ainsworth's father remark, "This boy has the makings of a pro," as he watched George play in an exhibition game. On the other hand, Mike was all thumbs when it came to baseball. Little Jacob Boner could play circles around him.

The Roberts family intrigued me. They lived about one mile west of the schoolhouse. They had three children, Iva Mae being the oldest. She was my age. She was in the second grade, one grade ahead of me.

We were different, different as day is to night. Even at age six I knew she was a girl and I was a boy.

One day I fell in love with her. Maybe it was a full moon that brought it on. I don't know. What I do know is that I fell head over heels in love with her. It happened all at once, like the sun coming out of a dark cloud.

She was a doll: small, dainty, long wavy blond hair like a little princess. No question about it, in my book she was a delight for sore eyes. I was truly smitten.

Not wanting to be called a sissy by my peers, I didn't approach her on the playground. Rather, I tried to get her attention by being the loudest one while several of us were playing games. She didn't seem the least bit interested.

I thought about writing her a note, asking if I could come to her home on a Saturday to play. A good idea, but I was too bashful to carry it out. So that idea went down the tube.

Many times that year Mr. Johnston called me down for daydreaming, he thought. In reality I was mooning over Iva Mae. Whenever he asked me what I was thinking about, I lied. I'd respond that I was memorizing my lesson so it would be perfect, come my turn at the recitation seat. Somehow he bought the whole bit, hook, line, and sinker. Otherwise, he would have given me a good dose of hickory tea.

Next, I began to fantasize. I could see Iva Mae and me taking in a movie in Benton (six miles away). Neither of our parents would take us, I knew, so we'd walk. That, too, was a figment of my imagination. Again, our parents would never permit it. Finally, I gave up the idea.

I had no peace of mind, even as I slept. I'd dream about my love for her during the nights. It was always so clear: We would grow up. Then we would marry and live happily ever after.

The following year I enrolled in a city school. Before long she began to drift further and further out of my mind. Finally, I forgot about her altogether. I suppose that's the way most puppy love ends.

The day before Halloween Teach made a few small announcements. Then he made a final announcement that really surprised us.

"Tomorrow is Halloween, as you well know. What you don't know is that we'll have a Halloween party tomorrow afternoon."

"That's remarkable," said Mary Conway. "We've never had a Halloween party before at school! I'm just tickled pink."

"Now, Mary," Teach admonished, "don't get taken away with the idea."

Just then Jacob leaned over to me, whispering, "The old goat must be slipping. He never said a thing about Mary's violation of rule number three."

"I am giving all of you the same assignment for tomorrow afternoon: Write an original Halloween story of not more than two hundred words. How many of you can bring a pumpkin with eyes, nose, and mouth cut out?"

All hands raised high.

"Good, that's settled then."

Mary raised her hand to speak.

"What is it, Mary?"

"How should we write the story?"

"Make it as ghostlike as you can. I want to see how different one story is from another.

"Yes, Henry?"

"What are we going to do about candles? We are going to put lighted candles inside the empty pumpkins, aren't we?"

"Certainly. How many——"

Just then Susan Hunter interrupted Teach. Again, no reprimand.

"We have four or five boxes of candles. I'll bring a box, one candle for every pumpkin."

"Thank you, Susan. that's very nice of you."

Susan saved the day for Jacob and several other pupils, none of whose parents could spare money for candles. They were lucky if they had enough money to buy the essentials of life and candles were not one of them.

I began to daydream. Soon I visualized another difference among people. Susan's parents owned a beautiful two-story Victorian house located on three hundred acres of fine bottomland. On the other hand, Jacob's parents owned a three-room shack covered with black roofing paper located on 140 acres of poor yellow clay. At the time I didn't think much about the difference between the two families. However, in later years I realized there was a great economic difference among different families. Our minister in one of his sermons referred to them as, "The havers and the have-notters."

Then I began to think about another difference. George Summers and Mike Epstein were about the same age, but their physical differences were great. George outweighed Mike by twenty pounds. Three weeks ago at the county fair, both entered a weight lifting contest. George easily picked up a hundred-pound weight and held it above his head for thirty seconds. Mike couldn't lift the same weight off the ground.

"Now that tomorrow afternoon is taken care of, let's talk about preparation for the party," said Mr. Johnston.

Suddenly, I was brought back to reality.

"I have arranged with Mr. Salinger, Grand Mogul of the Ancient Knights, to lend us thirty folding chairs," continued Teach.

"Yes, Sylvia, what is it?"

"Why do we need folding chairs for our party?"

"Well, Sylvia, I was keeping a big surprise for later in the day, but if you must know, I'll let the cat out of the bag now. When you leave for home at four o'clock, I'll give each of you a handwritten invitation for your parents, inviting them to the party tomorrow afternoon.

"Loren, can you bring your team and wagon to school in the morning?"

"Why, yes, Teach, but why?"

"Good. At nine o'clock tomorrow morning, take four boys of

your choice, drive to Mr. Salinger's house, pick up the folding chairs, bring them to school, dust them, and then stack them in piles in the back of the room for use tomorrow afternoon.

"What is it, Sadie?"

"That ain't fair, Teach. The five boys get out of school, while the rest of us must stay here and study. Just ain't fair!"

"I agree. There will be no classes tomorrow morning. We'll spend the time making ready for the afternoon program.

"Bring your false faces to school. Those who don't have one can spend time making it. I have the material. Also, I have lots of red crepe ribbon material. Those of you who have nothing to do can string up the ribbon, giving our classroom one grand party appearance. Halloween would not be complete without some jack-o'lanterns. I'll furnish them. Those of you who have finished your work can help me make them. You won't have to bring any material from home as I have everything required in my desk drawer."

Since the coal mine was idle that week and there was no pressing farmwork, every parent came to the party. Parents not finding an empty folding chair shared a seat with one of the pupils.

The program began at one o'clock with Mr. Johnston reading the following account on Halloween.

"Halloween is the name given to the evening of October 31 preceding the Christian feast of Hallowmas, or All Saints' Day. The ancient Celts set aside Halloween, the last day of their year, to examine the warnings of the future. They also believed the spirits of their dead relatives and friends revisited their earthly homes on that evening.

"The Celtic tradition of lighting huge fires on Halloween lasted until modern times in Wales and Scotland. As all of you know, the concept of ghosts and witches is still with us on Halloween. Both the United States and Great Britain still follow the Roman custom of the harvest festival along with playing games involving fruit, such as dunking apples in a tub of water. Other original celebrations are the decorative use of jack-o'lanterns and hollowed-out pumpkins carved to resemble hideous faces and lit by candles placed inside. You will see a demonstration of all these ancient customs as we move along through our program."

Next, we came to the front of the room to read our stories, beginning with first grader Jacob. When the fourth graders finished reading their stories, Mr. Johnston called a halt so we would have time to play several games of dunking apples in a tub of water. Then the games were followed by the reading of the remaining stories.

At the conclusion of the last story, Mr. Johnston said, "I think Mr. Summers has an announcement."

Standing up, Mr. Summers, much on edge and ill at ease, said, "I haint much on makin' speeches, but here's what I and my old woman want you all to hear.

"Mr. Johnston, you made us-ins most proud when you promoted George yesterday. We'll never forget that, and I mean it. Another thing, Mr. Johnston, we were proud of you for not making fun of George like the other teachers did. You're a damn good teacher, and if you ever need help, just call on us. We'll be mighty pleased to oblige. Oh, yes, one more thing. This morning I bought George a miner's cap and carbide lamp, a pick, and a number two coal shovel. He'll be sixteen tomorrow. I hate like hell to make him quit school, but it is a must. When the mine starts work Monday, me and him will be loading coal side by side."

When Mr. Summers sat down, the parents and pupils gave him a standing ovation. Then Mr. Johnston thanked everyone for coming and the party ended.

Mrs. Sallie Upjohn had a reputation for being a party pooper. And she proved she was in good stride that day of the Halloween party.

I have no idea how many women Mrs. Upjohn insulted that day. During the party Jacob and I sat together. We took a seat as far away from her as we could get, she on one side of the room, we on the other side.

As I was leaving the schoolroom, I heard Mrs. Upjohn say, "Mrs. Neal, it must be nice to be able to make your own clothes."

"Yes," replied Mother as she walked out the door. "It is especially nice when you don't own a sewing machine." Not true, but she made her point.

Jacob was right behind me. He whispered in my ear, "That set old blabbermouth on her haunches."

Mother was a happy, even-tempered person. She was sympathetic and understanding. She cared for people, and she was always there to give Father and me a helping hand when it was needed.

However, she could dish it out as well as the next person when it came to handling busybodies like Mrs. Upjohn.

Yes, Mother sewed many of our clothes. She was an excellent seamstress, as evidenced by garments sewed on her Domestic sewing machine. Sometimes she sewed things by hand with needle and threat. I can still see some of her stitches, short and evenly spaced. They would have been a credit to any professional tailor.

To me, her Domestic sewing machine was the marvel of the age. The machine was housed in a stained and varnished oak cabinet. Four small casters made it easy to move from place to place. Raising the lid and lowering it in place made a worktable. This operation also brought the machine up out of the cabinet and locked it in place. It was a foot-powered machine. Pumping your feet up and down on a wide pedal at the bottom of the machine furnished power for the machine, causing the threaded needle to go up and down. The faster you pedaled the faster is sewed. A rod connected the pedal to a twelve-inch flywheel. A small round belt connected the flywheel to a smaller pulley fixed to the head of the machine, causing foot power to be transferred to the machine.

Mother's Domestic sewing machine is, at this writing, eighty-seven years old. I have it still in my home office. Of course, Mother has long since gone over the divide. However, when I look at it, then close my eyes, I can see her making it sing as she sews garments for Father and me and sometimes for a sick neighbor woman.

Halloween night was a far cry from the school Halloween party. It took a 180° turn. Vandalism ran rampant. Some of the boys and a few of the girls went to the village for a window-soaping spree. First, they would knock on a house door. Then they would shout, "Trick or treat." If the occupants obliged with candy or apples, the youngsters thanked them and moved on to another house. If the response was, as one grouchy old man said, "Get lost, or I'll turn my dogs loose on you," he found his windows soaped the following morning.

Also, there was a more vicious form of vandalism, as evidenced on Harry McCaleb's farm. Several boys or young men, as you care to characterize them, ages twenty-one to thirty-two, paid him an uninvited one o'clock visit early Halloween morning. First, they pushed his new farm wagon to the edge of his horse pond. Next, they removed the four wheels. Then they turned the wagon bed upside down and shoved it into the pond. That done, they tied each of two wheels together with a big piece of rope, leaving about six feet of space between them. With a long rope tied to one wheel, and with the aid of two men on the roof, each pair of wheels were hoisted upward, coming to rest straddling the ridge of the roof.

With the help of neighbors, Mr. McCaleb spent the major part of a day pulling the wagon bed from the pond and reassembling the wheels. And the young men called such acts fun!

When we returned to classes the next school day, Mr. Johnston had marked each of our stories "100." I never could figure out whether he gave us a high mark because our stories were that good or because he felt sorry for us.

Chapter 6
An Atypical Day

Several days dragged by with nothing eventful happening. Then one day in the middle of November was the day of all days. Everything about it was different from any other day that year.

As I walked along the clay road to the schoolhouse that morning, huge, black clouds began forming in the west. *Should I return home?* I wondered. Before deciding what to do, Jacob and I met at the *T*.

"Think it's going to storm, Jacob?"

"Not for a while. If we run, we'll get to school before it rains."

"What if we get soaking wet?"

"So what? What better excuse to return home do you want?"

We arrived at the schoolhouse in the nick of time. Heavy rain began pouring down just as we entered the building, and the thermometer, fastened to the outside door casing, registered 70° Fahrenheit, much too hot for the middle of November.

At nine o'clock sharp, Teach took the roll. Everyone was accounted for except Mary Conway. Since she was a punctual pupil, always on time, I thought she must be ill.

Recess came none too soon. The rain stopped, the sky cleared of clouds, and the sun came out bright and clear.

Later that morning I looked at the wall clock. It was 11:22. Just then Mary Conway and her mother walked in. Mary took her seat, while Mrs. Conway greeted Teach as she walked toward his desk.

Gee, I asked myself. *What's wrong? Both of them look terrible.* I wondered if someone had died.

"Mr. Johnston, I came with Mary this morning to tell you why she is late. We had a very destructive storm this morning," said Mrs. Conway, shaking as if she had a chill.

"Mrs. Conway, I can tell you and Mary are terribly upset about something. Take it easy. Start at the beginning and tell me your problem," said Mr. Johnston with a pained expression on his face.

"Thank you, Mr. Johnston. I really appreciate your concern."

Mrs. Conway went on to describe the storm in detail. She said she and her husband were watching a jet-black cloud moving out of the southwest. Thunder and lightning made conversation almost impossible. Everything was still. Not a leaf moved. Just then a funnel-shaped cloud began descending from the jet-black cloud. When the tail hit the ground, it bounced up in the air. It bounced and hit the ground for several yards. Then it moved along the ground, leveling everything in its path. The destruction lasted only a few minutes. Then Mr. Conway went to assess the damages. When he came back to the house, he said the only damage suffered was the barn roof. It was lifted up in the air and dropped about a hundred feet from the barn. All of the ninety acres of cornstalks were broken off even with the ground and blown away. Since the corn was gathered, no financial loss occurred.

The Boswell family, on the other hand, suffered extensive damage. The tornado tail ran right through the middle of their farm, clearing a path seventy-five yards wide and extending half a mile beyond the farm's northeast boundary. Trees were uprooted, fences blown down, and one prize bull was killed, having had a broken tree limb blown right through his body. The Boswell house itself suffered only minor damage from the wind accompanying the twister. Three windows were broken, and the kitchen chimney was blown off the house onto the yard. Fortunately, none of the Boswells suffered personal injuries.

Teach thanked Mr. Conway for taking time to describe the tornado damages to us. Then he invited her to visit for a while, since Mary's history class was next. Mrs. Conway thanked him. Then she said she couldn't stay because her husband needed the horse and buggy. Just as soon as she returned home, he was going to see his insurance agent in Benton to file a claim for barn damage.

Ever since Teach had us write his seventeen rules of negative behavior, the older boys and I tried to figure a way to beat them without getting caught. So far several rules were broken, and each time the violating pupil received a dose of hickory tea.

It was noon. Jacob and I were playing catch when we noticed

Otho, Jason, Jack, and Loren standing in one corner of the school yard with their heads together.

"I wonder what's going on, Jacob. They're cooking up something. Know what it is?"

"Naw. I don't know anything."

The way in which he answered led me to believe he knew more than he was willing to tell.

"Come on now, old buddy, we've been friends too long to keep secrets from each other."

"Well," he remarked as he walked up close, "I'll give you a hint. Ever notice those brown streaks on the sides of the coal house as well as those on the schoolhouse steps?"

"Sure," I said. "What caused them?"

Jacob laughed. "A word to the wise is enough," he said. "You'll find out one of these days. Unless you figure it out for yourself, forget it. If I tell you more, Jason will beat hell out of both of us. Let's finish playing catch until Teach rings the bell."

The first thing after lunch Teach told us someone had drilled a small hole through the girls' privy back wall and removed the door latch. Also, someone drew obscene pictures on the walls inside the coal shed. He said it was hard to believe any of us would stoop so low, and hoped we would cooperate with him in repairing the damages, as well as in removing the obscene drawings.

"What can we do about it?" Jimmy Shaw inquired.

"I'm really sorry to ask this of you, because I know that all of you have chores to do on Saturday morning, but I really need help," pleaded Teach.

"I didn't do anything wrong," blurted Andy Detweiler. "But I'll volunteer to help."

"Put me down as a volunteer, Teach. I'll do whatever I can," I said as I sat proudly in my seat.

"So will I," spoke up Marvin Lucas.

"I'd like to but I can't, answered Joe Perkins. "Dad has me lined up to cut sprouts all day Saturday and Sunday."

"That's remarkable," chided Hiram Chasteen. "You old hypocrite, working on Sunday."

"Let's cut the baloney!" shouted Teach. "I need two more volunteers."

Hiram and Mike Monroe responded almost as one.

With a sparkle in his eyes, Teach proudly accepted them. "I'm grateful to all of you. I'll borrow Mr. Westermeir's two-horse surrey and pick up the four of you between eight and nine Saturday morning. We should finish in a couple of hours."

"Jason, are you chewing tobacco?" Teach inquired.

Everyone laughed and turned to look at Jason.

"No laughing matter!" Mr. Johnston shouted, frowning and squinting those large eyes of his as he quickly walked back to Jason's desk.

"My old man raises tobacco, but I don't chew it because it's too strong," said Jason boastfully.

"Open your mouth!" Mr. Johnston demanded.

"What for?" Jason scornfully replied.

"I want to see inside your mouth, Jason."

Most of us knew Jason chewed tobacco and that he was biding his time until he could swallow the cud. So when Teach finally looked inside his mouth, he saw nothing but a bright red tongue and a set of pearly white teeth. Just then Mr. Johnston spied some dried, brown spittle near the inkwell. Each desk had an inkwell about two and one-half inches in diameter. It was covered with a black lid. The inkwell fit loosely in a hole drilled in the upper left-hand corner of the desk.

When Mr. Johnston lifted the cover, he wasn't too surprised to find it full of spittle. Jason had been using it for a cuspidor. We called it a spittoon.

When Jason told Mr. Johnston that he did not chew the tobacco raised on his father's farm, he told the truth. Because the tobacco was too strong, he chewed Kentucky twist, bought from one of the village grocery stores.

"Jason, take your inkwell outside this very instant, clean it well, and I don't ever want to catch you using tobacco again," Mr. Johnston ordered. "Another thing, when recess comes around you remain in your seat!"

Jason knew what was in store for him when we were dismissed for our afternoon recess. Mr. Johnston had Jason come up front and lean over the big desk whereupon Mr. Johnston laid on twenty-five heavy licks with his large hickory switch. However, the punishment failed to cure Jason's tobacco-chewing habit, and he said as much when he met Jack in the school yard.

"Did it hurt?" Jack inquired with a silly grin on his face.

"It's not a damn bit funny!" Jason answered sharply. "I didn't know the old devil could hit so hard. However, I'd never cry if the old goat had beat me until school let out. You can lay bets on that!"

"Oh, heck, Jason, forget about it. Let's play catch until books."

Teach dismissed us promptly at four o'clock with the usual one, two, three, and four. Everyone went through the ritual except Jack. He just sat in his seat stone-faced and angry looking. We knew something was brewing, but what?

"Aren't you ready to go home, Jack?" Mr. Johnston inquired.

"Not 'til I do my job," Jack replied sullenly.

Several of us, boys and girls, knew the fireworks would begin any moment. What they were, we weren't sure, but we were going to hang around to find out.

"Jack, what job are you talking about?"

"I'm going to whip you! That's what I'm talking about."

"What reason on earth do you have for fighting me?" Mr. Johnston inquired as if he couldn't believe his ears.

"I don't have a reason."

"Then why in the name of heaven do you want to fight?"

"I don't have a single reason. I have four reasons."

Mr. Johnston looked perplexed as he said, "What are they?"

"To begin with, most of the older boys feel the same way as I do about you."

"I'm sorry to hear that, Jack."

"Here are four reasons to show how we feel about you: one, tradition; two, you can't teach; three, I just don't like teachers; and four, making eyes at Gloria Van Clever."

"I'm sorry you boys feel this way about me," said Mr. Johnston as he put down his book, stood up, and walked over to Jack who was now standing up.

"I'll answer your reasons, beginning with number four. Then if you still insist on fighting, we'll fight.

"Making eyes at Gloria is the most ridiculous thing I've ever heard. I thought everyone knew that I'm engaged to Mary Musgraves, English teacher at the Benton Township High School. We are to be married next June 4. Yes, I help Gloria whenever she comes to my desk with a problem. However, if you paid attention to what goes on instead of going to sleep or just holding your hand over your eyes, you would see that I help many pupils with their problems. Another thing, young man, if you would stoop so low as to ask for help when you have problems, I wouldn't be forced to give you so many failing grades. Just keep up your stubbornness and you'll fail the seventh grade again. Case closed on number four.

"Three: Not liking *all* teachers is a pretty big order. Have you ever given consideration to the fact that if you worked harder and procrastinated less, teachers just might give you more consideration? It works both ways, you know. You could show a change of heart tomorrow by coming up to my desk and asking the meaning of the word *procrastinate*. I know you don't know its meaning.

"Two: You say that I can't teach. I'm a high school graduate, have two years at the university, and passed the county teachers' examination with flying colors. Who do you think in this land of ours is going to believe that you know more about evaluating a teacher's qualifications than I do? *Evaluating* is another word you can bring to my attention tomorrow if you decide to see me about your school problems.

"One: Tradition. Yes, Jack, I did my homework on this one. During the past five years, seven teachers were whipped by one of the pupils. You, by the way, hold the record. You beat up two teachers last year so badly that they never returned. The third teacher threatened to quit, but one of the school directors begged him to finish the term. From the beginning of the school term, I've been expecting one of you older boys to tangle with me. Why did you wait so late in the term to pick a fight with me?"

"Us boys we just couldn't agree on who should fight you. Yesterday, we agreed that I was the one to beat you up."

"Now that we've had this little talk, how about letting bygones be bygones and just forget about the fight?"

"Naw, I knew you was a fraidy cat all along. I'll not sleep well until I mop up the ground with you," Jack snarled.

"Well, have it your way. Let's go outside and get it over with."

As the two came out on the playground, we moved in as close as we dared. We were anxious to watch the fireworks. Jacob began taking bets on who would win.

"Better take that silk shirt and pretty tie off, or they'll be torn to shreds when I mop up the ground with you," Jack said as hatred clearly showed in his large round eyes.

"Jack, want to call it quits and forget all about it?" pleaded Teach.

"Naw. I knew you was an old fraidy cat the first day I laid eyes on you."

"One more thing, Jack, before we start to fight. I just happen to have two pairs of boxing gloves under my buggy seat. How about fighting with them?"

"Oh, goody, goody. Let's do it. Then I'll beat you up like a real prizefighter."

"Jacob, will you get the boxing gloves while I take off my shirt and tie?" requested Mr. Johnston.

"Sure thing, Teach."

Mr. Johnston used a horse and buggy to get to and from school. The horse was a beautiful animal, light brown in color, five feet, six inches tall, large eyes, and as gentle as a lamb. The school directors were too tight, everybody said, to build a small shed to protect the horse from the weather. However, Mr. Johnston solved the problem with a waterproof horse blanket. The girls dearly loved old Nellie, as she was called. They took turns during the noon hour to feed her oats and give her fresh water placed in a number two washtub provided by one of the neighbors.

Jacob handed each contestant a pair of boxing gloves. Then one of the older boys tied the gloves securely to the combatants' wrists.

"What are the rules?" Mr. Johnston inquired.

"Hell, they ain't no rules. Hit, bute, gouge, tackle, and anything else you can think of."

That said, Jack rushed Mr. Johnston as he tried for a shot at his nose. Mr. Johnston sidestepped, causing Jack to lose his balance and go sprawling on the ground. When he arose, his muddy face reminded me of old Salley, our pig, when she finished rooting in the mud. Jack was really mad now. He tried for a right to Mr. Johnston's stomach. Mr. Johnston sidestepped Jack again as he landed a solid blow to Jack's left jaw. It rattled him, but the fight was far from over. Next, Mr. Johnston stuck out his nose, as if to say, "Hit me!" Mr. Johnston blocked Jack's punch and landed another haymaker to the side of Jack's head, knocking him to the ground. He immediately got up. Then Mr. Johnston really went after him, landing blow after blow to his body. Another haymaker to the jaw and Jack went down again. But he wasn't knocked out. He just lay there for a few minutes recuperating. So far Jack hadn't landed a single blow on Mr. Johnston.

Getting up, Jack said, "If you'd stand still and fight like a man, I'd whip the daylights out of you."

"Remember, Jack, you said no rules."

Jack waded in, striking wildly. Teach followed through with several short jabs to the chin. Teach was working Jack over good when suddenly Jack landed a right uppercut that sent Teach reeling backward. Jack rushed in for the kill. Mr. Johnston sidestepped him, coming back with a five-six punch barrage to the head that closed Jack's right eye and skinned his lip, causing it to bleed profusely. Mr. Johnston shook Jack with a left-right, then landed three more punches to the head, knocking him out cold.

"Oh, you've killed him!" I cried.

"No, not at all. He'll come around shortly. Jacob, bring the water bucket out here." Mr. Johnston soaked his handkerchief in the cold water. Then he bathed Jack's head. Finally, Jack came to.

Rising to his feet a bit wobbly, Jack said, "Teach, you're by far the best man. I have never taken a shellacking like this before, and I've been in a lot of fights. Are we still friends?"

"You bet your Sunday boots we are," said Mr. Johnston.

After shaking hands, Jack started for home. Mr. Johnston hitched his horse to the buggy and started for his boarding house.

Father wasn't surprised when I told him about the fight that evening. He told me that Mr. Johnston was the college boxing champion the two years he attended college. In fact, Father said that was why he was hired. Apparently, the board of directors was sick and tired of having one teacher after another whipped and, in most cases, run out of the community.

"Dad, I have just one question. Why did Mr. Johnston allow Otho to bluff him early in the term when Jacob was not given a dose of hickory tea as promised?"

"Good question, son. Being early in the term, Mr. Johnston tried everything in the book to get along with his pupils, especially the older boys. When he discovered they took him to be a softy, he used Jack as an example to show all of you that he was running the school, not the pupils. And I can assure you he made his point."

Chapter 7
Visitors

More days dragged by with nothing remarkable happening. Then on Friday afternoon, the last week in November, Teach told us the county superintendent would visit our school the following Monday.

"What time is he coming?" asked Susan Hunter as she pulled her skinny hand through her long, brown, wavy hair.

"Good heavens, Susan, I haven't the slightest notion when he'll arrive. All he told me was that he'll visit next Monday," said Teach as he shook his head in disgust.

"Should we put on airs?" Mary Sloan wanted to know as she turned up her nose, showing the dimple in her chin more prominently.

"I want all of you to have perfect lessons and be on your very best behavior. That is all I ask," said Mr. Johnston as he walked over to the recitation seat to start his next class.

It was ten-thirty on Monday morning when the door opened and in walked the county superintendent. I looked at the man as he went to the front of the room. I had never seen him up close. He was large, muscular. His right shoulder stooped slightly as he stood and extended a hand to Mr. Johnston.

"Glad to see you again, Mr. Johnston." They shook hands, each smiling from ear to ear like two lost brothers having found each other after years of being apart.

"Boys and girls, this is our county superintendent, Mr. Newhouse," Mr. Johnston announced, keeping that big smile from ear to ear.

"Good morning, Mr. Newhouse," we responded in unison, for we were coached many times on just how to meet visitors.

"Is there anything special you want to see or hear today?" asked Mr. Johnston as he nervously stood on one foot then the other.

"No. Just go through your regular schedule," Mr. Newhouse responded as he occupied an empty seat in the back of the room.

As Mr. Johnston called, "First grade arithmetic class come to the recitation seat," Mr. Newhouse arose and walked to the front of the room as he said, "Mr. Johnston, go out to the buggy and keep my driver company. I'll teach this class."

Our class was scheduled for fifteen minutes, but Mr. Newhouse held it over for half an hour. We were never asked a single question about numbers. Instead, he wanted to know how we liked school. Did we like Mr. Johnston? How many days we were absent and why? Did we have all our books, tablets, pencils, and art supplies? None of us had art supplies, because we never had classes in art.

At eleven o'clock, Mr. Newhouse sent for Mr. Johnston. After a handshake, Mr. Newhouse said, "Congratulations! You are running a splendid school. I'm most proud of you and your pupils. I must run now as I'm scheduled to visit the six-mile school this afternoon."

It happened on a Monday, the second week in December. This was a day I'll never forget. Dark black clouds hung heavy overhead. The wind came out of the northeast with strong gusts, making it almost impossible to stand upright. Then shortly after nine o'clock, snow began falling, and it continued falling for the rest of the day. Mr. Johnston began the day by telling us we would have a Christmas party, and all the parents would be invited to share in our joy.

"This morning we will draw names from my hat. I am sure you have done this before. There is only one rule: No gift is to cost more than twenty cents."

Cheap! Yes, according to prices today. However, in 1914 union shop haircuts cost only fifty cents. Doctors' charges ranged from seventy-five cents to one dollar for an office visit.

"Mr. Johnston," Sylvia Slavins spoke up, her dark eyes looking straight at Teach, "my mommy don't have no money to buy presents."

"Sylvia, you mean to say, my mother doesn't have any money—"

"Yes," she interrupted with tears in her eyes. Her tear glands seemed always to be overloaded.

"I can't buy a present either," sighed Sadie Tatum.

"Don't worry about a thing. I know crops haven't been good this year, and the coal mine has been idle more days than it worked. However, nothing is going to keep all of us from having a glorious party. Those of you who don't have money to spare, remain in your seats during recess. I have a solution, so don't worry about a thing," replied Mr. Johnston.

On the playground during recess, Jacob remarked, "Charles, wonder why Egghead had the pupils not able to buy presents stay in? Do you think he is going to whip them because their parents are poor?" Then he gave out with a loud, roaring laugh.

"Jacob Boner! Don't be a silly ass! Sometimes I get the feeling you're plain daffy.

"However, to answer your first question: I simply don't know, but Mr. Johnston is getting soft. I almost fell out of my seat the other day when he said, 'When we have room discussions where all classes are involved, you will no longer be required to raise your hand to speak. We lose too much valuable time that way. From now on, just take your turn. Then speak your mind.'"

"I don't know what has come over the old goat. He doesn't whip as many pupils as he did at the beginning of school," said Jacob.

"Not only that, Jacob, he doesn't whip as hard, and he lets most first offenders off with a good scolding. I wonder what's come over him."

"Maybe being in love with Miss Musgraves is making him a saint," Jacob said, laughing so hard his little, fat tummy bounced up and down like a rubber ball.

Later that morning the eighth graders were reciting their arithmetic lesson. There was a knock at the door. This was nothing unusual, for the village store was two miles away and many of the local residents came to the school to borrow something. Some borrowed a pencil, a stamp, a bucket of coal, or a book from our big library of twenty-five volumes, including a set of *The Books of Knowledge*. Jacob, to this day, insists that he learned to swim in Little Silver Creek from instructions given in volume five. Others came to have Mr. Johnston read and interpret a document and other materials that came in the mail. Still others came to get his opinion on some personal problem.

When Teach opened the door, there stood the McNeal boys. All of us pupils knew them. They were good old boys, fresh from the backwoods. Billy was six feet tall, fat as a butterball, wearing a tattered felt hat, a long overcoat that saw too many winter seasons, and a pair of leather knee boots. Glenn was five feet, five inches tall, skinny as a rail, wearing a coonskin cap, a short topcoat with holes in both elbows, and a pair of rubber boots.

"Top of the mornin' to you, Mr. Johnston," greeted Billy. "I'm Billy. This is brother Glenn."

"Glad to meet both of you," Mr. Johnston said as he shook each of their hands. "What can I do for you?"

"Well," spoke up Glenn, "we-uns got ourselves a problem. The folks 'round these parts that knows you, claims you're damn good at helping poor folks with what 'er ails them. So that's why we come to see you."

"Please come inside and warm yourselves by the potbellied stove. I don't want you standing out there in this blustering snow."

As the three entered the building, Mr. Johnston called on Otho Boner to take over the arithmetic class. This was common practice whenever Mr. Johnston had visitors.

"Now what's the problem, fellows?" inquired Teach.

"Well, you see, it's this away," answered Billy, pausing to let his words sink in. "Me and Glenn inherited our parents' farm of three hundred acres and a house. Glenn has the house sittin' on a hundred acres of land. I have two hundred acres. Now I want to run a fence twixt our properties so when I start raisin' cattle this summer they won't stray off."

"Then what's the problem?" asked Mr. Johnston.

"We can't agree on the fence line place," said Billy. "The way Glenn steps it off 'tis twenty feet on my land and that haint f——"

"And when Billy steps it off 'tis twenty-five feet on my ground," interrupted Glenn.

"Fellows, you do have a real problem, but not one the boys and I can't solve," boasted Mr. Johnston as he put on that knowing smile of his.

"As you know, our crops didn't do nothin' this year. I only got ten bushels of corn to the acre, and Glenn didn't do no better," said Billy. "So how much is this all gonna cost us-ins?"

"Absolutely nothing, fellows."

"Now looky here, Mr. Johnston, we're poor folks, but we-uns

don't take charity from nobody, and you can bet your socks on that." He paused to let his words sink in. "How you planin' on doin' it?"

"Billy, you can't build your fence until spring. Right?" said Mr. Johnston.

"Right."

"I'll hold off teaching a unit on linear and square measures to the eighth grade arithmetic class until the January freeze sets in. Then I'll br——."

"What on earth is lin-air?" interrupted Glenn.

"That means measuring along a line, such as measuring the distance around your farm. Before your question, Glenn, I started to say that I would bring a couple of eighth grade boys, and any other pupils who care to come, to your farms on a Saturday morning. We will take the necessary measurements. Then bring the data back to the classroom where we will solve your problem as a class project. Right now I'd say you will be hearing from us about the middle of January."

After Mr. Johnston escorted the McNeals out the front door, he returned to finish teaching the eighth grade arithmetic class.

It was Monday, a week before Christmas. I chuckled to myself as I watched Archie Tucker enter the schoolhouse a few steps ahead of me that morning. I wondered what he wanted as I sat in my seat pretending to study today's reading lesson.

"Good mornin', Mr. Johnston. My name is Archie Tucker and I'm twenty-one years old."

"How can I help you, Archie?"

Archie was six feet tall, weighed 182 pounds, wore a tattered blue suit and a bright-colored bow tie. He walked with a slight limp due to a runaway horse-and-buggy accident.

"Well, Mr. Johnston, I just come back home from St. Louie because I couldn't get no good job. You see, I kaint read nor write, so no-uns would hire me. I was wonderin' if you would help me larn to read and write and cipher a liddle. I'd be glad to pay you for your time. What you say?"

"There won't be any charge, Archie. You see, my teacher's contract specifically states that I cannot charge for teaching in addition to my forty-dollar monthly salary for a seven-month term."

"That's mighty neighborly of you, Mr. Johnston, but there's one problem."

"What's that, Archie?"

"I'd need to come to school more like a visitor. You see, I kaint come every day. I have to hep Pa do some fense mendin' and other fixin' up 'round the place to pay for my board."

"How often can you report for class?"

"Sometimes I'll be here every day. At other times most likely two or three days a week. I kin start 'morrow mornin' if that's hunky-dory with you."

"That will be fine, Archie. Books begin at nine o'clock."

"Oh, there's one more thing, Mr. Johnston. Will I haf to sit with the liddle first graders?"

"No, not at all! That third seat from the rear of the second row over there is yours," said Mr. Johnston as he pointed his finger in the direction of the eighth graders' seats.

"What'll I bring with me?"

"A tablet and a pencil."

"I'll pick them up this afternoon at the village store. One more thing 'fore I leave. Must I start readin' out of a liddle ol' first grade reader?"

"No, of course not! There is nothing in the first grade reader that is of interest to you. The first page reads like this: 'I see a bird. I see a tree. The tree has limbs. The bird flew to a limb on the tree.' You would be bored to tears reading things like that."

"Then what will I read, Mr. Johnston? I'll do anything you say."

"I'll write your reading lessons, since you are my special pupil. Shortly, you will be reading subjects like hitching up a horse to a buggy, weather forecasts in a daily newspaper, items in a mail order catalogue, instructions on operating farm equipment, and any other topics that you and I come up with that are of your interest."

"Gee, Mr. Johnston, I don't know how to thank you. I know Ma and Pa will be glad, too. I jest know they'll say a prayer for you every night from tonight on. I jest can't wait to get home to tell them the good news."

"That's all for today," said Mr. Johnston as he walked with Archie to the door.

Just as Mr. Johnston turned around, Archie touched him on the right shoulder as he said, "Jest one more thing. I heard you beat the living daylights out of Jack Reeves. That was a good thing, because you're the first teach that wasn't whupped good and proper. Another thing: If any of the boys ever gang up on you, I'll jump in and twixt the two of us we'll beat the tar out of 'em."

"Thanks for your offer. I'll remember that. So long 'til tomorrow morning, Archie."

Chapter 8
Teacher Gives More Invitations

During the humdrum days that followed nothing out of the ordinary happened. Then as Christmastime was just around the corner everything took on a brighter look.

'Twas the morning before Christmas and all through the classroom the pupils were hustling and bustling in hopes this Christmas party would be the best ever.

Promptly at 8:45 A.M. Mr. Johnston and the eighth grade boys brought in a seven-foot white pine Christmas tree fastened firmly to a wooden stand.

Susan Hunter brought candles, each with an alligator-clip holder to fasten them firmly to the tree branches. With the help of volunteers, the candles were placed throughout the tree, ready to be lighted at the beginning of the party.

Mary Sloan brought a twelve-inch silver star for the very top of the tree.

Sadie Tatum, Sylvia Slavins, and Henry Ainsworth brought long strings of popcorn to help decorate the tree. Other pupils brought a variety of glass Christmas tree ornaments.

The rest of us were busy stringing red and green strips of crepe paper throughout the room.

Miss Musgraves was busy with colored chalk. She was drawing a large, beautiful picture on the blackboard, showing Santa Claus with a pack on his shoulder going down the chimney.

Some of the boys, finishing their jobs, set up the folding chairs provided by Mr. Salinger, Grand Mogul.

It was 11:30 A.M. Mr. Johnston surveyed the decorated room. Then, beaming with pride, he said, "Boys and girls and Miss Musgraves, you have done an outstanding job in decorating our classroom. I have never seen anything quite so beautiful. You have all worked hard, so let's take a long lunch hour. See you back here in one hour."

At 12:30 P.M., the parents began arriving. Mr. Johnston stood at the door, greeting each one personally and shaking his or her hand.

The women were astonished at the classroom. Then there was so much chattering that I could hardly catch a word. As they took their seats, I was able to pick up a few conversations.

"My, my, did you ever see such beautiful decorations for Christmas? I well remember when the old log schoolhouse was demolished and the new one built. Never had we anything like this," said Granny Talley to Mrs. Reeves. Granny was ninety-two years old, gray-headed, skinny as a rail and walked with a slight limp.

"Isn't Granny amazing?" said Mr. Conway to Mr. Shaw.

"Did you know she reads the daily paper without using glasses?"

"No, I didn't know that. There is something else that is most amazing. It is said she has never seen a doctor in all her ninety-two years."

"Most amazing! Most amazing!"

"Who is that beautiful young lady talking to Mr. Johnston?" Mrs. Monroe inquired of Mrs. DeWees.

"Why that's Miss Musgraves! Didn't you know?"

"No, I guess I don't get around as much as I should."

"You don't wonder Mr. Johnston sparkin' her, do you?"

"I don't know when I've seen such beautiful blond hair and sky blue eyes," said Mrs. Monroe as she pushed her fingers through her own stiff, peroxide blond hair. "If I were Mr. Johnston I'd never sleep a wink until we tied the knot."

"Me, too," sighed Mrs. DeWees.

Looking at Jacob I said, "I heard some of the boys in Benton call her a 34-32-34. I don't know what that means, but I suppose it's a compliment."

"I don't know what it means either. I'll ask Otho after the party. He knows everything about girls."

At one o'clock sharp, Mr. Johnston called our party to order. He beamed, smiling one of his big smiles as he said, "Parents, it's a genuine pleasure to have you as our guests this afternoon. The children and I extend the best of holiday greetings to all of you. We hope you enjoy yourselves." Then he asked us to bow our heads while he led us in prayer.

It wasn't healthy for anyone to mention separation of church and state as a reason for not having church services in school back then. I was playing with friends in the Benton Township play area when a stranger found that out the hard way after he complained about the Benton Township High School beginning assemblies with prayer. He filed a complaint with the board of education.

Coming out of the schoolhouse, he was seized by six men, their faces covered with red bandanna handkerchiefs.

These men scared me. I hid behind a corner of the building. Peeping around the corner, I saw a sight I'll never forget.

"Wh—— what you going to do to me?" asked the stranger as sweat ran down his face.

"How many times have you got in trouble butting in other peoples' business?" a six foot, six inch vigilante inquired.

Before he could answer, another tough laughed. Then he said, "How'd you wind up in Benton? Couldn't you get enough trouble from where'er you came from?"

"Boys, what'll we do with the old meddling son of a bitch?"

"Please, please, men," he begged, now down on his knees, "I beg of you. Don't hurt me, and I'll get out of town, never to come back."

"Oh, shut up, you whining bastard!"

"Let's take him out to the edge of town and string him up on the old hanging tree," said another one of the masked men.

"Sometimes I don't know why I put up with you knuckleheads! No one has been hanged on that tree since the turn of the century. Another thing: If you guys want to end up in the pen, that's your business," said the more passive one of the group as he started to walk away.

"Come back here, Bill. What do you suggest?"

"Look what's coming down the street, and you'll see what I sent for earlier this evening."

I looked, too. Two men were approaching the group. One had a pillow under each arm. The other one was carrying a gallon bucket of roofing tar and a wooden fence rail.

"Please, please," begged the stranger as the men tore off his clothes, leaving him, as they say, "naked as a jaybird."

While four men held the stranger spread-eagled on the ground, the fifth man poured roofing tar on his body from his feet to his neck. All the while the sixth man was covering him with feathers. Then he was ordered to straddle the rail, whereupon he was ridden out of town and ordered to never return.

Back to the party, my daydreaming over: Following prayer service we and the parents sang Christmas songs and played games. The most popular game was dunking for the apple. At three o'clock Mr. Johnston surprised us by passing out candy, oranges, and bananas. The climax of the day was giving out the presents. No one was left out, for Mr. Johnston bought several extra ones. Therefore, we all received presents whether our folks could spare the money or not. All of us could see that Mr. Johnston was mellowing.

Mr. Johnston was also full of surprises, as evidenced one morning when he invited Pvt. Henry Atkins to present his firsthand experiences in the American Civil War on the same day that the eighth graders were to begin a unit on that subject.

It was the first Tuesday in February. Promptly at nine o'clock, Private Atkins walked through the door, straight as a ramrod. Although he was seventy-two years old, hair starting to turn gray, he was still every bit the soldier after an absence of forty-nine years from military service.

After the two men exchanged greetings, Mr. Johnston introduced us to Private Atkins. Because he lived in Benton, few of us had ever seen him. Then Mr. Johnston told us all to put away our books and to listen to what Private Atkins had to say.

"Boys and girls, it's my pleasure to visit with you and Mr. Johnston this morning. I'm not going to talk about the great generals, such as Grant, Lee, Pemberton, Rosecrans, and other great officers and brave soldiers. You will be reading about them in your history books. I'm going to spend my time doing two things; namely, first, talk about happenings that, for some reason or other, never reached the history books; and second, allow you to ask questions. As I talk I want you to ask questions about anything you don't understand or want more information about.

"By the late 1850s there was heated talk about the possibility of war between the North and the South. If war came no one could predict whether southern Illinois would fight for the Union or the Confederacy. By early 1860 there was much confusion and bitterness within families; ours was no exception. Brother John, two years my junior, was a strong supporter for the South, while I was headstrong for the North. Many a time Father stepped in just about the time John and I were ready to come to blows. This wa——"

"Why didn't you just shove your father aside and slug it out?" I interrupted.

"The thought never crossed our minds, because both of us had too much respect for Father. What I started to say was that fighting never settles anything. All of us found that out after the war was over; four years of fighting and neither side really won.

"One June day, 1861, found John and me in the Benton town square. Since we lived on a farm, it was always a treat to come to town. That trip had an exceptional treat for us as we noticed a huge line of men going into a store with a huge poster overhead stating '30,000 Volunteers Wanted for the Union Army.' Below the poster on the ground was a real cannon and a man with a bull-tone voice begging men to volunteer. I signed up. When I came out, John was gone. I was to see him only one more time alive. He ran away from home to join the Confederate Army."

"Good heavens, if you knew that your brother was going to fight for the South, why didn't the two of you stick together? Why didn't you flip a coin to see which side both of you would join?" said Susan Hunter.

Shrugging his shoulders, he replied, "We had strong convictions in what we believed. Father said we were bullheaded; and I'm sure he was right.

"This is the rifle I carried for four years," he said while proudly showing us how it worked.

"Is it loaded?" I asked, excitement showing in my eyes.

He paused to let his words sink in. Then he said, "A gun is always loaded." Scanning our faces he went on. "It's the unloaded gun that kills people. I remember well the two men occupying a tent next to mine. They cleaned their rifles one Friday evening just before retiring. Of course, both rifles were put away empty. During the night one of the men couldn't sleep. He arose, put a shell in his rifle, and put it down where it had been placed earlier in the evening. The next morning his buddy, always the joker, picked up what he thought was an empty rifle. Laughing, he aimed it at a soldier passing by. 'If you were an enemy, I'd shoot you,' he said. With that he pulled the trigger of the empty gun, killing the soldier instantly."

"Was he punished?" Jack Reeves eagerly inquired.

Private Atkins laid down his rifle, folded his arms, and said nothing for a moment. "Yes, he was punished. He was given a military trial, found guilty, and shot the following morning at sunrise."

"Did he die?" quipped Joe Perkins.

"You don't live very long when six soldiers use your heart as a target," he said with a downcast look in his eyes.

"What I'm going to tell you now is morbid, but it is a part of history," he said as he pulled out a cord about three feet long tied with three knots.

"Oswald Kerner joined our company late in August. Like all of us, it was necessary for him to change from a quiet farm boy to a fighting man—if he were to survive. Somehow, he was different from the rest of us in one respect: He was sadistic. Returning to camp one evening, dancing and singing an old Indian war song, he proudly showed everyone this cord with one knot tied on it."

What did it mean? I wondered. I didn't have long to wait.

"This here, fellers, is my record cord. I know I killed one of the enemy today, so I tied a knot in this here cord. I'm going to do my best to have the whole cord tied in knots before the war ends.' However, he never had a chance to complete his project. A week later, while doing scout duty, he killed an enemy picket. A second picket nearby shot him right through the middle of his forehead."

As he was putting the cord in his left trouser pocket, he said, "I found his body the next day with this cord in both hands. He had just finished tying his third knot."

"What's a picket?" inquired Henry Ainsworth.

"A picket is a soldier placed on a line forward of a position to warn of an enemy advance."

"Other than using spies and pickets, wasn't there any other way to study troop movements?" Marvin Lucas wanted to know.

"I was coming to that, young man, when you raised the question. We used hot air balloons stationed back out of range of enemy gunfire. I was an observer in one such balloon. We fastened one end of a seventy-five-foot length of rope to a large stake driven deep into the ground, with the other end of the rope fastened to the bottom of the basket.

"Two of us ascended. As the observer I would study enemy troop movements through a spyglass, then relate them to my buddy seated next to me. He would write them on a sheet of paper, tie them around a small rock, and toss them over the side of the basket. Then a messenger, stationed on the ground, retrieved them for the commanding officer."

"That sounds good for daytime observations, but what about nighttime?" quizzed Jimmy Shaw, always the one to muddy the waters.

"Observations were satisfactory on moonlit nights. Even on pitch-black nights, we would go up to observe the location of enemy campfires.

"The history books fail to mention a very important American Civil War event known as Grant's Pass. The Confederates stretched huge log chains across the Mississippi River about sixty miles south of Memphis, Tennessee. How was Grant going to get ships past the blockade? He couldn't get men close enough to cut or dynamite the chains.

"The river was constantly shifting its course, cutting across a bend to leave behind a small lake. Moon Lake was formed by one such shift in the river. It was located only a few miles west of the blockade. Grant ordered his men to dig a canal from Moon Lake to the Mississippi River, bypassing the chains. Then he sent his ships down a small river that emptied into the lake. They moved through the canal to the river. To this day the people in Mississippi call the canal Grant's Pass. Now the ships had fairly smooth sailing until they were only a few miles from New Orleans. Here they were blocked by another set of log chains stretched across the river. With his heavily armed ships, Admiral Farragut blasted any enemy soldiers or ships that dared come near. Then he commanded his men to cut the chains, giving the Union full control of the entire river."

Mr. Atkins described several engagements he and his company fought, and commented on the number of men killed and injured on both sides. Then he said, "In every barrel of apples, there are always a few rotten ones. The same thing can be said about a group of men. Both sides had a few men that were rotten to the core. These men sacked and plundered every home and store of both sides, the North and the South. Word soon got around of these ludicrous acts.

"The men were away at war, so the women buried the silverware and small artifacts in their garden plots. There was one bright side, however. When our captain discovered such deplorable acts, he made the guilty return every item they plundered. He personally went with them to see that the job was done. Then he had the men return to camp for food, blankets, and anything else the women needed. You may be interested to know that this order of generosity originated from no other one than your own southern Illinois general, John A. Logan."

We sensed the lecture was nearing the end, when Jacob Boner jumped out of his seat and blurted, "Private Atkins, how many enemies did you kill?"

Standing first on one foot then on the other one, Private Atkin's smile changed to a face of sadness. After a few moments of silence, he said, "Killing and injuring splendid young men is a subject I dislike talking about. As the years go by, I dislike it more and more. War is hell! Right at this very moment many young men in Europe are finding this out firsthand in their own war.

"When you and your buddies are shooting at the enemy, standing only seventy-five yards or less apart, and the enemy is shooting at you, it's hard to tell who shoots whom."

Holding up his left hand, he said, "Can you see this scar in the palm of my hand? I'm one of the lucky ones. After four years of fighting, this is what I have to show for it.

"One night I was doing picket duty when a Confederate took a potshot at me, hitting the palm of my left hand. The lead slug never went through. We were too far from base camp to get medical help, so I bandaged it the best I could. The slug is still there, and it doesn't cause any pain."

He concluded his lecture by congratulating us on being a very attentive audience, shook hands with Mr. Johnston, and then walked out the door the same way he came in—straight as a ramrod.

As Jacob and I were walking down the lane that afternoon on our way home, neither one of us was saying anything. Then, out of the blue, Jacob blurted out, "Why do you think old Egghead softened up? Do you think it's because he's in love?"

"No, Jacob, I don't think so."

"He was an old battle-ax for about two months. Since his fight with Jack, he's getting soft as apple pie."

"That's it, Jacob."

"What's it, Charles? I don't see the connection."

"Remember when I told you he was hired primarily because he was a boxer?"

"Yes, but what has that got to do with it?"

"Everything, Jacob. I see it this way. He started out tough and mean, hoping one of the older boys, sooner or later, would start a fight. Then he would give him a good whipping. That finished, he would put fighting on the shelf and devote full time to being a good teacher."

"Well, Charles, if that's so, why didn't he challenge Otho when he threatened Teach the time I was due for a paddling?"

"That was my question, too. So I put it to Father for an answer. He said a fight that early in the term would have worked against Teach. The parents would have thought of him as a mean, mean old skunk. By the time the fight came around, most of the parents had a soft spot in their hearts for him."

By this time we had reached the *T*. I turned to the right as I said, "See you in the morning, Jacob."

"Same here, pal. Sleep tight tonight. Don't let the bedbugs bite," answered Jacob grinning like a possum eating persimmons.

Chapter 9
Education beyond the Classroom

During the past few days, other than a big snowstorm, everything was unremarkable. Then, suddenly the sun popped out. The temperature climbed to the midseventies.

It was a beautiful Saturday morning near the end of February. Mr. Johnston, the eighth grade pupils, and a few of us stragglers went to the McNeals' property. First, they measured the total acreage. Next, they measured the number of acres each brother was entitled to own. Then they went Glenn's house.

"Good mornin', Mr. Johnston and all you fine young-uns. Come inside and sit a spell. There's room for all of you in the parlor," greeted Glenn.

"Mr. McNeal, we c——"

Mr. McNeal interrupted Mr. Johnston. "Please call me Glenn and call my brother Billy. We're just ole plain country folks."

"OK, Glenn. Since it's going to be a clear, warm day for February, we came to finish our job. I know we promised to visit during the middle of January, but the weather was too bad for us to do a good job for you and Billy."

"Oh, make no never mind of that. Billy won't build the fence until next month no how," said Glenn.

"Shall we go to Billy's house?"

"No. We'll send for him to come here."

Since no telephones were in our community, other than in Royalton, I wondered how Billy would know. I didn't have long to wait.

Glenn opened the back door as he called, "Here, Gyp. Come here, boy."

The most beautiful dalmatian dog I ever saw came on the double, wearing a beautiful collar and walking as proud as a peacock. Glenn said he was six years old. Glenn wrote a note, and tied it to Gyp's collar.

"Go to Billy's house," said Glenn as he pointed his right hand in that direction.

Gyp leaped off the porch. Then he dashed, straight as an arrow in flight, toward his destination. Glenn returned to the parlor.

"Does Gyp understand English?" queried Mr. Johnston.

"I don't rightly know, Mr. Johnston. He's been carryin' messages now well nigh on three years. Gyp is only half of it."

"What's the other half?" Mr. Johnston inquired.

"Billy owns Gyp's brother, named Simon. He brings messages to me from Billy in the same way."

All Mr. Johnston could say, was, "I'll be doggone."

In a matter of minutes both Billy and Gyp entered the house. All of us wanted to pet the dog, but Mr. Johnston put a stop to that, saying, "We must get down to business.

"Gentlemen," said Mr. Johnston, "you never inherited three hundred acres."

"I don't want to 'barrass you in front of the young-uns, but Daddy wouldn't lie to us," said Billy.

"That's right," agreed Glenn.

"Glenn, let me see your abstract," Mr. Johnston requested.

"Just as I suspected. It says, in part, 'three hundred acres more or less.' That means you have x number of acres over three hundred or x number of acres less than three hundred. In your case, it's less."

"How many acres did we inherit?" Glenn wanted to know as he fidgeted in his chair.

"We took accurate measurements. Both of you inherited less than three hundred acres between the two of you. There is no need to return to the classroom to figure your problem."

"How'd you know that from a few ole measly measures?" Bill inquired.

"Really, Billy, it is not complicated at all. Our measurements show both of you inherited 44,800 square rods. There are 160 square rods in one acre. Therefore, both of you together own 280 acres, not 300.

"Your share, Billy is 186 2/3 acres, while your share, Glenn, is 93 1/3 acres."

Before we went home, Mr. Johnston, two of the boys, and I took measurements to show Billy the correct fence line location.

I have no way of knowing the reason, but Teach had begun to treat me as if I were one of the older boys. This did much to swell my ego.

It was the last week in February. The weather was warm. The rain poured down on the schoolhouse's tin roof.

I should study my lessons, I thought, *not sit here wishing that I was at some other place, anyplace but school.*

Soon I was staring straight at my reader, but not seeing a single word. I was reliving the spelling match we had the last Friday afternoon with the Nine-Mile School pupils. Throughout the year we had a total of eleven spelling matches among our own pupils to prepare for the big match.

"Charles!" Mr. Johnston barked, "you are spending a lot of time reading that one page. What's the problem?"

"No problem, Mr. Johnston."

For the remainder of the study period, I turned a page now and then, but I never saw a single word. All that was in my mind was the spelling match.

Reverend Brown officiated. As one would expect, he was fair, honest, and impartial.

It was two o'clock when we took our seats on the north side of the room. The Nine-Mile School pupils were already seated on the south side when we entered. Reverend Brown was seated at the teacher's desk. Mr. Johnston and the host teacher, Mr. Applegate, sat in adjoining seats near the door.

"Time to begin," announced Reverend Brown. "Stand and form a line on your side of the room."

Jacob and I were worried. We knew we could not spell as well as the "big kids." However, Reverend Brown took care of that. He gave us smaller children easy words to spell, saving the more difficult ones for the seventh and eighth graders.

The match went on for more than an hour, pupils taking their seats when they misspelled a word. Now, only Michael Epstein, our champion speller, and Andy House, the opposition's champion, remained standing.

Everyone was tense, yet a sense of calm settled over the room.

You could hear a mouse running across the floor. Everyone wanted his champion to win. But who would win was the question.

"Is anything wrong?" Reverend Brown asked Andy.

"No, of course not."

"Your hands are shaking. Are you feeling well?"

Andy laughed nervously. "I'm not sick! Let's get on with it!"

"OK. Here's your first word," he said as he looked at Andy. "Remembering."

"Remembering," said Andy. "R-e-m-e-m-b-e-r-i-n-g."

"Correct." Looking at Michael the reverend pronounced the word *ostracize*.

"Ostracize. O-s-t-r-a-c-i-z-e," said Michael as quickly as I would have spelled *cat*.

"Correct."

This battle of wits went on for about thirty minutes, each champion as sure of himself as if he was reading the words right out of a dictionary. Then it happened!

"Mississippi," said Reverend Brown, looking straight at Andy.

"Mississippi. M-i-s-s-i-s-i-p-i," responded Andy.

"Sorry son, that is not correct. Take your seat. Mississippi."

"Mississippi," said Michael, beaming with pride. "M-i-s-s-i-s-s-i-p-p-i."

"That is correct, and you, my boy, are the new champion speller of the day. Congratulations!"

Everyone stood up, giving Michael a big round of applause. All of us began to leave when Mrs. Epstein stood up. There were about twenty-five parents in the audience, but Mrs. Epstein had something she wanted to say.

"I have here in my hand an order signed by Mr. Epstein to present to the winner. However, since my son won the match, it wouldn't be right to give him the prize. Come here, Andy. You are the winner of your school. You deserve the prize."

"Thank you, Mrs. Epstein. I know my mother and father will thank you, too. They were sorry they could not be here this afternoon."

"That's understandable, Andy. Don't give it another thought," said Mrs. Epstein.

Mr. Applegate stood up and walked briskly to Mrs. Epstein. "This is a very noble thing you did today. I really appreciate your generosity. You are a kind and gentle lady, and all of us are glad to have you, Mr. Epstein, and Michael in our neighborhood."

"I agree with everything Mr. Applegate said, and I wish you, your husband, and Michael nothing but the very best," said Mr. Johnston.

"You are most kind, Mr. Johnston. I'll certainly relate both of your gentlemen's kind words to my husband."

The order was a splendid prize, indeed. It called for a pair of trousers, a shirt, a tie, and a cap, all for free.

A knock on the door brought me back to reality. The spelling match was over and done with. *Forget it*, I thought.

"Answer the door, Loren. I'm busy completing a report for the county superintendent," said Mr. Johnston.

"Aw, heck, Teach, why do you always call on me to answer the door when you're busy?"

"I call on you because you know how to welcome guests, and you're a pretty nice guy, most of the time."

We got a bang out of that, and I laughed until I thought my sides would split.

"Oh, all right, I'll do it this time!" Loren was mumbling something inaudible as he stumbled along to open the door. It wasn't complimentary, that I'm sure.

"Mornin', Loren. I wants to see Mr. Johnston," said Ella Mae Taylor.

"Come on in, Ella Mae," shouted Mr. Johnston seated at his desk.

Everyone knew Ella Mae. She was eighteen years old, never went to school a day in her life, wore a plain gingham dress, a light brown sweater, and her curls set off her beautiful face as they dropped just below the brim of her brown hat. All of us admired her as she walked ladylike toward Mr. Johnston.

"How can I help you, Ella Mae?"

"Do you all have any rotten pepper?"

"Well, Ella Mae, what on earth do you want with rotten pepper?" queried Mr. Johnston as he was momentarily at a loss for words.

"Wal, it's this away. Mommy wants to rot a ledder to her sis over there in Ohier. But she doesn't have none of those rotten things to rot with."

"I see. I see," he said, as if he didn't believe what he was hearing. "Ella Mae, do you remember that fire sale Hanson's General Store had last August in Benton?"

"Oh! Sure enough. I members it. Mommy bought a real pretty set of pillars there for well nigh nothin'."

Mr. Johnston was silent for a few moments as he shuffled through the bottom drawer on the right side of his desk. Then he placed a tablet, three pencils, and a sheet of two-cent stamps on top of it.

"Ella Mae, I bought some real bargains there also. When I asked for a tablet and a pencil, the clerk said, 'This is a fire sale, mister. We don't make small sales. You'll buy in large lots, or do without.' So I bought in large lots," said Mr. Johnston as he laughed more to himself than to us.

"Now looky here, Mr. Johnston, if you're figgerin' on giving me somethin' for nothin', I won't hanker to it. My daddy won't take no charity. No, sir, he won't!"

"Ella Mae, I have no intention of giving you anything."

"You don't?" said Ella Mae, slightly bewildered.

"No, I don't. Just listen to me for a moment. Hear me out. Then if you don't agree with me, we'll forget the whole thing, just act like nothing happened."

"I 'pologise, Mr. Johnston. I won't butt in again. I won't say nary a word."

"Michael, get your pencil and tablet out of your desk. Then bring them here."

"I left my tablet at home. May I bring my slate?"

"Certainly. Take your place on the recitation seat, and write down the figures I give you. We'll make this an arithmetic lesson. Twenty tablets, $.80; fifty pencils, $1.50; twenty two-cent stamps, $.40; fifty envelopes, $.25. Michael, let's see how quickly you can tell me the cost of each item."

While Michael was working on his assignment, Mr. Johnston inquired about Ella Mae's mother's and father's health, the crops they intended to plant this year, and, of course, the weather. It seems that everyone talked about the weather, but no one could do anything about it.

"I'm finished," said Michael proudly. "Here's the cost of each item: one tablet, $.04; one pencil, $.03; one stamp, $.02; one envelope, half a cent."

Michael beamed as brightly as the morning star as he stood up, ready to return to his seat.

"Not yet, Michael. I have another assignment for you. Figure the cost of six tablets, three pencils, twelve stamps, and one dozen envelopes."

"Now, looky here, Mr. Johnston. If you're planning on giving me them thar things, I hain't 'bout to take 'em for nothin'."

"You're not getting these for nothing. At forty dollars a month for seven months, there is no way I can give things away. I just can't afford it."

"I'm glad to hear you-all say that. We just don't take no charity."

"Ella Mae, did you ever hear of barter?"

"No, I don't rightly say I have."

"Barter means to exchange one thing for another thing. For example, the other day Jack Reeves traded one agate for two of Curtis Talley's apples. Now, do you understand the meaning of barter?"

"Yes, I think so; but how can we-uns all barder?"

"I'm glad you asked that question, Ella Mae. Michael, how much does Ella Mae owe me?"

"The way I figure it, Ella Mae owes you a total of $.63: six tablets, $.24; three pencils, $.09; twelve stamps, $.24; twelve envelopes, $.06. total $.63."

"Ella Mae, you owe me sixty-three cents. Is that satisfactory with you?"

"That's mighty fair. Now, how are we going to do that thar barder, Mr. Johnston?"

"Well, Ella Mae, I happen to know that your mother's cherry pies took blue ribbons at the county fair for the past six years. Cherry pies cost thirty cents each at the village bakery, and I like nothing better to eat than a cherry pie. How about exchanging two of them for these writing materials?"

"That's more than fair. I'll bring you-all three pies, one for good measure."

"No! Ella Mae, I too, don't take charity. Two pies or the deal is off!"

"OK," said Ella Mae as she picked up the writing materials and skipped out the door.

As usual, I did my assignments at home the previous evening, leaving nothing to study at school. So I spent my free time either staring off into space or daydreaming. Seeing Ella Mae reminded me of my visit with Father last August to the Taylor home where we were to pick up a pointer bird dog pup. I began daydreaming again.

We rode horseback. As Father was tying old Ned to the rickety hitching post, the front door opened.

"Come in, come in, gentlemen, and a welcome to you all," called Mrs. Taylor. Shaking our hands, she invited us into the house.

"Thank you, Mrs. Taylor. I know you folks are busy, so if you will show us which pup to take, we'll be on our way."

"Nonsense, nonsense. Come in and sample my fresh cherry pie with a cup of java. Jed's out in the barn. I'm sure he seed you all a comin'. So he'll be here in a jiffy. In the meanwhile, you-all come into the parlor while I heat some water to make coffee."

We heard the back screen door squeaking followed by a bang. "I'll fix that door one of these days!" Mr. Taylor said angrily as he slammed the door.

Mr. Taylor smiled as he came into the parlor. He was barefoot, had on a pair of overalls and a blue work shirt.

"Long time no see," he remarked as he shook Father's hand. "Glad you brought the young-un along. While you are here, I'm gonna larn him somethin' he ain't never gonna larn in that school."

I thought he was a strange one. I wondered what I could learn from him that I couldn't learn in school. *Oh, well*, I thought, *just wait and see.*

"When's the pie and coffee gonna be ready, Ma?"

"Now jest hold your horses, Jed. Give me five minutes more, give or take a minute."

"How 'bout a little snort while we-uns are waitin'?" asked Jed.

"Don't mind if I do," replied Father with a gleam in his eyes.

Mr. Taylor left the room, returning with a gallon crock jug. "Take a swig of this," he said as he passed the jug to Father.

"I've never tasted better whiskey. Is it bottled and bond?"

"Hell, no! It's some of my good ole moonshine. Make it myself. Taste mighty good, don't it? Take another——"

Just then Mrs. Taylor brought in the cherry pie and coffee. After taking the first bite, I could well understand how her pies always won blue ribbons when she entered them at the county fair.

When we finished eating, Mr. Taylor was quick to say, "How 'bout another snort?"

"No, thank you, Jed. We'll pick up the pup and be on our way, if you don't mind," said Father as he stood up and started for the door.

Mr. Taylor smiled and gave us a knowing glance. "Come out to the smokehouse if you-all got a minute. Got somethin' out there I'm most proud of," he said as he led us out through the back door.

As we entered the smokehouse, I got the shock of my life. I had never seen anything like it. *What is it?* I wondered. *Is this what I'm going to learn about?* There was a coal-fired kitchen range connected to a crude brick chimney. In back of the range, almost touching it, was a wooden barrel. I would guess it to hold about forty gallons.

"This is half-full of mash," Mr. Taylor said as he proudly pointed his finger toward the barrel.

"It looks like brown water. What's it made of?" Father inquired as he looked inside the barrel.

"I mixes ground corn, yeast, and water. When hit ferments, I puts hit in this here still," he said proudly as he pointed to a large boiler he called a still.

The twenty-gallon still was made of copper with an inverted conical cover. Three clamps held it firmly to the boiler. The still sat on top of the range lids. A copper pipe fastened to the top of the boiler led to a washtub. Inside the tub the copper pipe was formed into a coil with the lower end extending through the bottom of the tub. Also, there was a gadget fastened to the top of the boiler. Later, I learned this was a pressure gauge, removed from a pressure cooker.

"When the mash boils, steam travels through this here copper pipe tubin'. The cool water in the tub changes the steam to whiskey and drains into a gallon jug settin' on the floor," explained Mr. Taylor. Then Mr. Taylor told us the water used to cool the coil came from a sixty-gallon steel barrel firmly anchored to a five-foot wooden stand placed just to the right of the range. A hand-operated pitcher pump, firmly fastened to the top of the barrel, supplied the water from a cistern located outside the smokehouse. The bottom of the barrel was connected with a three-quarter-inch water pipe to the top of the tub, mounted on a wooden stand in such a way that the top of the tube's

For having a whiskey still in his smokehouse, Jed Taylor was arrested, convicted, and sent to the county jail for six months. The sheriff confiscated the still and destroyed it. Shortly after Mr. Taylor was released from jail, he installed another still similar to the one shown above, in the thick of Black Bottom Swamp.

rim was slightly lower than the bottom of the barrel. A gate valve was used to control the water flow into the tub.

One end of a second gate valve was connected to the bottom of the tub with the opposite end connected to a three-quarter-inch pipe leading through the floor, then to the yard.

By operating the two valves Mr. Taylor could keep the water in the tub at the correct temperature required for the distillation process.

"My, my, what a setup," Father said as if he still couldn't believe what he was seeing.

"There's one more thing," said Mr. Taylor as he led us across the room to an oak barrel half full of charcoal mounted on a solid wooden stand. "When I gets me twenty or twenty-five full jugs of whiskey, I brings it over here and pours it into this here barrel. Then I opens this here spigot at the bottom of the barrel and drains out the whiskey. The charcoal takes out most of the not purities. This makes real good whiskey."

"Yes," Father corrected, "impurities."

"Next, I adds flavoring and coloring, makin' the whiskey look and taste damn near as good as store-bought. If I've a mind to make high-powered whiskey, I runs it through the still two or three times before I filters it in the charcoal barrel."

"Why do you do that?" Father wanted to know.

"Wal, every time it's stilled, the more alkyhol you-all gets. Run through once, gets you-all about 80 proof or about 40 percent alcohol. Run it through again, and you-all gets about 150 proof or 75 percent alcohol."

"So you see, my welcome visitors, what do you think?"

"Aahhh! I'm lost for words. In all my born days, I've never seen such a setup," answered Father, meaning every word of it.

"It's eleven o'clock," Father said as he looked at his large railroad pocket watch. "Let's pick up the pup. Then we'll be on our way."

"What's the hurry? Ma ud like to give you-all some more cherry pie and coffee before you leave."

"That's most kind of you," said Father. "I'd sure take you up on that offer, but I promised the wife I would dig a lettuce bed this afternoon."

With the pup in my arms, we mounted old Ned.

As we started for home, Father remarked, "Seeing exactly how whiskey is made is an experience added to your education, son. It's just something that isn't taught in school. And maybe it shouldn't be," he added more as an afterthought. "Son, what's the matter with you? Are you feeling sick?"

"No, Father, why do you ask?"

"Well, you haven't said a single word since we left Mr. Taylor's house. Usually, you talk the legs off the table."

"I've been wondering. That's all."

"Wondering? For God's sake, what about?"

"I was wondering how the two gate valves work that Mr. Taylor showed us. Do you know how they work?"

"Why, yes, I do. They control the flow of water from the barrel to the washtub then out into the yard. The amount of water flowing through the pipes is controlled by means of a gate inside each valve. Did you notice the small wheel on the top of each valve?"

"Why, yes. But what are they for?"

"They control the water flow inside the pipes. As Mr. Taylor turns the wheels, the gates inside the valves open, shut, or partially obstruct the opening in the passageways at his option. Comprehend?"

"Sure do. You do a better job of teaching than Mr. Johnston does. You should be a teacher instead of a coal miner."

"Hogwash, son. Flattery won't get you anywhere. You're still going to clean the living room rug this afternoon."

My daydreaming over, I spent the remainder of my study period reviewing material for my next class.

Chapter 10
My Final Month as a Pupil

Classes ended and classes began day after day. All I could think of however was one more month and I'd be free of the spider's web.

"School's out, school's out. Teach let the monkeys out," shouted Jacob as he jumped from the porch to the ground. Scooping up both hands full of snow, then forming it into a hard snowball, he pelted Mary Sloan in the back of the head.

"You dirty little devil, Jacob Boner!" she screamed.

Whirling around, she took after Jacob. Being a tomboy and as quick as a deer, she soon caught up to him and overpowered him.

"This 'ill teach you to mind your manners, you little sawed-off runt!" she said as she threw him to the ground and rubbed his face in the snow. "You ever do this again, I'll mash your face to a pulp. Now, get up and get the heck out of here!" she admonished him as she picked up her books and started for home.

I just stood by, paying little attention to the scrap between Jacob and Mary. My thoughts were focused on the development of the day thus far. This was the first school day in March, and it came in like a lion. Snow began falling around eleven o'clock that morning, and the wind began blowing harder and harder as the day wore on.

Because of the blustery weather and the eighteen-inch snow, Mr. Johnston dismissed school at 3 P.M. He warned us of the dangers accompanying a blizzard if one developed and told us to go straight home and not to loiter on the way.

Jacob arose. Brushing the snow from his face, he said, "I'll get even with that she-devil Mary, if it's the last thing I do! Ready to go home, Charles?"

"I'm in a hurry to get home, so I'll not be walking down the lane with you today."

"Which way are you going?"

"I'm taking the shortcut across Jim Snider's field," I answered.

"Are you crazy? I wouldn't be caught dead in that field."

"Why not?" I wanted to know.

"Why not? Old Man Snider's bull won't let a living thing trespass. That's why."

"With the snow blowing so hard, I don't think the bull can see his hoofs below his face. And, besides, with this kind of weather, he is probably in the barn with the rest of the animals," I said as I crawled over the fence and began trudging across the field.

For the next twenty minutes everything was OK, or so I thought. Then the wind began picking up speed and the snow began falling faster than ever. If the bull was in the pasture, I was now certain he couldn't see his hoofs below his face, for a full-scale blizzard was moving in fast.

I began to worry. *Am I walking in circles?* I wondered. I knew that when people are lost, they generally walk in circles, and I was lost, no doubt about it.

Seconds later, I fell head-on into a ditch full of snow. Getting to my feet I realized I had walked too far to the east. I had fallen into a drainage ditch with only my head sticking above the snow. The blizzardlike wind had completely filled the ditch with snow.

I knew my life was over if I didn't get out and get out soon.

Walking along the bottom of the ditch, I put both hands on the bank, feeling for something to hold onto, a sapling, a weed, a rock, anything. No luck. No matter how hard I tried to climb out, I always slipped back to the bottom. I was trapped, no doubt about it.

After what seemed like hours, I began to feel sleepy. *No, no, I mustn't fall asleep*, I said to myself. *Could this be a dream?* I pinched my cheek with my right hand. *No, it is not a dream.* The temperature was getting colder and colder. The blowing snow was blistering my face and my hands were getting numb. I could hardly feel the top of the bank as I continued searching for something to grip.

Soon I realized that getting out on my own was impossible. With what strength I had in me I began to shout, "Help, help, help!"

Knowing the possibility of anyone hearing me was very remote, I kept on shouting for help anyway. I had attended Sunday school regularly, and I had faith in the Lord. This faith, I'm sure, gave me added strength to shout louder and louder as I became weaker and weaker. Then I saw them through the swirling snow: two figures. Was I dreaming or was this for real?

I shouted with all the strength left in my ebbing body. "Help! Help! Help me!"

"Did you hear that?" said one of the figures, his words almost inaudible.

"No, I don't hear anything but this cursed blowing wind. Let's get out of here and get out fast!"

"No, no. Over there. I think I see something. Come along, Harry. Let's have a look-see."

"All right, Arvin, but let's make it quick. This weather isn't fit for man or beast!"

Nearing the ditch Arvin shouted, "I know him. That's the Neal boy."

Both men leaped into the ditch. In a matter of seconds they boosted me to safety.

My voice was so weak I could hardly talk. I never was so glad to see anyone in my life, including Santa Claus.

When both men climbed out of the ditch, Arvin pulled off his heavy woolen topcoat and wrapped it around my body. At the same time Harry jerked off his woolen stocking cap and pulled it down over my head. It went all the way down to my shoulders, so he rolled it up around my ears, leaving my nose and eyes exposed.

I was so weak I couldn't stand up. "Am I going to die?" I said.

"No, of course not," said Arvin laughing as he picked me up off the snowbank. "We are taking you home."

Arvin and Harry took turns carrying me until they turned me over to Mother. By that time I was as warm as a bug in a rug, and I had completely regained my voice.

When Father came home, he told me that both Arvin and Harry were coal miners. They were on their way home from work when they found me. Had school been dismissed at four o'clock, the usual time, the miners would have been long gone. Then I would have frozen to death, no doubt about it.

"Father, are you going to pay them a reward?" I inquired.

"No, of course not! You should know better than to ask. They would feel highly insulted if I so much as offered them money."

"You mean you're not going to give them anything for saving my life? I think you're real m———"

Father broke in. "I didn't say that. Harry and Arvin don't have a garden. So I'll send each one a bushel of apples and a bushel of sweet potatoes this fall. This is the way we repay kindness around here."

As Jacob and I walked to school that Thursday morning following the snowstorm, I wasn't much company. I hadn't slept well the night before. I was bothered. I couldn't make heads or tails out of my assignment on fractions.

"What's the matter, Charles? We're halfway to school, and you haven't said more than two words."

"There's nothing the matter!"

"Nothing?"

"No, nothing!"

"Now don't hand me that baloney. I've known you too long not to know when something is bothering you. What is it?"

"Well, if you must know, I can't understand my assignment on fractions. I could kill Teach for promoting me to second grade before the end of the term!"

"Couldn't you get help from your parents?"

"No. Father went only to the third grade, and Mother is in bed suffering from the grippe."

"Couldn't you learn from the examples given in the book?"

"No, and neither could Father. He said the instructions were confusing, and the examples given were only for the easy problems."

By this time we were entering the school yard, and I was fearing the upcoming arithmetic class. I feared it and the whipping I was sure to get for not having learned my assignment. I feared it so much that I wore two pairs of trousers and two shirts to help lighten the blows that I was sure would come from Mr. Johnston's hickory switch.

Mr. Johnston rapped on the desk. "Second grade arithmetic class come to the recitation seat."

We all shuffled forward and took our places on the big seat.

"Ida, what is the answer to one-fourth plus one-fourth?"

"Two-fourths, I guess?"

"Don't you know for sure?"

"Yes, I'm sure."

"One-half plus one-half?"

"One."

"One-half plus one-third?"

Ida was silent for several moments, hung her head, mumbled something, but really didn't say anything.

"Speak up, speak up, Ida!"

"Don't know."

"Does anyone know?" said Mr. Johnston, looking disappointed. No one answered.

"Class, take your place at the blackboard."

Teach dictated several problems dealing with fractions. There were only a few correct answers, and these were for the easy ones. It was self-evident that what we knew about fractions could be put on the head of a pin.

"Class, return to the recitation seat," he said as he shuffled around in the top drawer of his desk, finally bringing out a round piece of cardboard marked into six triangles. Then he said an amazing thing.

"I'm not disappointed with you for not learning your assignment. Your arithmetic books give the poorest instructions and examples of fractions that I have ever seen. So no one gets a whipping for not learning his lesson."

Ida Mae almost fell out of her seat laughing. Then she giggled. Everyone in the room bit his or her cheeks to keep from laughing out loud. I felt as if a big load had been lifted from my shoulders.

"What's so funny, Ida Mae?" Mr. Johnston folded his arms as he said, "Ida Mae, I'm waiting for an answer, and my patience has just about run out."

"I am sorry, Teach. My laughing had nothing to do with you or the lesson. I just thought of a funny joke I read about last evening, and I couldn't hold back a laugh."

"Tell us about it. Maybe we'll all get a laugh."

"Reverend Brown was driving his new Model T Ford on a country lane when he saw Egbert Stein looking over his cornfield.

" 'Good morning, Brother Egbert. You and the Lord are raising a fine field of corn, the best I've seen in these parts.'

" 'Yes, sir, Reverend, but you should have seen this field when the Lord had it by himself.'

"Laugh and get it over with," said Mr. Johnston as he gave out with a big horselaugh. "Now let's get down to business. Charles, how many triangles do you see in this circle we'll call a pie," Mr. Johnston said as he handed the piece of cardboard to me.

"Six."

"What is the name of each piece?"

"One-sixth."

"Correct."

"Now, Charles, what is one-sixth plus one-sixth?"

"Two-sixths."

"Look at the piece closely: What part of this circle is two-sixths?"

"One-third."

"Correct. Later, I'll teach you formulae for solving problems in fractions. You will be doing addition, multiplication, and division of fractions long before the term ends. For a few days, we'll solve them by looking at parts of the circle. I'll be bringing in pies made up of different fractions, such as thirds, fourths, sixteenths, etc. These kinds of devices are called 'seeing aids.' I learned about using them when I attended the university."

There was no doubt about it. Mr. Johnston had a mean streak in him. But there was also a compassionate side hidden somewhere in that long, lean body of his. He must have spent hours after school preparing visual objects to better present his subject matter.

As I reflect on my first year in school, I cannot recall a time that Mr. Johnston dealt in abstractions when concrete examples would present a clearer picture. Also, I remember him spending numerous recess periods and noon hours helping slow learners with their lessons.

The following Saturday was a beautiful, warm sunshiny day. The robins were pulling worms out of the ground. The mockingbirds were chattering their usual pirated songs. The redbirds, all decked out in their bright plumage, were chirping as they flew from treetop to treetop.

"What a beautiful day," I said to Jimmy Shaw as we began a marble game in his front yard.

It was such a pleasant day that Mrs. Shaw was doing the family ironing on the front porch. I looked at my watch. It was 10:45 exactly when she stopped ironing to bring Jimmy and me some lemonade and cookies.

"Charles, who's that roaring this way in a Model T Ford sedan?" Jimmy asked as Mrs. Shaw resumed her ironing.

"I don't know," I replied. "There's one thing for sure. He's driving wide open."

"Then he'll be doing thirty miles an hour," gleefully shouted Jimmy.

The car came to a sudden stop at the front gate. Two men got out and walked slowly to the front porch.

"Mor'n, Mrs. Shaw," they said as they removed their hats.

"Mor'n to you'all," she said as she kept right on ironing.

"We've some bad news," said the tall man, who was wearing a black-and-white checkered suit, black tie, black shoes, and a navy blue felt hat.

"Well, spill it out, mister! I've heard bad news before."

"Your husband committed suicide. He drowned himself in the big swimming hole in Little Muddy River."

"Well, it's about time. He's been talking about it for six months," said Mrs. Shaw as she kept right on with her ironing.

"We're so sorry, ma'am, to bring you this bad news. What can we do to help?"

"Call the undertaker in Benton. He'll know what to do."

All this time Jimmy was crying his heart out. I did what I could to comfort him, but what can one say at a time like this that is really helpful.

The thing that bothers me to this day is the horrible memory of Mrs. Shaw continuing to iron, not once trying to console her son.

Arriving home, I said to Father, "Did you know Mr. Shaw committed suicide?"

"Yes. In fact, I was asked to help remove the body from the creek."

"What happened? Did he accidentally fall in?" I couldn't believe he committed suicide.

"No. You know that steep hill on the east side of Little Muddy River just above the big swimming hole, don't you?"

"Why, yes. That's where Otho taught me how to swim."

"Do you think you could lie down on the hill about twenty feet above the water, wrap bailing wire around your legs, arms, and hands, then roll down the hill into the water to drown yourself?"

"No, I sure couldn't, and I don't think Mr. Shaw could have either."

"Exactly. He didn't."

"Then what happened?" I inquired curiously.

"It was murder, and I'm confident I know who did it. However, I don't have enough evidence that would hold up in court."

Then Father explained the facts of life to me. He told me that Mr. Shaw was, in the coroner's opinion, "poor white trash." By calling the death a suicide, neither he nor the sheriff had to spend time making an investigation. He told me further that Mr. Shaw was a habitual gambler, that it was common knowledge he was head over heels in debt to the professional gamblers in Benton. Being a poor dirt farmer, there was no way he could obtain enough money to pay his debts. Since a gambling debt was illegal, it could not be brought to court. The other alternative was murder. This was one way to teach petty gamblers not to bet more than they could afford to lose.

One cool March morning I came to school with a bursting headache. Mr. Johnston felt my forehead.

"Your head is hot and your eyes are watery. Stay inside until books. If you're not feeling better, I'll have one of the older boys take you home."

"Dummy, dummy, dummy, Mike Monroe is a dummy," shouted Marvin Lucas as Mike ran into the front door of the schoolhouse, crying on his way to his seat.

For Mike, life had been full of hard knocks from the beginning. He was still crawling when other children his age were beginning to walk; he was two and a half years old before he learned to talk. At an early age children began picking on him, including his sister and two brothers.

Mike was destined for difficulties even before he was born. His genes played tricks on him. He weighed six pounds at birth; his face was long and narrow; he was underweight and had club feet.

When he started school, the teacher noticed another problem: Mike couldn't recognize numbers or pictures on flash cards unless they were held close to his eyes. He was fitted with glasses. They didn't help too much, since he was almost blind in one eye. Later eye surgery corrected that.

Looking up from a book he was reading, Mr. Johnston said, "Mike, come up here and sit beside me."

Mike began to cry. Wiping tears from his eyes he shuffled down the aisle. "Am I stupid?" he asked Teach.

"No, no, of course not! Why do you ask?"

"Marvin always calls me a dummy. Yesterday, I looked up the word in the dictionary. It said a dummy is a stupid person, that's why I asked."

"The definition is correct. That's why you are not a dummy."

"How come?"

"You are not stupid. Every person is different from every other person. No two people are exactly alike in looks, in weight, in personality, in intelligence, and in athletic accomplishments."

"I never knew that. I feel better already."

"Let's face it. You don't make passing grades all the time. However, when I present a subject to you several times, you get the message. The same is true when you read your lessons a number of times. Then you get passing marks. This proves you are not dumb. With a little more effort on your part, you can do as well as anyone else in your class.

"Mike, there are many more things to learn than reading, writing, and arithmetic. Who's the fastest runner in your class?"

Bowing his head and looking sheepish, Mike said, "I am."

"Who guessed the weight of the fat lady and won the prize at the county fair last August?"

Grinning from ear to ear, he said, "I did!"

"Do you know why Marvin calls you dummy?"

"I guess because he doesn't like me."

"How many friends does he have?"

"None that I know of. Almost everyone hates him."

"OK. How many friends do you have?"

"I guess everyone but Marvin."

"You see. He's jealous of you. That's why he calls you a dummy. I'll take care of him," mumbled Mr. Johnston as if talking to himself. "Mike, remember this for the rest of your life: Making friends is just as important as making 100 in arithmetic, maybe a great deal more important. Now, run out and play. You have seven minutes 'til books."

Just before Mr. Johnston dismissed us for recess, he asked Marvin to remain in his seat. After laying on the hickory switch for twenty-five whacks, Teach said, "Marvin, I trust I'll never hear of you calling Mike a dummy again. This kind of behavior is contrary to everything I've tried to teach all of you about being compassionate and understanding of your fellow human beings."

A few days later, I told my father about Mr. Johnston's conference with Mike.

"There's a sequel to your story, son," he said as he related what he heard at the village grocery store that very morning. According to the scuttlebutt, Mr. Johnston called on the Monroe family on one of his home visits. In the privacy of the living room, he pointed out that Mike was not getting parental or sibling support at home. This lack of support, he pointed out, was the cause of many of Mike's problems. Lack of such support he said, "Makes my job harder and is certainly going to warp Mike's personality if not corrected." Before the end of the visit he explained a number of ways in which the family members could help Mike.

Neither of the Monroes realized just how much damage they were doing by treating Mike as if he were the fifth wheel on a wagon. They thanked Mr. Johnston for coming. Then invited him for next Sunday's dinner.

Dividends are always in the offing when teacher and parents give children extra support. I discovered that later when I was a teacher. This was evidenced in Mike's case. He went on to high school, then to college. While in medical school a kind benefactor paid for an operation on his club feet. Today, he is a physician in a hospital considered one of the ten best in the United States. Mike wasn't dumb. He was just a late bloomer.

It was 9:45 that Friday when we heard a gentle knock on the front door.

"Answer the door, Jacob," directed Mr. Johnston.

"Yes, sir," said Jacob as he arose from his seat, skipped up the aisle, and opened the door.

"Hello, young fellow. May we——"

"Come in, come in, gentlemen," Mr. Johnston called as he stood up from his chair and walked forward to greet his guests.

"I'm Capt. Alexander Palmer and this is Cpl. Matthew Little," said the taller of the two men.

"How can I be of service?" Mr. Johnston inquired.

"We're Spanish-American War veterans, and we have a favor to ask of you," said Corporal Little.

"If I can help, I'll be glad to do what I can. Exactly what is it you want?"

"Well," said Captain Palmer, "Decoration Day comes long after school is out. Our veterans thought it would be educational for the children, as well as show respect for all of our war heroes buried in Orthodox Cemetery, if we held a special memorial of our own. What do you think of the idea?"

"Naturally, I haven't had time to consider the idea, but at the moment it seems like the patriotic thing to do."

"Then you'll do it?" said both men in unison.

"Why not? I think it's a marvelous idea. How about next Friday, beginning at one o'clock?" Mr. Johnston inquired.

"One o'clock next Friday it is," said Captain Palmer. "We'll get the word out. Everyone in the village and the people in the country will be thrilled. There will be a turnout like you've never seen before, Mr. Johnston.

"There is one thing we failed to mention, Mr. Johnston. Most of the people will bring a basket lunch and start eating dinner [lunch] around 12:30. Care to join us for vittles?"

"Splendid idea, fellows. I'll dismiss school early and we'll all eat together. Pupils, what do you think of the idea?" quipped Mr. Johnston.

"Sure thing, great idea," we shouted and screamed. Anything was great if it meant getting out of school.

Mr. Johnston shook hands with the two veterans, thanked them for their thoughtfulness, and bid them farewell. Then he took time out from his pedagogical duties to explain our part in the forthcoming memorial.

"Jack Reeves and Curtis Talley, as soon as I finish my announcement, go to the Orthodox Cemetery and count the number of veterans buried there. Don't overlook the Civil War veterans' graves."

"I'll g——"

"Mr. Johnston," I broke in, "don't forget the Revolutionary War veterans. I know of three such graves."

"Thank you, Charles, for reminding me.

"I'll pick up some small American flags and some crepe paper while I'm in Benton tomorrow. I'll have Miss Musgraves come here to help us make some beautiful flowers from the crepe paper. We want to be sure of having one flag and a few flowers for each veteran's grave."

Next, Mr. Johnston gave us some insight on Decoration Day. He told us that the commander in chief, Gen. John A. Logan, believed in decorating the graves of those veterans who died in defense of their country. In 1868, three years following the American Civil War, he issued an order designating May 30, 1868, as the day to decorate the graves. He called this day "Decoration Day."

Concluding his remarks, Mr. Johnston sent Jack and Curtis on their way to the cemetery. Then he called his next class to the recitation seat.

The following Friday didn't come any too soon. I don't believe I slept more than two hours the night before. Mother packed two extra pieces of angel food cake, an extra orange, and three extra apples. "These extras," she said, "are for any of the pupils that might not have dessert."

Mr. Johnston dismissed school promptly at eleven o'clock. Then all of us marched to the Orthodox Cemetery. I was dressed for the occasion in my miniature soldier's uniform.

After lunch we listened to Captain Palmer give a rousing speech on America's role in the Spanish-American War. The only thing I remember about it is that following the war we were recognized as a world power.

Following the speech we placed a flag and a couple of homemade flowers on each veteran's grave. Jack and Curtis did an excellent job in locating them. None was overlooked. The village and country adults did their part. They cleaned the cemetery of debris and placed flags and flowers on the graves of their relatives.

On the next to the last Saturday morning before the end of the term, I was lying on the grass under a partially leafed-out soft maple tree. It was a beautiful day just to daydream and think about the forthcoming vacation. The sun shone brightly through the leaves. The 75° temperature was delightful. Cold winter weather with its icy blasts were over and done with. I felt like I was in heaven.

"Charles, come inside and get dressed. I want you to go to the village and get a haircut."

"Aw, gee whiz, I don't need a haircut! Can't I wait 'til school is out?"

"No, you can't! You're getting to look like that longhair hobo we saw last week camped by the railroad track."

"I thought such homeless people are called 'bo jacks.'"

"True. That's what some of the people around here call them, but the correct name is hoboes."

Forty-five minutes later I was walking down the village street toward the barber shop. Looking across the street I saw a sign in Haskin's Grocery Store window. It read, "Boy wanted for Saturday work."

I crossed the street, went into the store, and approached Mr. Haskins, who was behind the counter wearing a white apron and looking every bit like a boss.

"When do you want me to start work, Mr. Haskins?" I inquired.

"Well, well, but aren't you a fast one, Charles?"

"No, not at all," I replied. "I just want the job, and I could use the extra money."

"Really, I was hoping for an older boy."

"What kind of work do you have in mind?"

"The hours are from eight o'clock 'til five on Saturdays. The work consists of sweeping the floor, cleaning the counter and shelves, carrying out groceries for the ladies, and any other little things that need to be done. The pay is fifty cents a day. Also, there may be a few workdays during school vacation."

"I'll take it," I said eagerly.

"Hold on a doggone minute. I didn't say you had the job."

"Look Mr. Haskins, I'm strong for my age. I can do everything you've mentioned."

"Well, I don't know," he said, hesitating. "I'll have to think about it."

"Tell you what I'll do. You give me the job. I'll work for you next Saturday. Come five o'clock you be the judge. If you like my work, pay me fifty cents. If not, I'll work the day for nothing, and you can look for another boy."

"Fair enough. I'll look for you next Saturday at eight. You're a fast-working salesman, I'll say that for you," he said as he turned to wait on Mrs. Harris who just walked into the store.

Walking into Hartman's Barbershop, I noticed the following sign painted in letters one foot high on the window: U.R. NEXT

Shortly after I took a seat in the barber chair, a stranger entered.

"Is Mr. Next in?" he said as he looked at the two empty chairs.

"No, he isn't. He stepped out a few minutes ago. Can I help you?" inquired barber Hartman.

"Naw. I want Mr. Next to cuts my har. A feller down the street said he could cuts my har jest lak the one in this here pitcher," he said as he showed Mr. Hartman a picture of a well-known movie star.

"Are you going to be in town very long?" barber Hartman asked.

"Wall, I'd say tolerbly long. I got to get me some grocers, and buy some parts for my ole tin lizzie. I'll do my buyin'. Then I'll come back to see if this feller Next come back. I shore wants him to cuts my har because I've got me a date tonight with Sally Smothers. Do you-all know her?" he asked with a twinkle in his eyes.

"Can't say that I do," replied barber Hartman.

"She shore is purty. I can't wait to get to kiss 'er," he said as he walked out of the shop grinning.

"All through, Charles. If you were a bit older you could go dancing tonight," said barber Hartman as he turned on his big smile.

I paid twenty-five cents for the haircut, walked out the door, went home, and played outside for the rest of the day.

"Last day of school," I said as Jacob, his cousin, and I met the following Friday at the *T*.

"So it is. This is my cousin, Sylvester Travelstead," Jacob said as he introduced us. "He's from St. Louie. He is out of school for a week. He——"

"It's called a spring break," interrupted Sylvester.

We had walked down the lane about two hundred yards when Sylvester spotted a rabbit running into the woods.

"I'll get him," shouted Sylvester as he gleefully took off on a run.

Jacob shrugged his shoulders. "Isn't it remarkable, Charles?" Jacob said with a look of disgust in his eyes. "Just look at him! Isn't he a pretty sight to behold? High button shoes, socks up past his knees, knee britches, a white shirt and tie, and that damn silly looking sissy hat sitting on top of his head. Would you believe it, Charles? He's two years older than me, and he looks like something the cat dragged in. There's more. I have to take *that* to the village tomorrow! I'll be laughed off the street."

"Oh, don't feel too disgusted. That's the way kids dress in St. Louie. My cousin lives there. He's my age. He dresses exactly like Sylvester, with one difference."

"I can't wait to hear it," Jacob said sneeringly.

"Every morning his mother pins a fresh flower onto his coat lapel."

"Well, I'll be a monkey's uncle," he said as he roared with laughter.

Just then Sylvester joined us, not too worn looking from his adventure. Naturally, he returned without the rabbit.

"Jacob, what was so funny? What were you laughing at?"

"Oh, nothing really. You see, I have these laughing fits occasionally. Why just last Sunday I had one in church right in the middle of Reverend Brown's sermon."

"What causes them, Jacob?" Sylvester inquired.

"Hell, I don't know! Pa says my mother was scared by a laughing hyena just before I was born," Jacob said as he went into another long-drawn-out laughing seizure.

When we reached the schoolhouse, we joined a merry crowd of our peers and most of their parents. Everyone was anxious to get the program started, for it was planned for the whole morning.

Several of the children gave readings. Susan Hunter played a violin solo, "How Can I Forget Thee."

Jason DeWees was all geared to recite, "The Face on the Barroom Floor." Mr. Johnston put the brakes on that one long before the program began. A good thing, too, for a good many members of WAD-AB (Women Against Drinking Alcoholic Beverages) were present. It's anyone's guess what would have happened had Mr. Johnston allowed Jason's recitation.

A ciphering match was the final number. Loren Barker and Curtis Talley chose up. All of us knew which side would win, for Loren was an arithmetical whiz. He knew his multiplication tables up to the fifties. I've seen him add three columns of numbers as quickly as I could add simple one column numbers. So it was no surprise, when the match ended, to see Loren standing alone. He took his win like a true gentleman. Then he took his seat.

On our way to the picnic area on the bank of Little Silver Creek, Sylvester noticed some beehives on the other side of a barbwire fence. They belonged to Jim Bolen.

"What's them white boxes doing out here?" Sylvester inquired.

"Why those are beehives," said Jacob. "See the bees going in and out? When it's a nice warm day like today, they search for nectar."

"How do they know where to go?" Sylvester wanted to know.

"Well, as soon as spring arrives, Mr. Bolen takes them out in his wagon where he shows them the best flowers to work for choice nectar," said Jacob, frowning and looking down at his shoes as he held back one of his belly laughs.

I bit my cheeks to keep from giving out with a big horselaugh. *What a pity to bring a city dude to the country*, I thought.

"Well, Jacob, how does Mr. Bolen talk to the bees?"

"Aw, just forget it," he said irritably. "Let's be on our way."

Some of the older boys came early. They had a roaring bonfire going when we arrived. After dinner, all who could brave the cold water went swimming. We had to walk about a mile along the creek bank to get away from the girls and women. None of us had bathing suits. In fact, I was fifteen years old before I knew there was such a garment as a swimming suit.

After the swim, Mr. Johnston handed out the report cards. Everyone was promoted. I was promoted from the second grade to grade three. Archie Tucker was promoted to the eighth grade. Mr. Johnston made a little speech about him.

"Archie was a part-time pupil this year because of his farmwork. What he lacked in attendance, he made up a hundredfold in hard work and burning the midnight oil. When he first came to school, he couldn't read his name. Now he reads the daily paper. He has read every book we have in our small school library, as well as other books he has been able to borrow."

Archie thanked Mr. Johnston.

After shaking everyone's hand, Mr. Johnston dismissed us saying, "I'll see you all next fall."

An amazing thing happened the previous evening at the school directors meeting. For the first time in the history of our school, Mr. Johnston was hired back for the following year. Not only was he reemployed, he was given a ten-dollar raise. His new contract read "Fifty dollars a month for a seven-month term."

Jacob, Sylvester, and I began a slow walk homeward bound. Just prior to reaching the lane, I began walking toward the back of the schoolhouse.

"Where are you going?" Jacob inquired.

"Follow me and see for yourself," I said with a twinkle in my eye.

Walking to the rear of the coal shed, I picked up Mr. Johnston's hickory switch.

"What you got there? Looks like Teach's hickory switch," Jacob said, giggling.

"How right you are," I said proudly.

"When did you hide it?" he said, not believing what he was seeing.

"During the ciphering match when everyone was in a frenzy, wondering who would win, I snatched the switch off the top of the bookcase and quickly stuffed it down my pant leg and up my shirt. Then I slipped out and hid it where you saw me pick it up."

"Boy, I wouldn't want to be in your shoes next year if Teach finds out about it," Jacob said, frowning as if he bit into a sour pickle.

"Won't do him any good if he does," I said boastingly.

"How come?"

"I'm going to the village school," I said.

"Can't do that. You don't live in that district."

"No, but the boundary line cuts through our farm. I can go to either school I please," I replied.

"Just why do you want to change schools?" Jacob inquired.

"The village school has a good music program, and I want to play in the band. As you know, Jacob, I've been playing the clarinet for more than a year."

"Yeah, I know," he said, "that little dinky clarinet looks like a toy."

"It's an E-flat clarinet. It's no toy! My fingers are not long enough to play a B-flat clarinet," I shot back rather exasperated at his musical ignorance. "My parents are buying me a new clarinet, and I start taking lessons again next week."

By now, we reached the *T*. I said good-bye to Jacob and Sylvester. Then I walked down the country road toward home. School was out and the summer vacation was beginning.

In retrospect I don't want to leave the impression that we were a weird bunch of hoodlums, always looking for a fight. We were not.

True, boys fought boys, and sometimes they fought girls. Older boys fought their teacher. Men fought each other.

No man, woman, or child would even think about engaging in fisticuffs without first observing the following unwritten rules:

1. Never start a fight without having a good reason.
2. Never take undue advantage of your opponent.
3. Never use knives, guns, or clubs unless your opponent plans to use them.
4. Never fight a handicapped person.
5. Never walk away after a fight without shaking your opponent's hand.

Why didn't we settle our differences in the courts, you may well ask. Almost all of us looked upon the courts with suspicion. We had little respect for judges and lawyers. Therefore, we believed fighting was a quick way to settle an argument, and it didn't cost a penny.

I don't want to leave the impression that we were a bunch of heathens. I knew of no one who did not belong to a church and attend services regularly. When the Epstein family came from St. Louis, they affiliated themselves with the synagogue in Benton. Both Mr. and Mrs. Epstein fostered a religious understanding between Jews and Christians, even though they had no intention of converting to the Christian faith.

That's the way it was when I attended the first grade, my only school year as a pupil in a one-room country school.

It was sixteen years later that I was inside another one-room country school. I was no longer a pupil. I was the teacher.

PART TWO

THE TEACHER

Chapter 11
From Flunky to Teacher

The year 1930! One year after the stock market panic of 1929 brought an end to the period of prosperity. High wages and increased production and consumption of goods came to a halt. The rise of stock prices had reached its peak during the first six months of President Hoover's administration. Billions of dollars were invested in the stock market. Get rich quick was the slogan of the day, and some people were getting rich—at least on paper. People from all walks of life bought stocks, borrowing from banks, selling sound government bonds, mortgaging homes and farms. By early fall of 1929 stock brokers were carrying more than 300 million shares of stocks on margin for their clients. By October of 1929 the buying fever came to an end, giving way to an equal selling fever. Soon prices hit rock bottom. Thousands of investors lost everything they had invested, leading to financial ruin. October 29 was the day of doom! The New York Stock Exchange, the world's largest, collapsed. By December 31 stock values declined to the tune of $15 billion.

The stock market panic was the introduction to what became known as the Great Depression. Soon it spread over the entire nation. By the early 1930s it spread over the entire world. In spite of well-known financial facts, President Hoover said, "Business is fundamentally sound." He predicted that a new era of prosperity was just around the corner. Instead, many factories closed, untold number of businesses went into receivership, mortgages on farms and homes were being foreclosed, banks were failing daily, and prices of commodities hit rock bottom. Wages for those lucky enough to have jobs, were cut to the bone. Soon 10 million men were unemployed. The national unemployment rate rose to 25 percent.

In southern Illinois coal mines were shutting down or, at best, working only one or two days a week. Here the unemployment rate was as high as 75 percent in many communities. Also, homes and industries nationwide were turning to gas and oil to supply their energy. This furthered unemployment for our coal miners.

Bank failures in southern Illinois were on par with bank failures nationwide. Prior to the depression one county supported nine banks. By 1932 only one bank was solvent, made so by careful management.

The afternoon train arrived at the Royalton Station at 1:36 P.M., exactly on time. Among the debarking passengers was a portly man dressed in a conservative brown business suit, handkerchief neatly folded in his coat pocket, wearing imported Italian shoes, a brown Stetson hat, and carrying a gold-headed walking cane.

He knew exactly where he was going. Looking neither to the right nor left, he headed for the bank, two blocks away. Upon entering he went directly to the teller's cage.

"I'm Sylvester Atwater, chairman of the Carbon Coal Corporation. I just arrived from Chicago. I have an appointment with President Dillard."

"Right this way, Mr. Atwater. Mr. Dillard is expecting you," the teller said pleasantly as she led the way to the president's office.

"Good afternoon, Mr. Atwater. We met two years ago when I was called to Chicago to bring the board an up-to-the-minute progress report on the bank."

"Pleased to meet you again," said Mr. Atwater as the two men shook hands. "If you have appointments for the next two hours, cancel them, for we have a good many things to discuss."

"Yes, sir, Mr. Atwater. I'll call in my secretary. She——"

"You won't need her," he ordered as he interrupted the president. "This is strictly a confidential meeting."

The two men spent the next hour and a half discussing general bank business. Then Mr. Atwater said, "I expect to take the 4:15 train back to Chicago. So I'll leave you with a few salient points that the board expects you to follow without question. So far your loans appear to be in good order, according to our auditor. Your job is to keep them that way. In the future supervise all loans personally. Under no circumstances allow your loan manager to have the final word. Make no loans where the collateral is less than 25 percent of the loan. This means at current prices. Land values are falling drastically. So keep up to date on car, farm, and home values in this section of the state. As a final word, remember this: the Carbon Coal Corporation owns 51 percent of the bank stock. Any robbery from the inside disguised as poor loans will be your neck. This bank is solvent, and it's going to remain so. If it doesn't, the corporation's five lawyers will take you to court; and, if this happens, you can bet your bottom dollar that you will face a ten- to twenty-year jail sentence plus a hefty fine. Now, do we understand each other, Mr. Dillard?"

"Yes, sir, Mr. Atwater, we sure do!"

"Good. I don't want to miss my train," reminded Mr. Atwater. The two men shook hands. Then he walked out of the office and headed for the depot.

Some bank failures were legitimate; others went bust by being robbed from the inside.

One beautiful fall day Joe Samples walked into the Benton Farmers and Merchants Bank to take out a loan.

"Good morning, Joe," greeted teller Loren Cunningham. "How are you getting along? Out getting a taste of this beautiful fall weather?"

"Oh, I'm fine." Then, with a laugh, "The weather is great, just great, but I do have a problem, Loren."

"What is it, Joe? Not getting married are you?" asked Loren as he winked his left eye.

"Nothing like that. I need to take out a loan."

"That's what we're here for. Everyone gets into a financial bind occasionally. How much are we talking about, Joe?"

"Dad said twenty thousand would put me in good financial shape," he said as he nervously ran his hand through his hair. "Do I need to get the president's okay?"

Laughing out of the corner of his mouth, Loren replied, "Why of course not, Joe! You're one of the good old boys, honest as the day is long. Your family has had roots in this town ever since the American Civil War. In fact, your father telephoned me this very morning, telling me you were coming. I intend to take care of you."

"What do I have to do to get the money?"

"Nothing. Nothing at all, Joe. Just sign this note that I have already completed. It says, in part, that you will repay the money within six months. Is that satisfactory?"

"Sure sounds okay to me, Loren."

The teller gave Joe Samples $20,000 without requiring either collateral or a cosigner.

Was Joe a good risk for the bank? You be the judge. Joe attended high school for four years without earning a single credit. He was now twenty-two years old, married and divorced, and jobless. Likely as not he never had more than ten dollars to his name unless his father gave it to him. It's no secret why the bank closed its door two days later when the bank examiners discovered numerous loans made to irresponsible borrowers.

The day the bank examiners ordered the bank closed, Pres. Harry Goodall sat in his office staring at a picture on the wall, next to the door, showing him being honored as the new bank president. *How could things have gone so wrong in nine years?* he wondered. He stood up and in a stupor looked around the office. Next, he went to the front door, locked it, and hung up a "closed sign. Then he went out a side door, got into his blue-colored sedan, and drove to his farm northeast of Benton. He passed his house, driving to his forty-foot grain storage silo adjacent to the red barn. Getting out of his car, he went inside, climbed the stairs to the top, opened a ventilating door, and jumped out. His body struck a stack of concrete building blocks, killing him instantly.

President Goodall was an honest man. No one would deny that. He just couldn't take life anymore, knowing that his bank was robbed from the inside by an unscrupulous teller making unsound loans.

Two weeks later Benton's First State Bank failed to open its doors by request of the bank examiners. Bert Johnston lived at 22-110 North Main Street in a beautiful two-story brick home. Bert was a newcomer, having lived there for only nine months. He was a secretive person, but one day while mowing his grass, he told a neighbor he was from Chicago and had moved to Benton to retire. That same neighbor six weeks later called Bert, telling him that the First State Bank closed its doors that morning. Bert thanked his neighbor. Then he drove to the bank parking lot in his new black Lincoln touring car. Entering the bank he knocked on the glass-paneled door marked "closed."

A bank teller cupped his hands over his mouth and shouted, "Bank's closed."

Bert cupped his right hand over his right ear. He, too, shouted,

"I can't hear you." At the same time he motioned for the teller to come closer.

The teller moved close to the door, shouting, "The bank's busted. Go away."

Just then Bert whipped out a .45, pointed the barrel toward the teller's head, and yelled, "You bastard, don't move an inch or your wife will be going to your funeral in a couple of days. Now unlock this damn door and be quick about it!"

The teller quickly unlocked the door. Scared out of his wits, he could scarcely talk. "The safe's open, take all the money you want, but don't hurt me. I've got a wife and two small children at home."

"Get this and get it straight! This is not a robbery. This is a withdrawal of $45,280, all that I have in my savings account. Now, get over to that safe, count me out $45,280, not one dollar more or one dollar less, if you know what's good for you."

"Yes, sir, Mr. Johnston. Just don't hurt me."

Bert unfolded a large shopping bag, then he placed the money, all in large bills, inside the bag. "Now, Mr. Teller, when I leave, you make out a withdrawal slip, backdating it. Just one more thing. Don't get any bright ideas of calling the sheriff. Yes, he can put me in jail, and the judge can refuse me bond; but if this happens, your wife and kids will sooner or later be going to your funeral. It's this way, my friend. I have several buddies in Chicago that owe me favors. Nothing would please them more for one of them to come to Benton and help me out. Unless you are tired of living, my advice to you is to follow my instructions to the letter."

Apparently, the teller followed Bert's instructions to a tee. No robbery ever appeared in the *Daily Bugle* and Mr. Johnston continued to live unmolested in the beautiful two-story house on 22-110 North Main Street.

There were no national welfare or relief programs until Pres. Franklin Delano Roosevelt took office in 1933. Then it took approximately two years to get the program in full swing. In the meantime, people had to strive for themselves. Friends, relatives, and neighbors were not of much help, not because they didn't want to help, but most were in the same boat: flat broke, with little or nothing on the pantry shelves. In the cities some men and boys stood on street corners selling apples at five cents apiece. In front of one Chicago soup kitchen men stood in line four abreast and two blocks long. In

St. Louis evicted tenants and families no longer homeowners shacked up along the Mississippi River. Having no money to buy building materials, they raided dump sites, gathered driftwood and boards along the riverbank, and, in some cases, removed siding and other building materials from vacated houses. The settlement of some seventy-five shacks was a disgrace to humanity, through no fault of the occupants. Some men simply dug a rectangular hole in the riverbank the size of a room. Then they constructed a roof of rusty sheet metal or used boards covered with used linoleum or pieces of roofing material found in some junk dump. Others built a single room on top of the ground, making use of any scrap building materials they could find. All in all the little village was a sorrowful mess. Some wit never lost his sense of humor, however, for he placed a large sign, facing the river, for all to see. On it was one word: HOOVERVILLE. "I dedicate this poor man's village to President Hoover for the mess he has made of this country," he would say to anyone who cared to listen.

With the exception of his closing remarks, I remember very little of what my high school commencement speaker said on that May evening in 1927. "Go forth tonight," he expounded "and seek your fortune. Opportunity is knocking at your door. Don't let it slip through your fingers."
With our nation in turmoil and no one knowing what tomorrow would bring, opportunity couldn't knock. The wolf at the door wouldn't let it come anywhere near the premises.
My parents couldn't afford to give me a college education, so I joined the hundreds of graduating high school seniors in southern Illinois looking for work.
I pounded the pavement looking for work, any kind of work. Nothing was available. Some merchants rubbed salt into the wounds by placing signs in store windows reading, "No help wanted, please don't ask." I was totally disgusted and on the brink of giving up. At one time I even contemplated suicide. However, that didn't seem the way to go either.
On one hot July afternoon as I was walking home with my head bent down, my mind a total blank, Ed Parker greeted me from the steps of his country store.
"Hi, Ed," I said begrudgingly as I continued to walk.

"Got a minute, Charles?"

"Hell, yes," I replied sarcastically as I came to a halt. "I've got a minute, a day, a week, or a month. That's all I've got left is time! So what's cooking, Ed?"

"I'm going broke! My customers aren't buying. I'm not even making expenses."

"Join the club, Ed. Everybody I talk to is disgusted, irritable, and fearing the future. If things get too bad, console yourself. You can always shoot yourself."

"That's very funny, Charles. How is it I'm not laughing? Now, let's get serious for a change. There's one more shot I'd like to try. Want to help me?"

"Why not? Since I'm a complete failure, I have nothing to lose. What do you have in mind, Ed?"

"I'd like to give you a job. It's——"

"Whoopee doozee! A job! Don't tell me, Ed, that you are actually offering me a job? I can't believe it!"

"It's just a flunky job," Ed said, "but it is a job. I want to try a take-order delivery system. Your main job would be to go house to house in the morning, taking grocery orders, and make deliveries in the afternoon. During your spare time you would stock the shelves, keep the storage room in good order, and sweep out the store after closing time. I'll pay you fifteen dollars for a six-day week. Will you take it?"

"You bet your boots I'll take it! When do I start?" I said, hardly believing I actually had a job.

"How does tomorrow morning sound?"

"Sounds good, Ed. I'll be here at seven sharp. I know your hours, and I'll make you a good hand."

That job lasted two months. Ed's "one more shot" idea never got off the ground, so he went bankrupt. I spent the next two weeks looking for another job without any luck. So I did what most of the unemployed did: I went to the city. I went to St. Louis where I could stay with my aunt, having to pay only for the food I ate.

To have a better shot at finding a job, I paid a fee of two dollars to a commercial job placement agency. If I accepted a job because of its help, my contracts called for an additional payment of 10 percent of my first month's salary. To further my chances of getting an early lead on vacancies, I made it a point to be at the *Globe Democrat* press building to check new edition advertisements as soon as they came off the press. In this way I could scan the want ads and be on my way to interview for a job long before the paper hit the streets.

One delightful fall morning the following ad appeared in the *Globe*:

> Wanted: Assistant Chemist. Applicant must have a high school education, including one year of Chemistry. Apply in person to Chemist Adrian Steinberg, Missouri Milling Company, 10012 North Grand Avenue.

That's for me, I said to myself. Full of hope and anticipation of a good job, I boarded a North Grand streetcar.

Mr. Steinberg was a good-looking man. He was about five feet, six inches tall, weighed 165 pounds, and had a pleasing smile. He was easy to talk with, and after I answered at least ninety chemistry questions, he said, "I like your frankness in answering my questions. You must have had one excellent chemistry teacher. The job is yours if you want it at eighteen dollars for a five-day week."

That job lasted three weeks before the Missouri Milling Company, too, went out of business for lack of orders. At least it didn't do as many other businesses did—hire its employees strictly on a percentage basis. If merchandise moved, everyone made a little money. However, if orders started falling off, everyone made less and less. For instance, a fellow I met at the YMCA said that some weeks his share was as low as $8.45. He was working on a percentage of the profits.

I was at liberty for twenty-two days before accepting a genuine flunky job with a large business firm at 816 Washington Avenue. As the office boy, I ran errands, carried the firm's newspapers to the executives' desks, and swept out the offices after closing time. Also, if any of the employees had need for a flunky I was it, all for ten dollars for a five-day workweek. This job lasted six weeks when I was again unemployed because, according to Vice Pres. Homer T. Shaw, his daughter married an unemployed bum.

Mr. Shaw handed me my final check for ten dollars, then he said, with saliva drooling from his mouth, "I can't stand his guts, but he makes my daughter happy. That's what counts." Then as an afterthought he barked, "I gave the scoundrel your job, and by the by he'll support my daughter or I'll know the reason why."

Unemployed again! I had it. City life wasn't my cup of tea. Upon leaving Mr. Shaw's office, I went to my aunt's apartment, packed my suitcase, and left a note for her when she came home. Then I took a Compton streetcar to the bus station where I bought a one-way ticket to Buckner, my hometown, in southern Illinois.

After I returned home, one evening about eight o'clock, my uncle William Neal, principal of a village school, and I were sitting on his front porch talking about the state of our nation, particularly as it was affecting our part of the country.

"Charles, do you have any leads on a job so far?" he inquired.

"No, I don't, Uncle Bill. Not too long ago I'd hear of a few job openings. Now I don't know of a single vacancy anywhere."

"Times are tough, Charles. I'm fifty-five years old and I've never witnessed our country in such a turmoil as it is today. Now that you are married, it's doubly important that you get a position that has a sound future."

Immediately, my mind went back several months to when I first met my wife. At age nineteen, I had no intention of getting married. What with the depression on, men losing jobs by the thousands, soup lines getting longer by the day, I could not see torturing a wife by exposing her to the great mess this country got itself into.

Then it happened. I fell deeply in love with a pretty blond eighteen-year-old, Fairy Berneice Bacon. She was an entirely different girl than I had ever known. In addition to being pretty, she had an outgoing personality. Having won a local beauty contest did not change her personality or give her the big head. I thought this was remarkable. The better I became acquainted with her, the more I thought she would make me the kind of wife most men would desire but seldom enjoy.

Even though times were rough, we agreed to tie the knot. Apparently, for once in my life, I made an excellent choice. As it turned out, it was the most intelligent decision I ever made. As I reflect back on our sixty-two years of married life, I recall the many, many times she shared my troubles, sympathized with me in periods of adversity, and always made my interests her interests.

Like me, she never smoked. Never used alcoholic beverages.

Nevertheless, she died of lung cancer, most likely from secondhand smoke.

"Charles, are you with me? You seem to be in a stupor. What's the problem?"

"No problem, Uncle Bill, I was just in deep thought."

"Okay. Have you ever thought about teaching?"

"That's a real laugh, Uncle Bill! What I know about teaching you could place on the head of a pin and have room to spare."

"I'm not so sure. The State Teachers Certification Board is giving a teacher's examination two weeks from this coming Saturday in the Lincoln School in Benton. To take the examination for a second grade elementary school certificate, a candidate must have at least an eighth grade education, be a United States citizen, and be of sound moral character. What do you say, Charles? Want to give it a try?"

"I really don't know, Uncle Bill. Do you think I can really teach school?"

"Sure I do, or I would never have mentioned it. Of course, even if you pass the examination no village or city school will hire you without some college credits, but the country schools are different ball games entirely. You see, Charles, most country school directors wait a few weeks before school begins to hire teachers. They want to hire the cheapest teachers they can get."

"Well, Uncle Bill, doesn't that mean they'll get what's left, the dregs of the teaching profession?"

"That's entirely right, but they also get teachers who will accept low salaries. 'Save us taxpayers a little money,' one trustee told me. Apparently, Charles, he couldn't have cared less about the kind of education children in his school district receive."

"Uncle Bill, would you help me prepare for the examination? If you will, I'll take it."

"Sure will! Next Monday I'll bring you several books to study during the day, and I'll tutor you every evening between now and the day of the examination."

I took the examination on the prescribed day. Nothing happened for three weeks. I didn't know whether I passed or failed. Then in the morning mail on July 3, 1930, I received a round cardboard package. Opening it, I was thrilled beyond belief. On a sheet of parchment my name stood out in Old English script. It was a second grade certificate good for teaching in grades one through eight, inclusive, provided I attended a college or university for a minimum of six weeks each summer for three years. After that time, the certificate required renewing.

"Hooray," I shouted to the housetops for everyone to hear. "I am no longer a flunky. Now I am a teacher." Then I gave Fairy a big hug and kiss. "I'll get a teaching job if I have to canvas every rural school district in southern Illinois," I promised her.

Chapter 12
Teacher Finds a Vacancy

Having a teacher's certificate without a teaching position didn't bring in the bread. I knew precisely what was next: fill my Model T Ford gasoline tank with fifteen-cent-per-gallon gasoline. Then hit the road, inquiring about country school vacancies.

For a week I had driven over country roads contacting directors in three different counties, only to find most posts taken or to meet with a curt, "Hmm, no experience." What was most degrading was, "You're too young." What really stirred my dandruff was, "We'll take your name, address, and the least amount you'll teach for. Then we'll contact you if we can't find a cheaper teacher."

As I went out the door from my last interview for the week, I felt frustration building up inside me. As I walked to my car, I shouted for all the neighbors to hear, "What unmitigated gall! Who do these directors think they are?"

Exactly who were these country school directors in the early 1930s? By Illinois law, rural school directors were three in number. They were elected by residents in their respective district in staggered terms of one, two, and three years. With such an arrangement, one would think the voters had an opportunity to avoid having a stacked board. And some did. However, local politics sometimes entered the picture, completely altering that which the law was supposed to prevent. For example, it was not uncommon for one farmer director to give part-time employment to the husband of a destitute farming family in the community. Since school elections were seldom contested, it was a simple matter to have the part-time employee run and be elected as a director, thus stacking the board two to one on every decision. The third director never complained because it was only a matter of time until he, too, would give the husband part-time employment, thus reversing director control.

Father takes his family for a Sunday drive in his Model T Ford. In 1930 the author drove a similar Model T Ford to and from school.

The Neals' 1930 Model A Ford, Fairy at the wheel, bought secondhand during the second half of the 1930–31 school term.

Theoretically, a director could be voted in or out each year, depending on the expiration of his term. And this did happen on occasion. However, most farmers were too busy during the Great Depression to be bothered with school elections. Their main concern was keeping the wolf from the door during the hard times.

The directors met monthly in one of their homes. The teacher was seldom or never invited to attend. It was common practice for the wife to serve coffee or iced tea along with pie or rolls, and some of them imbibed something stronger than coffee or iced tea.

Directors did a little more than just hire and fire the teacher. They issued him or her a written contract, set the salary, defined his or her outside duties as well as the teaching responsibilities, and made him or her the official janitor of the school.

Other duties of school directors were four in number, seldom carrying out the teacher's recommendations.

1. School directors purchased school supplies, including maps, library books, window blinds, wood and coal for the schoolroom's potbellied stove, floor sweep, brooms, chalk, erasers, pencil sharpeners, and any other supplies they saw fit.

    Most directors purchased none or very few school supplies. In most cases, if the teacher ran out of supplies, he or she either bought them or did without. If the directors were informed of a shortage of supplies, the teacher was usually cut off bluntly with, "We are out of funds for those budgeted items." Of course, this was an answer I could not accept, because the directors approved the budget in the first place.
2. School directors were responsible for maintaining the building and grounds. Here again frugality was the name of the game.
3. School directors set the tax rate for the county assessor. Most directors set a tax rate much too low to operate a respectable school.
4. School directors kept a set of books which were audited annually.

Following the annual school director election, an organizational meeting was held. The primary purpose was to elect one of their three members president, the other one secretary-treasurer.

I had no better luck the first part of the second week. Most of the directors I interviewed were friendly enough, some even offered me coffee or iced tea. However, I had to listen to the same song and dance as the previous week: "No experience? Much too young. What's your lowest salary?" It began to sound like a broken phonograph record, until I hailed a rural route mail carrier who was driving a one-horse buggy pulled by a beautiful jet-black horse with a white patch about the size of a baseball on his forehead.

"Whoa!" he shouted. The horse came to a sudden stop.

"Sir," I said, "may I ask you a question?"

"Sure thing, as long as it calls for an easy answer," he replied, with a twinkle in his eye.

"I'm a teacher. Do you happen to know of any rural schools looking for a teacher?" I inquired.

"Indeed I do. However, before I tell you, let's do away with that frustrated look on your face. I know these are hard times, but you look like you're going to a funeral instead of looking for a job. Cheer up! Put a smile on your face like this," as he demonstrated a big smile from ear to ear. "This is especially effective while you're talking to the director."

"How's this?" I said as I put forth a big smile from ear to ear.

"That's better, much better. Something else—play up to the directors' wives when you are being interviewed."

"Why? Do they have something to do with hiring the teacher?"

"You had better believe it! Not legally, of course. But they have a great influence over their husbands."

"You were about to tell me of a vacancy," I eagerly reminded him.

"Indeed I was. Two days ago one of the Four-Mile School directors told me they have as yet to hire a teacher."

"Where does the nearest director live?"

"Take this road for a mile and a half west to Bert Snider's place. His is the freshly painted white two-story farmhouse on the south side of the road. You can't miss it. Oh, yes, by the way, I delivered his mail about an hour ago. Most likely he'll be sitting in the front yard under a large green ash tree, reading." Then he shouted, "Get up" as he struck his horse lightly with a buggy whip to continue on his mail route.

"Thank you!" I shouted as I started the Model T Ford and headed for the Snider place.

Bert Snider, sound asleep, was sitting in an outdoor lounge chair. His mail and paper lay beside him on the ground. I judged him to be about forty-five years of age, probably weighing in the neighborhood of 180 pounds. He was wearing a pair of blue overalls, a blue shirt unbuttoned at the neck, and a pair of ankle-length work shoes. Gently touching his broad shoulder startled him awake.

Putting on that "mail carrier's smile," I said, "Sorry to disturb you, Mr. Snider."

Rubbing his eyes and yawning, he replied, "Reading makes me sleepy. Say, you look like a teacher! Am I correct?"

"Does it show that much?"

"No, not really, but only a teacher would be wearing a coat and tie on a beastly hot day like this."

"Yes, Mr. Snider, I am a teacher," I said as I introduced myself. "I am looking for a teaching position. I——"

"I wish you had come a day earlier. We were not able to find a man teacher. Against our better judgement, we hired a woman. Last year a seventh grade bully ran the woman teacher out of the school three days before school was out. She was so frightened she never returned. Unfortunately, this same bully will be in the eighth grade this year. By the by, the Dutch Hill School hasn't hired yet. You'll——"

"Mr. Snider," I said, "where does the nearest director live?"

"You'll want to see John Joe Pirka, secretary-treasurer. By the way, some people call him 'John.' Other people call him 'Joe.' Just thought you'd like to know."

"Thank you. Where do I find him?"

"He'll be at home. This summer's heat has burned all the field crops, ruined they are," he said sadly. "Take this dirt road west for two miles where it forms a *T* with the main north-south dirt road. Turn right for three-fourths of a mile. John lives in a one-story house painted green, the only green house on the road. You can't miss it."

"Thanks, Mr.——"

"Tell John I sent you. It won't do any harm."

"Thank you very much, Mr. Snider. I'll be on my way."

Mr. Snider was right. No one could miss that dreadful, faded, olive green house. Knocking at the front door brought Mrs. Pirka on the double—short; thin; wrinkled face; small, nasty almond eyes; and a crooked, leering mouth.

"We don't want any!" she said with a smirk. "On your way, or I'll sic my dog on you."

Putting on that "mail carrier's smile," I said, "I take it you are Mrs. Pirka."

"Yes! What's it to you?"

"Mrs. Pirka, I'm a teacher. May I see Mr. Pirka?"

"Hell, I don't know why anyone would want to see him. He's just a lazy bum. Sits on his ass all day complaining about one thing or another. But come on in and sit in the living room. I'll go fetch him. He's in the outhouse taking a crap for himself. He'll sit there all day if I don't go and fetch him," she said, angry as a hornet.

In a few minutes Mr. Pirka entered the living room, introduced himself, and asked how he could help me. He was the exact opposite of his wife—handsome, clever, intelligent, with a happy disposition. We talked for over an hour about everything from the terrible summer heat to President Hoover's shenanigans in Washington. Mr. Pirka may have been a farmer, but he was as informed on the state of the nation as any city person I had ever met.

"I'm going to be honest, Mr. Neal. What I like about you is your pleasant smile [*Thanks to the mail carrier*, I thought] and the fact you are a good listener. In over an hour not once did you break into my conversation. Would you like to meet the other two directors, Joe Taylor and Harry Rone, president?"

"Yes, I would, Mr. Pirka, if it isn't too much trouble."

"No trouble at all, I assure you. Oh, Maude," he shouted.

"What in hell do you want now?" she screamed from the kitchen.

By this time I was so embarrassed I couldn't meet Mr. Pirka's eyes.

"Take the buggy and fetch Joe and Harry. I——"

"Why, in the name of God, can't you take the man to one of their homes?"

"Maude, all of my director's books and records are here. It's too big a job to lug all that to one of their homes."

"No, that's not it! You're just too damn lazy. That's why! Besides I'm going to bake an apple pie."

"Maude, you know what I told you the other day, don't you?" he said belligerently.

I wondered what he had told her. Whatever it was must have

been potent, for she left the kitchen, and in less than a half hour brought the two directors into the living room.

Following introductions, Mr. Pirka went into the kitchen.

Mr. Rone said, "Pay no attention to Mrs. Pirka, Teach." I wondered if I had his vote. Was he trying to tell me something by calling me "Teach"? "She's a menopausal shrew. She seems to get a kick out of having a spat with anyone who will engage in fisticuffs of words."

Little did I know it then, but during the coming school year I would be a witness many times to Mr. Pirka's marital battles.

When Mr. Pirka returned to the living room, the three of them began talking about their farm problems and what they could or could not do about them. Farm help seemed to be the thorn in their sides.

"I know our corn crops are burned to a crisp, but we can't give up. The only way to survive is to look to the future, and that means hiring farm help. What are you fellows paying for farm labor?" Mr. Rone wanted to know.

"Well, Harry, I won't pay a cent over seventy-five cents a day," spoke up Joe Taylor.

"What are you paying, John?"

"All I can afford and stay in farming is seventy-five cents. Oh, I might go to eighty if the man looks like he can do a good day's work," answered Mr. Pirka. "Fellows, you'll get a kick out of this one. Last week a man applied for a job, said he heard I needed some help. 'How much do you want a day?' I asked. He answered without batting an eye, 'One dollar a day, or I don't work.' "

"That's the joke of the year," Mr. Taylor replied as he gave forth with a loud belly laugh.

"Enough farm talk for today," said Mr. Pirka. "Let's get down to business and start interviewing the candidate."

"You look awful young to me," chided Mr. Taylor. "How old are you?"

"Twenty-two this coming September," I answered.

"Age is relative, Joe," spoke up Mr. Rone. "Remember the teacher we hired four years ago? He said he had twenty years of teaching experience. You remember what we found out, don't you, Joe? He had one year of experience, taught twenty times."

"If we hire you, where will you live?" Harry Rone wanted to know.

"My wife and I would prefer to live in the community if a house is available. We——"

Mr. Taylor interrupted. "I have a house for rent. It belonged to my parents when they were alive. Only three-quarters of a mile from the schoolhouse, and it's the only vacant house in the community."

I thought if I played my cards right I just might get another vote. "How much rent are you asking?" I inquired.

"Ten dollars a month, in advance."

"It's a good house, Charles. You don't mind if we call you 'Charles,' do you?" Mr. Rone spoke authoritatively.

"No, not at all. I'd feel more at home if you did," I replied.

"You do have a teaching certificate, do you not?" Mr. Pirka wanted to know.

"Oh, yes," I replied. "I am a qualified elementary schoolteacher."

The directors shot question after question to me for forty-five minutes. Then Mr. Pirka said, "Gentlemen, are you ready to vote?"

"No, by God, not yet!" spoke up Mr. Taylor. "How much money are we talking about, Charles? We don't run the government mint."

"I believe a hundred dollars a month for an eight-month term is a fair figure." Quite frankly, I would have accepted any amount over fifty dollars a month. I observed each of their faces as I answered their questions. Mr. Taylor's Adam's apple jumped so high I thought it would pop out of his mouth at any moment. Mr. Pirka took in a big gulp of air as his face turned crimson.

Mr. Rone's eyes turned glassy as he stammered, "Charles, we never paid that much money to a teacher but once and that was during the world war. Is that the least you will accept?"

"Gentlemen, I know we're all going through traumatic times. Frankly, it's hard sledding for all of us. I don't want to seem obstinate. So I'll settle for ninety-five, but not a dime less."

"Are you planning to live in my house?" Mr. Taylor was quick to ask.

"Why, yes. As I said before, we want to be part of the community."

"What's your pleasure, Harry?" Mr. Pirka inquired.

"Yea."

"How about you, Joe?"

"Yea."

"My vote is also yea," responded Mr. Pirka.

After shaking hands all around, Mr. Pirka completed two copies of a contract. Then each of us signed in the designated places. Both Mr. Taylor and Mr. Rone left in a hurry, saying they had to mend fences. As I started to leave, Mr. Pirka motioned me back.

"You've a long drive ahead of you, Charles. Would you mind sitting down and having a piece of apple pie and a cup of coffee with me?"

"I sure would love that," I answered.

"Maude!" Mr. Pirka shouted. "Come in here!"

"What in hell you want now?" screamed Mrs. Pirka as she came into the living room.

"I want you to meet our new schoolteacher, Charles Neal."

"Hi. You won't last thirty days. Those Olivetti bullies will run you out of the school, or they just might beat the hell out of you. As for you, John, if you want the pie and coffee, get it yourself. You're no cripple, and I know damn well I'm not your flunky," she screamed as she raced back into the kitchen.

"Charles, pay no attention to what she says. She's all bark and no bite. Pardon me while I put a word in her ear."

I never found out what he said, but in less than five minutes she served us apple pie, coffee, cream, and sugar.

When she returned to the kitchen, Mr. Pirka said, "Charles, don't pay any attention to Joe Taylor's insulting remarks, such as the ones he usually makes. He's an egotist, plain and simple. Hear him out. Then forget what he says. He doesn't have a single friend in the whole community."

If he hasn't a single friend, how does he get elected to the school board? I wondered. The question bothered me. Little did I know it then, but I'd learn the answer before the end of the school term.

The apple pie and coffee were delicious. Having nothing further to discuss, Mr. Pirka and I shook hands.

"See you on August 18," I said as I went out the front door.

On the way to my car I wondered what insidious threat Mr. Pirka was holding over his wife. *I'll find out before the end of the term or my name isn't Charles Neal*, I said to myself.

All the way home I kept talking aloud, over and over saying, "I no longer do flunky jobs now that I'm a teacher!"

As I got out of the Model T Ford, I saw Fairy sitting on the front porch.

"All the running around is over," I shouted gleefully. "No more flunky jobs."

"You found a teaching job?" Fairy inquired.

"I sure did! The best part is my salary of ninety-five dollars per month, the second highest paid rural teacher in the county."

"You lucky so-and-so. Let's go inside where you can tell me all about it," Fairy said gleefully. "I'm so happy for both of us."

I showed her the contract, told her about the rented house, and described each of the directors.

"Your biggest surprise is coming."

"What's that, Charles? I don't think I can stand another surprise."

"Oh, you'll stand this one," I said. Then I described Maude Pirka the best I could. "She's really a scream a minute. Sounds like a bulldog but is harmless as a pussycat. There is, however, one thing I don't understand."

"What's that, Charles?"

"Mr. Pirka, her husband, has something hanging over her head. What it is, I don't know, but I intend to find out later on."

"Tell me about it."

"Really, I haven't much to tell, but when she rants and raves he whispers something in her ear. Then she is as calm and relaxed as a cucumber. Strange, to say the least."

The following morning I went to Murphysboro to register my teaching certificate with the county superintendent of schools.

As I stepped into the county superintendent's office, a peanut-shaped head shot up from behind a rolltop desk.

"You're the new Dutch Hill schoolteacher, aren't you?" he inquired as he stood up, came forward, and shook my hand.

"Yes" I said. "How did you know? There are no telephones in the Dutch Hill area."

"I have cooperative people in every community in the county. I was notified an hour and a half after you were hired. I guess you came to register your certificate. Is that right?"

"Yes," I said as I gave him my second grade certificate.

He described the kinds of problems I could expect as well as the general nature of the people in the community.

"You'll want to take along your county school supplies while you're here," he said. Then he provided me with a packet containing report cards and gold, blue, red, yellow, and white stars used to designate pupils' achievement. "Instead of giving letters, A, B, C, and D, give stars. Give gold for A, blue for B, yellow for C, and white for D."

"That's all good enough," I said, "but what kind of a star do I give for failing work?"

"Oh, man, heaven to Betsy. You don't have failures! This would be a reflection on you as a poor teacher. Never, never talk like that!

"By the way, there is a large class schedule in the packet. I want you to fill in the subjects by grade and length of each period. This done, you fasten it to the wall in plain view for all to see. I'll be on the lookout for it on my first official visit."

He returned my certificate, we shook hands, and he wished me the best of luck. As I left his office, I looked at my watch. It was 10:48 A.M. Then I headed for home in my Model T Ford.

Neal-Appendix-1

APPENDIX
TEACHER'S CONTRACT

It Is Hereby Contracted and Agreed by and between _Harry Rone,_ _John Pirka, and Joe Taylor_ the undersigned School Directors of District No. _one_, County of _Smithton_ and State of Illinois, and _Charles D. Neal_ a legally qualified Teacher, that the said _teacher_ shall teach the School in said District for the term of _eight months_ for the sum of _ninety-five_ Dollars per calendar month, teaching at least _five_ hours each day, commencing on the _18th_ day of _August_ 19_30_ Provided, that nothing herein contained shall require said _____ to teach upon the days excepted from the school month by the statute. And the said _teacher_ agrees faithfully to teach the said School according to the best of h_is_ ability, and to keep a Register of the Daily Attendance of each Pupil belonging to the School, and make such report of the School as is or may be required by law, or by the State Department of Public Instruction, and to observe and enforce all rules and regulations established by proper authority, for the government and management of said School.

And It Is Further Agreed By and Between the Parties Hereto, That the said _teacher_ shall use h_is_ best endeavors to preserve in good condition the School House and premises connected with it; also the Apparatus and Furniture thereto belonging, and also all Books and Records provided by the School Board for the use of said School, and to deliver the same to the Clerk of said District, or his successor in office, at the close of the said term of School, as in good condition as when received, natural wear and tear excepted.

And the undersigned, as Directors of said School District, hereby agree in behalf of said district to keep the School House and premises connected with it in good repair, to provide necessary fuel for the use of said School during the said term, and that for the services performed as above described, then and thereupon the undersigned Directors of said District agree to certify to the Schedule as the law directs, in favor of the said _teacher_ that the sum of _ninety-five_ Dollars is due h_im_ the same being the amount of wages agreed upon by the parties hereto.

Provided, That in case the said _teacher_ shall be dismissed from the said School by the said Directors for gross immorality, incompetency, or any violation of this Contract, or shall have h_is_ Certificate annulled or revoked by the County or State Superintendent, _he_ shall not be entitled to receive any compensation from and after such annulment or dismissal.

IN WITNESS WHEREOF we have hereunto subscribed our hands this _15th_ day of _May_ 19_30_.

John Pirka
Harry Rone   School
Joe Taylor   Directors
Charles D. Neal Teacher.

Chapter 13
Teacher's First Day

With my teaching certificate registered, Fairy and I didn't have much time to waste. She and I began planning for our move to Dutch Hill. She made many of the little things that women make to change a drab house into a beautiful home. I spent time packing furniture and getting bids from different moving companies.

It was a Wednesday prior to the beginning of school on the following Monday. Fairy and I moved into our ten-dollar a month four-room rented house. We spent the next two days cleaning, washing windows, and polishing each piece of furniture with TLC (tender loving care). Last but not least we filled our two kerosene lamps, since we had no electricity.

We stood back to survey our handiwork. The new lace curtains added a certain charm to the windows that made the old house have the appearance of a real home.

"You know, Fairy, I've been thinking," I mused.

"Thinking? Thinking about what?"

"How nice it will be to come home from school each day to a cozy little home, all our own. With the depression in full swing and hard times the rule rather than the exception, we certainly have been blessed by God. I have a good job and I will be paid in cash rather than in school orders."

"School orders? What's that, Charles?"

"As you know, many families can't pay their taxes. Tax money pays the bulk of teachers' salaries. As a result many school districts soon run out of money. When this happens teachers are given school orders. They are something like IOUs, meaning school districts will pay in full plus 6 percent interest when and if they get tax money or money from the state."

"Charles, that seems so unfair."

"It's grossly unfair! Teachers can't live on air. Some——"

"What do they do?" Fairy interrupted.

"Some banks and businesspeople buy the orders, discounting them from 10 to 50 percent on the dollar. When monies come in, either from state or from real estate taxes, the oldest outstanding orders are paid first plus 6 percent interest, a hefty return on their investments. Meanwhile, teachers must sell their orders at a discount to keep food on the table."

Looking at my watch I said, "Gee, it's 9:30! We have a lot of shopping to do between now and Monday. Let's hit the sack."

As I walked over the rise on the dirt road on the morning of Monday, August 18, 1930, the little one-room schoolhouse came into view. A porch (I estimated to be eighty-by-ten-feet), a vestibule with two small windows, and a belfry graced the east side, facing the dirt road. Walking around the building, I saw that eight windows, adjacent to each other, made up the west wall. The remaining walls were solid, consisting of six-inch wood siding.

Returning to the road, I turned around, facing the schoolhouse. Then I took a good look at it as I thought, *What a deplorable-looking physical plant for the children of this school district to call "school."*

Suddenly, something bordering that of a vision of the Chamness one-room, log schoolhouse came into view. It was built in 1860, now having stood vacant for many years. A woodstove heated the building during cold weather. The children sat on logs as they studied and recited their lessons. It was this building the pioneer children, living in Chamness Town (now extinct), Illinois, called their "school."

Staring off into space, I began comparing the two buildings. Then suddenly a good feeling came over me. I first thought the schoolhouse I was looking at was deplorable. By comparison with the Chamness schoolhouse, it seemed like a palace. Now I realized something important. During the past seventy years real progress was being made in schoolhouse construction.

As I unlocked the door I looked at my watch: 7:45. I sighed. Forty-five minutes until time to ring the first bell. In the meantime I had things to do. First, I fastened the class schedule on the wall exactly as the county superintendent had directed. Next, I placed the supplies in the teacher's desk. Finally, I took the water bucket with drawing rope attached and the common dipper from the teacher's cloakroom and placed them conveniently on the well curb outside

During the 1930–31 school year, the author taught in a one-room elementary school similar to the one shown here.

in the school yard. Everyone, including passersby, drank from the same dipper. Calling it repulsive was the understatement of the year. Hygiene was a required subject for all seventh graders.

How can I teach the germ theory in such a way so the pupils will want to have their own individual drinking cup? I asked myself.

My Uncle Bill had made me a present of my one and only professional book, Bagley's *Classroom Management*. Checking it, I found no answer to the problem, as I discovered with several other problems that arose during the school year.

According to my watch it was now 8:30. Stepping out into the vestibule, I pulled hard on the bell rope in long even strokes, ringing the first bell. In answer, children began coming into the schoolhouse. The first one was a little tot, perhaps a first grader, walking on crutches. As he passed by he said, "Teacher, I'm a cripple. Can a cripple come to school?"

"You most certainly can. You will always be welcome here," I said as I helped him to a small seat.

"Me glad. I've had roomtism fever."

Next, groups of children, thirty-one in all, came through the door. Here an older boy, perhaps a seventh grader, was leading a little one. I reminisced when I saw them, for they brought back memories of my first year in a one-room country school when Otho Boner brought his little brother, Jacob, my friend.

Last but not least were two boys much too big for elementary school. Since both boys had similar facial characteristics I assumed they were brothers. Looking them over I said to myself, *I'll bet a nickel to a donut these are the Olivetti brothers. A couple of bullies, unless I miss my guess.* One was overweight with a pockmarked face, brown eyes, and an overshot jaw. Head down, he snickered as he walked by. *Troublemaker or I miss my guess*, I thought. *He'll bear watching, for sooner or later he and I will tangle.*

Some of the youngsters stopped to make conversation; others simply passed, saying nothing as they made their way toward their seats.

It was nine o'clock as I pulled on the bell rope to ring in the beginning of a new term.

I was barely able to contain my enthusiasm as I walked to the front of the room. For a time it seemed I would never find a teaching position, but here I was at last a teacher, facing a roomful of eager faces. I wondered if my blue trousers, white shirt, matching tie, polished shoes, and a fresh haircut made me look professional.

"Good morning, boys and girls. I'm Mr. Neal, your new teacher," I announced. While I was printing my name on the blackboard, I could hear the sound of shuffling feet, a few guffaws here and there, and snickering from some of the girls.

I took their names, ages, and grade levels. Next, I assigned seats according to grades. Then I explained the class schedule posted on the wall.

"Any questions?" I inquired.

"Teach, how do you know that we gave you our correct grade?" a freckle-faced youngster about twelve years old wanted to know.

That question floored me for a moment.

"To begin with," I said, "I trust all of you boys and girls until you prove otherwise. However, I am required to check all the information you gave me against last year's teacher's record book."

"I don't have my books," said a blond-haired girl in the fifth row. "Mother said to wait until you told us what to buy."

"Your mother gave you good advice. We will have only a half-day of school today. Before you leave, I will give each one of you a list of books and supplies needed for your grade. As you most likely know, you can purchase new books and supplies from Browning's Bookstore in Royalton."

A blond-headed girl in the fifth grade section had a question. "Teach, can't we use secondhand books?"

"Certainly," I replied. "If they have all of the pages intact, they serve the purpose as good as new ones."

"Old four-eyes over there——"

"Hold it! Hold it! I shouted. "No name-calling permitted." Pausing briefly to let my words sink in, I said, "Now what did you start to say?"

"Harold over there," he said as he pointed his index finger toward a little chubby boy sitting in the fifth grade section, "wants too much money for his fourth grade reader. I won't pay it!"

"That sounds much better. Sounds like a gentleman talking," I said. "Now, to buy a book you must agree with each other. This is called a contract. In this case it would be an oral contract, which means the buyer and the seller agree on a certain price. Otherwise, no contract exists, as in your case; and no sale is made. It's as simple as that."

A hand shot up in the fourth row.

"What is it?" I asked.

"Teach, my father don't have no money to buy books. What will I do?" he inquired as tears came to his eyes.

By this time I could hear muffled laughs, snickering, and snide remarks. "Enough of that!" I demanded. I paused for a moment to let my words sink in. "One thing I will not tolerate is one student having fun at another's expense. Cut it out now!" I demanded. My statements worked like a charm. One could have heard a mouse walking across the floor.

"Son, come by my desk before you leave. We'll work out something so you will have books and supplies." I said this knowing very well the directors would not shell out the money for what they called "unessential expenditures." This would be another expense coming out of my ninety-five dollars a month salary.

Recess time: 10:15. The students all rushed out, glad for their release. Because it was the first day of school, I extended the play period from fifteen minutes to one-half hour. As I mingled with the pupils, they seemed happy and contented, not pent up as they were in the classroom.

Suddenly, from the other side of the schoolhouse, angry voices were building momentum as if a fight was in the making.

"You're a darned Hunky!"

"I'm not!"

"You are!"

"Am not!"

"Are too!"

"Am not!"

"My dad says if your name is Poloski, that makes you a Hunky."

When I arrived on the scene a boy had scraped a line on the ground with his shoe, then dared the other boy to cross it.

"Here! Here!" I shouted with authority.

Handicapped because I didn't know their names, I ordered them to immediately stop what they were doing.

"Now, what's the problem?" I asked as I pointed to the smaller of the two.

"He's——"

"I'm——"

"Cut it out! And I mean now! One at a time!" I barked. "You," I again pointed to the smaller one, "what's the problem?"

"He," pointing his index finger at his adversary, "says I'm a Hunky. He started calling me that last year. I looked up *hunk* in my dictionary. It says a hunk is a lump. I'm not a lump, and I won't take his insults any longer!"

"Did you call him a Hunky?" I asked.

"Yes, I did! He's Polish! Polish people are Hunkies."

"Now both of you hold it!" I demanded. Then I explained why America is called the great melting pot: Many of us come from different backgrounds, but we are all Americans and should treat each other with respect. "Let me give you a personal example. When my paternal grandfather came to America from Ireland, he settled in Boston. There were quite a number of fellow countrymen there. So he felt quite at home until he started looking for a job. Many of the factories and business places had signs posted on their properties, reading, 'Irishmen and dogs stay off the grass.' " Again pointing to the taller boy, I inquired, "Do you think that was fair treatment?"

"Heck, no!" he was quick to reply. "My mother is part Irish."

"Do you get the point?"

"I think so. If we wanted to fight everyone we meet who is of a different nationality, we would spend most of the day fighting."

"Right," I said. "I want both of you to settle down, shake hands, and from here on be friends. Will you do that for me?" They agreed, shook hands, and as far as I know remained friends from then on.

As I started to walk around the schoolhouse. I was startled to see a man coming toward me, hobbling. *More trouble*, I thought. He was short, frail, and white-haired.

"I want a word with you, Teacher!" he demanded angrily.

"How can I be of help?" I inquired.

"Those damned Olivetti boys and their buddies! You've got to put a stop to their stealing."

"What are they stealing?" I wanted to know.

"Eggs! That's what! They play some kind of tag game. They run all over my farm. I don't care none about that. It's when they go into my chicken house, steal some eggs, eat them raw, and leave the shells. That's what makes me mad."

He seemed more calm, now that he had his say. I introduced

myself. He said his name was Ed Simpson and that he owned the 160-acre farm adjoining the school ground.

"Mr. Simpson," I said, "if you will remain right here, I'll get the Olivetti boys. I think we can get to the bottom of this in a hurry."

"I hope so," he said.

The boys did not deny Mr. Simpson's accusations.

"Boys," I said, "tell us about the tag game. Also, tell us why you must run so far away from the playground."

The one with the pockmarked face acted as spokesman. "We play on Mr. Simpson's farm because his end isn't cultivated. His land is full of bushes and weeds. That's what we need to play our game. We call it tag, tag you are caught.

"First, we draw straws to find out who's It. Then the three of us hide in the weeds and bushes. The one who is It waits until one of us shots, 'All set.' Then the one who is It slips into the brush. The game is for him to find us one at a time, then to sneak up and tag on the back before we see him. So as not to be tagged we often run a quarter- to half-mile to hide on Mr. Simpson's farm.

"You are It until all three are tagged. Then the three who were tagged draw straws to see who is It next. That's all there is to the game."

"But why do you run as far as my henhouse?" Mr. Simpson wanted to know. "There are no bushes or weeds to hide in within two hundred yards of the henhouse."

"We don't run there to hide. We run there to eat raw eggs because we like them. Why should——"

"OK," I broke in. "Mr. Simpson, how does this sound to you? In the morning these two boys and I will step off two hundred yards on your property. There we will drive a tall stake. Beyond the stake is off-limits. This will give the boys plenty of hiding area as well as keep them away from your henhouse."

"If the boys do that, I'll have no objections," quickly answered Mr. Simpson.

"Boys, what's your answer?"

"Well, I don't know," replied the one with the pockmarked face.

"That's not good enough. Mr. Simpson has been more than fair in this matter. And I expect you to do the same. What will it be?"

"If we have to, I guess we'll do it," spoke up the leader.

"Now, boys, Mr. Simpson is busy, and it's almost time to end recess. So here's what we will do. We will drive the stake as agreed by Mr. Simpson. You boys will play tag in the designated area. If I get a report that any of you have violated our agreement, all four of you will be confined to the school yard property. I'm holding you two Olivettis responsible. So explain our agreement to your tag playmates. You are excused."

Mr. Simpson thanked me. We shook hands. Then he headed for home. I went to the vestibule to ring the bell, ending the recess period.

The children trudged in. They took their seats. Being noisy and restless was understandable. Being free as the breeze all summer, it was a drastic change in pace for them to be bound to single seats inside a schoolroom on a beastly hot August day. It was only 10:45 A.M. The temperature already registered 101° F in the shade.

"Come to order, boys and girls," I said. "The quicker we get down to business, the quicker we finish what I have in mind for the remainder of the morning."

A hand raised high. It was from the little crippled youngster.

"Yes?" I said. "What is it?"

"Mr. Teacher, I have a dog named Rover. Will——"

"That's nice, sonny. I too, have a dog. Because of his long chin whiskers we call him 'Whiskers.' "

"But, Mr. Teacher, will I learn how to write and spell his name?" he wanted to know.

"You surely will. Also, you will learn to write and spell many more things before the end of the term. By the way, sonny, have you been in school before?" I inquired.

"Nope! This is my first day."

"I see you know all about school. You knew how to get my attention by raising your hand. Where did you learn that?"

"My mamma told me," he said with a show of pride on his small face.

I thought how pleasant teaching could be if more parents took an interest in their children's education.

Since none of the children, as yet, had their books, I spent the remainder of the morning reading short stories and telling them stories of my own creation, being ever so careful to include stories interesting to the girls as well as the boys.

At noon I said, "Children, I'll look forward to seeing each and every one of you tomorrow. Be sure to bring your books, a pencil, and a tablet. Tonight, I'll make out a seating chart, showing each of your names as well as the seat you are to occupy for the rest of the term. So beginning tomorrow, I'll show my respect to you by calling you by your names." Then I announced, "School dismissed."

After sweeping the floor and closing the windows, I called it a day. As I walked home, I thought about the happenings that morning. We had some problems that could have spelled disaster, but they didn't. This gave me a feeling of a success and a glow of satisfaction.

Chapter 14
Tom "Skunk" Costello

Down in southern Illinois in the late 1920s and early 1930s, a stranger could find most of any kind of company he desired.

A gangster by the name of Charley Birger was hanged in Benton on April 19, 1928. Some people thought of him as the Al Capone of southern Illinois. Other people thought of him as another bootlegger just trying to make a dishonest dollar.

The Birger hanging didn't slow the flow of illegal booze. Now that he was out of the picture, more small-time hoods came to the front, each one trying to get control of the bootlegging business.

The Ku Klux Klan had flourished over the years, but it was gradually fading out. However, it was a long way from being dead.

Seeing white sheets and pillowcases with eyeholes cut in them hanging on clotheslines was no longer a novelty. Neither were fiery crosses burning during open meetings held in large fields with hundreds of hooded members going through their rituals.

Then there was the other side of the coin. Every little town supported one or more churches. One village with a population of only five hundred hosted seven churches.

Into this scene drove Tom "Skunk" Costello in his Model T Ford touring car. At that time no one knew whether he was a retired businessman, an outlaw, or a coal miner out of a job. He drank with the boys in the Old Diamond speakeasy and played poker with them on Saturday nights if he was in Buckner.

No one dared to ask him from whence he came, and none called him Tom "Skunk" to his face. It just wasn't healthy to ask a stranger personal questions. He died with his boots on. This is his story.

My wife and I had the pleasure or displeasure, whichever way you want to look at it, of meeting Tom Costello on the last Saturday in September 1930. It was 8:30 in the morning. We were in the

Bootlegger and gangster Charley Birger hanged in Benton, Illinois. Just prior to the hood being placed over his head, he smiled as he shouted, "Bury me in a Catholic cemetery. The devil will never look for me there." Then he gave a big grin as he shouted, "Let her go." Three minutes later he was pronounced dead.

Woodway Store giving our grocery order to the clerk when someone tapped me on the shoulder. Turning around I looked into the face of a man two inches taller than I and outweighing me by twenty pounds. He had on a conservative blue suit, a blue shirt, a harmonizing tie, a wide-brimmed felt hat, and cowboy boots.

"Howdy, Teach," he said with a broad smile as he extended his hand. "My name's Tom Costello."

"Glad to meet you, Mr. Costello," I said as I started to introduce my wife.

"No! No! Call me 'Tom.' That's what my friends call me. I'll not tell you folks what my enemies say about me, and there are plenty of them," he said, following with a healthy laugh.

After the introduction, my wife said she would handle the grocery order while I talked to Tom.

"Glad to have met you, Mrs. Neal," said Tom as he politely tipped his hat.

"Mary Ann Sullivan pointed you out the other day when we drove by the schoolhouse during morning recess. I'm sure you know Mary Ann," he said to me.

"Certainly do. Her twelve-year-old daughter, Susan, is in my fifth grade class. A most commendable child."

"Both of them think the world and all of the both of you."

"That makes me feel real good, Tom. This is my first teaching job, and I need all the compliments I can get."

"Mary Ann told me that she literally had to drag Susan to school last year. She would play hooky at every opportunity. She had trouble with grammar and arithmetic. When Mary Ann asked the teacher why, she said nothing could be done to help Susan because she was stupid."

"Tom, did the teacher actually use the word *stupid*?"

"She most certainly did. This year Mary Ann can't keep Susan away from school. She sits around Saturdays and Sundays pouting, saying, 'I wish it was Monday so I could go to school.' You folks have done wonders for that little girl."

"At the beginning of the school term we found that Susan was far behind in her studies, so we had her stop by the house after school three times a week for extra help."

"How did you make such a change in her so soon?"

"Fairy took a real interest in Susan. Actually, she is a better teacher than I am. Susan took to her like a duck takes to water. She's a wonderful child, easy to teach. We taught her many little tricks or shortcuts in learning arithmetic and grammar."

"The only shortcut I ever got in school was a cut across the behind with a paddle if I didn't have my lessons. A trick to learning! That's interesting! Can you give an example?"

"One day she made a complaint during the noon lunch period. Here's the way she said it: 'John hit Mary and I,' she said with tears in her eyes."

"What's wrong with that?"

"Plenty. I took care of Johnnie. Then I called Susan over to where I was sitting on the schoolhouse steps. 'Susan,' I said 'would you say Johnnie hit I?'

" 'No,' she replied. 'I'd say Johnnie hit me.'

"Would you say Johnnie hit Mary?'

" 'Yes, of course!'

" 'OK. Repeat your complaint, using the necessary words from your last two sentences.'

" 'OK, you mean I should have said, "Johnnie hit Mary and me?" '

" 'That's right, Susan. Next year you will learn all about agreement in case. For now, however, the crutch I just gave you will serve you well.' "

"I'll be damned! No wonder that kid likes school," Tom said as he turned around to leave the store.

"Nice meeting you, Tom. Feel free to visit school anytime."

"One more thing," he said as he turned around to face me and motioned me to come closer. "Anybody giving you any trouble?"

"No, I can't think of any right now," I said as I wondered why that question was raised.

"OK. That's the way it's going to be. If anybody, and I mean anybody, gives you a hard time, you tell old Tom. I guarantee you'll never be bothered again. You can depend on that," he said as he wheeled around and went out the front door.

While the clerk was completing our order, I jotted down some of the following prices posted on the wall:

Eggs	10¢ a dozen
Grapefruit	5¢ each
Strawberries	20¢ a quart
Center cut pork chops	10¢ a pound
Pork sausage	7¢ a pound
Round steak	12¢ a pound
Bread	8¢ a loaf
Irish potatoes	4¢ a pound
Lettuce	5¢ a head

With the clerk paid, the groceries sacked and in our arms, we headed for the boondocks for another week of isolation.

One evening about 7 P.M., we had finished eating supper. I was sitting in the living room half-asleep in an easy chair. I was startled awake by a loud knocking at the front door. Rubbing my eyes, I arose and staggered to the door. Opening it, I saw a cheerful-looking man about five feet, two inches tall with sideburns almost down to his mouth and only a tuft of hair on top of his head. He wore a pair of overalls, a blue work shirt, open at the neck, and a pair of clumsy-looking work shoes.

"I'm Paul Crain," he said cheerfully as he offered his hand.

I shook his hand, said I was glad to meet him, and invited him into the house.

"I been aimin' to meet you folks sooner, but jest didn't get 'round to it. Would have brung the old woman with me, but she's plumb tuckered out from doin' a washin' an' ironin' today. Pay no never mind though. You-uns will see a lot of we both before the school year is over. We-uns live on the old Tucker place a mile and a half north of the crossroads."

"Have a seat, Paul." All the time I was wondering what was coming.

"Don't mind if I do. I gets tolerable tired standin' on my feet all day."

"What can I do for you, Paul?"

"It's not what you can do for me. It's what I can do for you. Talk has it you-all bin talkin' to Tom Skunk.'"

"Well, yes. The wife and I met Tom in the Woodway Store a few Saturdays ago. What's wrong with that?"

"Well, the good folks 'round here thinks you should steer clear of him. He's a bad egg."

"Oh? In what way?"

"Well, every time he leaves Royalton for a week or two, a bank robbery happens within sixty to hundred miles from here. Before Tom Skunk drifted into here, we had nary a bank robbery in these here parts. He has no job, yet he's always got plenty of money to throw 'round. Looks right funny to us folks."

"From what you say, Paul, it looks like weak circumstantial evidence at the best."

"Then there's somethin' else."

"What's that, Paul?"

"Have you-uns met Pete Pagano?"

"No, we haven't."

"Pete runs a poker game on the second floor of the Miners Hall every Saturday night. 'Bout every other Saturday I goes there to play with the boys. You don't play poker does you, Teach?"

"No," I said laughing at the thought of a teacher gambling. "Paul, as a teacher I'd be fired on the spot if I did. The good folks would claim that I was a bad influence on the children."

"Bull! No harm in a little gamblin'. What I come to tells you is there is bad blood gettin' to the boilen point twixt Pete Pagano and Tom 'Skunk.' They've had plenty words so far. Tom says Pagano once in a while deals hisself an ace from the bottom of the deck. Then agin Tom claims that Pete marks the cards as the games move along."

"How can he do that with the players watching everyone's move?"

"That Pete's a fast son bitch. Tom claims he uses a sharp fingernail to mark the high cards."

"What's going to happen, Paul?"

"Well, Pete's a mean hombre. Tom's a bad egg. Both of them have just about had a fill of each other. I predicts there's gonna be some blood spilt sooner or later."

"Let's hope not, Paul."

"Well, Teach, that's what I come to tells you. Since you're new to these parts I thought I should come and tells you what's cookin'. I'll be goin' now. The old woman should have supper ready 'bout now."

I bid Paul good night. Then I went back to my easy chair to finish my snoozing.

After Tom Costello had been a resident of Royalton for about six months gossip had it that he planned his criminal activities with a methodical thoroughness. Most of the time he worked alone, people said. He never talked about what he was doing. If and when he worked with a partner that person kept mum for fear of his life.

Although Tom Costello and Pete Pagano both lived in Royalton, they spent most of their time in Buckner, giving it as their mailing address. It was here they passed the time of day and most of the night playing cards, rotation pool, and wooing the same girl.

A number of poolroom barflies claim they saw three notches on the butt of one of Tom's .45s and five notches on the butt of his second revolver. When asked how they knew, they said they saw them when he was target practicing one morning in the alley behind the poolroom.

John Slade said he knew for a fact that Tom drove to the hills of Kentucky with four empty suitcases in his car. When he returned, each suitcase held four one-gallon jugs full of moonshine. Then he made deliveries to several roadhouses in southern Illinois. When asked how he knew, he would reply, "Why Harlan Been, the moonshiner in Kentucky, is my cousin."

Perhaps the rumors had some merit. Who really knew? One thing we all knew: Tom was never indicted on any of the charges brought against him.

None of my pupils were very good as baseball players, but marbles was another game entirely. Melvin Swartz and Robert Dean were the best shots I ever saw. Both boys made up my seventh grade, and both boys had powerful fingers, knocking all of the marbles out of the big ring in a matter of minutes.

One day Robert approached me during morning recess. "Melvin and I would like to play against the boys in other schools. Could you help us, Teach?"

"I'm sure I could. We are having a teachers institute next Sunday morning. I'll poll the teachers and see if we can't come up with some interschool play."

Five city school principals were interested. We scheduled a semitournament of five games to begin playing at 2 P.M. on the

Jefferson School grounds in West Frankfort. Each school was allowed two players per game. Ours was the smallest school represented. Our whole student body of thirty-one pupils was less than any one single class in the competing schools.

Getting approval from Melvin's and Robert's parents was granted shortly after I arrived at their homes. Both boys were outside doing chores. I said I wanted to surprise them by taking them to a movie after the games and promised I'd have them home by 10 P.M. The parents gave their approval.

The boys met me at the schoolhouse at 1 P.M. We piled into my Model T Ford and took off with a jerk, arriving at the Jefferson School playgrounds at 1:45.

The tournament started promptly at two with janitor Dennis Hamilton as referee. He was in his sixties but he was no slouch at the game. Before game time, he demonstrated his skill as an expert player. He was plenty good; age didn't seem to affect his ability in the least.

We lost the first game, coming in third, won the second and third games, lost the fourth game, coming in second, and won the last game to win the semitournament.

There were no prizes for the winners, but the handshakes and congratulations from the attending principals were all the rewards Melvin and Robert needed.

"Boys, how about an ice cream soda and a milkshake?" as if I had to ask.

It was 5:30 when we sat down and placed our order in Molly's Little Restaurant.

The movie was our next stop. *Tarzan the Apeman* was on. I never saw two happier boys in my life. They saw it twice, then wanted to see it a third time.

"Boys, I, too, would like to see it again," I lied. "But I promised your parents I'd have you home by ten, and a promise is a promise."

We were nearing the rickety wooden bridge over Big Muddy River. A car ahead of us was about to cross when a car, with lights on bright, started to cross from the opposite side. There was scarcely room for two cars to pass.

I parked, wondering what would happen if one of the cars sideswiped the other one.

Suddenly the car ahead of us came to a screeching halt. The

driver stuck his pistol outside the driver's side window, took a quick aim, and shot out the headlights of the approaching car.

Going to the disabled car, he said to the driver, "What the hell is the matter with you, you damn fool? Don't you know the law requires you to dim your lights when meeting an oncoming vehicle! I'll say this once and once only: If I ever meet up with you again at night and you don't dim, I'll shoot out both of your eyes just like I shot out your car lights. Now get the hell out of here before I lose my temper!"

That driver lit on down the road. When he passed I couldn't see his face, but I'll bet it was as white as chalk.

When the shooter turned around, I was surprised to see it was Tom Costello. Recognizing my car, he walked to where I was parked. "Teach, I'm sorry you had to see this. The son-of-bitch gentleman shouldn't be driving if he doesn't know the law."

"I never saw a thing, Tom, but the boys have something to tell you."

"We won the marble semitournament this afternoon," said Robert, swelling with pride.

"Yeah, and we represented the smallest school," bragged Melvin.

"Congratulations, boys! What was the prize?"

"Teach took us to a restaurant. Then we went to a movie and saw *Tarzan the Apeman*," replied Robert.

"You really made a day of it." Then Tom pulled out his billfold from his left hip pocket and gave each boy a crisp one-dollar bill.

When the boys thanked Tom, he said good night and walked to his car.

We followed Tom (lights on dim) to Royalton where he left the highway at Oak Street. Then I took the boys home, arriving a little before ten o'clock at Melvin's house.

Several weeks passed. Then three men came to Market Street early the afternoon of April 15, 1931. Apparently someone passed the word along that Tom Costello was coming to Buckner later in the day. Harley Cannon—age sixty-one, six feet, two inches tall; cold steel eyes; a man of few words; wearing a light raincoat sat down on the liar's bench in front of the bakery shop located on the west side of Market Street. ("Liar's bench" was a name given to every bench that was located in front of a business.) Jim Cannon, Harley's son—

age thirty-eight, six feet tall, cold steel eyes like his father's—was with him and was very nervous, as shown by his constant pulling of his right earlobe. Pete Pagano, Harley's son-in-law—age forty-two; five feet six inches tall; nerves of steel; as arrogant a man that ever lived—completed the trio. Jim and Pete were wearing light suit coats. Both men sat down on the bench in front of Singer's brick building, a speakeasy, located across the street from the bakery.

Since Pete Pagano and Tom Costello hated each other, people on the street guessed that an encounter was about to take place. They quickly cleared the street, ducking into the nearest business establishment where they could watch with safety. They had not long to wait.

At exactly 2:55 P.M., Tom Costello drove over the railroad tracks in his Model T Ford touring car. As he neared the speakeasy, Pete and Jim jumped up, pulled out pistols from under their suit coats, and fired at him. Both men missed.

Tom stepped hard on the brake pedal, coming to a sudden stop. Jumping out of his car, coat thrown open, making a conspicuous figure with two .45s strapped to his thighs, he approached the speakeasy.

Jim and Pete ducked behind the wall when they saw Tom ready to do battle. Then Tom cut loose with a .45 in each hand. To this day one can see chipped bricks on the corner of the building due to Tom's expert shooting.

The ambush plan worked perfectly. Harley sat still, with head bent downward, during the first firing at Tom. Tom's full attention was directed at Pete and Jim. He had no idea a third party was involved in the ambush.

When Tom was directly opposite Harley, Harley arose slowly. Then he walked over to one of the steel support posts holding up the extended bakery roof. Leisurely he pulled a long-barrel .45 from under his raincoat and held it firmly against the post. He carefully took aim, getting off one shot, hitting Tom in the temple. The bullet came out on the opposite side of Tom's head. Tom never did see Harley, or the story might have had a different ending.

Tom lay in the street with blood oozing out of both sides of his head, his two .45s still gripped in his hands.

The coroner checked the body at 7:10 P.M. and pronounced Tom dead. Since no one claimed the body, the county placed it in a pine box, burying it in potter's field.

The following day the sheriff came to Buckner. He interviewed a number of people. Everyone that was interviewed said they were glad to be rid of Tom.

The sheriff's report stated: "Tom Costello was killed in self-defense by a party or parties unknown."

When people in Buckner and neighboring villages heard of Tom's sudden demise, they shrugged it off and in a few weeks forgot about it.

One day, about a year later, the mayor of Buckner received a letter from a Mrs. Janice Costello, Boise, Idaho. She was Tom's mother. In part, her letter stated that the last letter she received, more than a year ago, had a Buckner, Illinois, postmark. Could the mayor please tell her what happened to Tom? The enclosed photograph, when shown around, identified him as the person she sought.

The mayor, Felix Tucker, did not reveal the nature of Tom's death when he sent a consoling letter to the mother. He stated that the untimely death of Tom Costello had caused deep regret in the town. It was indeed unfortunate that a fatal accident had cut short the life of one of Buckner's most revered visitors.

Mr. Tucker told his friends that the contents of the letter was definitely a lie. But what kind of man could reveal the truth to a loving mother?

Chapter 15
Suicide or Murder?

With Tom "Skunk" Costello dead and buried, most of the people in Royalton and nearby communities felt relieved. Soon they got back into the swing of things, doing just as they always did before Tom rode into town.

The next few weeks passed quickly. One morning when prayers were over, we stood and sang "The Star-Spangled Banner." The voice quality was poor, but the patriotism could not have been better. Some of the youngsters referred to singing as hollering. I couldn't have agreed with them more, although I kept this little secret to myself.

Little Addison Wainright beamed with pride during all the singing sessions. His voice was a typical monotone and stood out head and shoulders above the rest of us. He was happy. *So why tinker with success*? I thought.

Just then a hand shot up. "What is it, Vivian?"

"My aunt from St. Louis visited with us last weekend. She said we can't have prayer service in school. I couldn't understand what she meant. It was something about separation of church and state. Teacher, do you know what she meant?"

Here was a question I had to sidestep. I thought for a moment. Then I said, "Vivian, the school directors instructed me to hold prayer service the first thing every morning. As you know this community is highly religious. Until they instruct me otherwise, we'll continue with morning prayer. Now, all of you get ready for your next class while I mark attendance in the teacher's record book. By the way does anyone know why Alex Giles is absent?"

"Yeah, I do," spoke up Ricardo Olivetti. "His old man kicked the bucket."

"Kicked the bucket," I said. "Did he kick over a paint bucket or a milk pail?" Some of the children began snickering. The others laughed out loud.

"No, no, Teacher! His old man killed himself yesterday afternoon. He went kaput, gone, gone, gone to another world. The undertaker is bringing him home about four o'clock today," answered Ricardo.

"I'm sorry to hear that. My wife and I will call this evening to pay our respects." Home visits were on my schedule. However, this was one home visit I dreaded to make.

Alex, round face, pug nose, and blond curly hair, was a likable youngster. He studied hard, always had his lessons done, and was never in trouble, at least so far this year. My heart really went out to that little boy.

"Seventh grade History class come to the recitation seat," I announced. "Gladys, when did the Civil War begin?"

"The North d——"

"The North declared war on April 15, 1861," interrupted Jake Monroe.

"The question was not addressed to you, Jake, but how did you know the answer?" I inquired.

"When I was in the third grade, I listened a lot. Gee, Teacher, I know all about the Civil War, the whole ball of wax."

"That's nice, Jake. Your turn will come later. Right now this period is for the seventh graders."

By having all of the grades in one room the open classroom concept was born years before its time, not conceived by some educational theorist but by necessity. All of my six grades, one through five and seven, were taught in one room. The classes were separated only by the fact they sat in different seats. In Jake's case, while the teacher was instructing the seventh graders, he became interested in the Civil War and learned about it himself.

During the course of the year, I found hearsay learning so prevalent that I gave a short oral quiz to the fifth and seventh graders before making new assignments. It was surprising how much the fifth graders had learned just by listening.

Without any more interruptions, I continued asking questions relative to the assignment. Then I closed the class with a short personal story.

"Class, I have a personal interest in reading about the American

Civil War. My paternal grandfather was an infantryman, fighting for the North.

"One evening, just about dusk, they were advancing on the enemy when all of a sudden the enemy opened fire. My grandfather's buddy on his right was killed instantly. Grandfather was shot in the palm of his left hand. His regiment didn't have a doctor. When they were camped for the night, he and two other soldiers tried to remove the lead ball to no avail. They cleaned out the wound. Then using whiskey as an antiseptic, they followed up by bandaging the hand the best they could. Next morning Grandfather was again on the firing line.

"He came through the remainder of the war without as much as a scratch, carrying that lead ball in his hand until he died forty-five years later."

" 'That must have been a freak accident, shot in the hand,' I said to him.

" 'No, no, not at all. Several of my buddies were shot in the legs, hands, arms, or feet,' he responded as his face saddened. He refused to talk any longer on the subject."

I couldn't get the Giles suicide off my mind. Somehow though, I was able to call class after class to the recitation seat for the remainder of the morning, with time out for recess, of course.

The first thing after lunch, I drilled the beginners on the alphabet. Then the third graders went through their reading lesson, and I spent the last twenty minutes before the afternoon recess having the seventh graders practice their Palmer Method penmanship. This, in my opinion, was the height of folly. It seemed so ridiculous to have all the pupils learn to write exactly like the illustrations shown in the Palmer Method book. If it were left up to me, I would have allowed each child to develop his own freestyle writing. Not so with the county superintendent. When I gave my opinion to him, you would have thought I was some kind of heretic.

"Under no circumstances will you discard the Palmer Method!" he said. "That's a tried-and-true method, and you or any other teacher in my county had better not try to change it. Freestyle writing! Bah! Humbug."

"Fifteen after two," I said. "Recess time." The children stood up and walked out of the schoolhouse in an orderly manner. I couldn't see lining up little children like soldiers, then having them march lockstep in and out of the building. However, this was the practice in all of the other county schools.

When the last pupil exited the building, Mr. Snider, director of the Four-Mile School, walked in.

"Mind if I visit a little while?" he said. "I'm on my way to the college to bring my son home for a few days."

"Not at all. Glad to have you," I greeted him as we shook hands.

"Mr. Neal, I've been a school director for fifteen years, and I've never seen a group of pupils walk out of a schoolhouse so quiet and orderly without marching like little tin soldiers."

"Mr. Snider, I firmly believe that education should be life itself, not a preparation for life. We as adults and children don't line up and march in and out of church. So why should children do it at school?"

"I never thought of it that way before, but it does make a lot of sense."

Hearing much loud talking on the playground, I said, "Mr. Snider, I think we have a problem. Want to come along and see what's taking place?"

"Sure thing. You lead the way."

As we stepped out the door, we heard a boy's voice poking fun at a girl who was crying her heart out.

"Susan's mother has a boyfriend, Tom Skunk, Skunk, Skunk, Pew, Pew, Pew. Stinky Tom, that was his name. If she had married him, you would have become 'Little Skunk.' Then we would have called you 'Stinky Susan.' Ha, ha."

As we approached the two, Susan was still crying and Jake Monroe was doing the teasing.

"Jake!" I commanded. "Stop it this second!" He started to leave. "Stay put, young man. I want a word with you. This is the second time I've caught you calling little girls bad names. The first time I gave you a warning. I see you've paid no attention to it. Now I'm giving you five recess detentions. For five recess periods you will sit in your seat by yourself with no one allowed to visit with you. Detention begins with tomorrow morning's recess. Now you're excused.

"Susan, come here." I took my handkerchief and dried her eyes, "Pay no attention to remarks like that. But if he bothers you again. I want you to tell me. Will you do that?"

"I sure will, Teach. Thanks."

"Run along now, Susan. Go play with the other girls."

"I see you are a law-and-order teacher," said Mr. Snider. "I like that. In fact, I like everything I've seen here today and like everything I've heard about your teaching ability."

"It's 2:30, Mr. Snider. Time for me to ring the bell to end recess. Want to come in and visit for a while?"

"I'd like nothing better, but I promised Tom I'd pick him up at his boarding house around five o'clock. So I'll just run along."

Mr. Snider got into his Dodge touring car and headed for the college. I walked into the schoolhouse to teach five of my remaining classes.

Three of my classes moved along as usual. The children had done their homework. Then I made assignments for the next day.

Near the end of the seventh grade English class, I announced a test for the following day. A groan permeated the recitation seat.

"Why a test tomorrow?" Yetlo wanted to know.

"A good question, Yetlo," I answered. "From its results, I'll find out two things: One, how much you, the class, learned about the unit of work; and two, how effective my teaching has been. So in reality I'll be testing both of us, the class and myself.

"Any more questions?"

"Yes," inquired Agnes Harper. "Will it call for long, written-out answers, or will it be true/false, fill in blanks, etc.?"

"It will be the essay type where you have an opportunity to express yourself in complete sentences."

I used the Socratic method of teaching more often than not. With paragraphic answers, I had the opportunity of checking sentence structure, spelling, and usage as well as knowledge of the subject. With the fifth and seventh graders, I paid particular attention to the manner in which they developed a subject.

As the first grade reading class approached the recitation seat, little Henry Meeker had his hand raised.

"What is it, Henry?"

"Me write a story about Rover. Want to hear it?" he anxiously asked.

"Now that we are all seated, I sure do. Let's hear it."

"I have a dog. His name is ———"

I interrupted him to ask the children a question. "Boys and girls, just a short time ago Henry didn't know one letter from another. Now he has written a whole story about his dog. Would you all like to hear it?"

"Yeah. Let's hear it," spoke up Wayne Roberts.

"I think it's nice, Henry, that the boys and girls want to hear your story. Would you like to read it to them?" I asked.

"Yes," he said, showing a bit of nervousness.

"OK. Stand up tall, face the children, and speak loud and clear."

"I have a dog. His name is Rover. Rover is kind. We play together. We make perfect pals."

"Wonderful!" I said. "Boys and girls, should we give him a big hand?" I asked as I started clapping my hands. Soon the whole room of youngsters was clapping their hands loud and furiously. Henry took his seat; a prouder little boy I've never seen.

Looking at my watch, I said, "It's five minutes 'til bell time. We have all had a busy day. You have earned an early dismissal. School dismissed!"

Sometimes when the children were on edge, not paying attention or just plain noisy, I would keep them in five or ten minutes past dismissal time. So I thought it only fair to dismiss them five or ten minutes early when they were exceptionally good all day.

I started to close the windows when I saw Yetlo Olivetti still sitting in his seat."Yetlo, are you waiting for someone?" I inquired.

"No, Teach. I know something that you just might be interested in knowing about," he said.

What could he know that I'd be interested in hearing? I wondered. "What is it?" I asked.

"You'll teach the eighth grade next year. There are three answers in the eighth grade arithmetic book that are wrong," he said as he approached me with Miles's *Eighth Grade Arithmetic*.

"Last year our teacher found the mistakes and gave us the correct solutions. I thought it would be embarrassing to you as a teacher, if some pupil showed you up," he said. "These answers are correct because she was good at figures."

The Miles book had been on the market for several years and had gone through three revisions. It was hard for me to believe there was a single incorrect answer on the answer sheets, let alone three.

Yetlo loaned me his book. Late that evening I planned to work the three problems and find out if the former teacher was as good in math as Yetlo claimed.

That evening at six o'clock, Fairy and I left the house to pay our respects to the Giles family. When we arrived, people were milling about inside and outside the house. As in most rural communities, almost everyone was there.

As we were walking to the front door we noticed several men sitting on the porch telling jokes. Whether the punch lines were humorous or not, each one was followed by big horselaughs. I felt frustration building inside me. I couldn't figure out whether these men were just ignorant or whether they had no respect for the Giles family.

The body lay in a bronze casket in the bedroom. Visitors entered through the living room, went into the bedroom, passed by the casket, then left through the bedroom door. With such an arrangement, the small four-room house was never overcrowded.

Poor Alex was walking around like a lost soul. Both of our hearts went out to him. When he saw us he came over, tears in his eyes. He blurted out, "My father didn't commit suicide like everybody says. I know he didn't. Next Saturday is my birthday, and he promised to take me to Royalton to the picture show. He never went back on a promise he made to me. He was murdered!"

Mrs. Giles came over, excused herself, and took Alex to the kitchen. Fairy was talking to one of the Sew and Stitch Sewing Circle ladies. Director Harry Rone motioned me to the door.

"Let's go outside, Charles, and sit in my car. I have something to tell you," he said, "Our wives are good mixers. They will take care of themselves for a few minutes."

"Harry, I just talked to Alex. He doesn't think his father committed suicide. He says that he was murdered."

"That boy's right! Giles was murdered! Here's the story. Because it was a warm autumn day, two young coal miners went to Deep Hole to swim in the Little Muddy River. They were about to dive in when they spotted a body floating near the opposite bank. When they approached it, they could tell it was dead. They were shocked when they recognized it was Giles. They dragged the body up the bank. Then they left the scene, stopping at my house on the way to the coroner in Royalton. I went with them. The coroner called the sheriff. As soon as he arrived, the five of us rushed to what we thought was a suicide.

"The body was tied with bailing wire, legs and arms. You know,

Charles, bailing wire is used in hay bailers to hold the flakes of hay together, forming the bail."

"Why, Harry, no human being could tie his arms next to his body, then roll down the bank into the water. That's impossible!"

"Of course. That isn't the whole ball of wax. When Dr. Flemming did a postmortem, he didn't find water in the lungs. What do you think of that, Charles?"

"It's nothing short of murder. What does the sheriff think?"

"The sheriff always take the line of least resistance. He put suicide in his report to the Royalton newspaper. By doing that, he eliminates an investigation. Why the people elect him term after term is more than I can understand."

"Who do you think did it, Harry?"

"My story is based on facts up to this point. From here on it is a matter of conjecture. Hearsay has it that the Giles's boarder, Amos Ainsworth, was too chummy with Mrs. Giles. On Saturday while Giles was working in the coal mine, Mrs. Giles sent Alex on an errand. Instead of going on the errand immediately, Alex hid in the barn. After several minutes passed he quietly slipped into the house. What do you think he found, Charles?"

"I haven't the faintest idea, Harry."

"He found Amos and Mrs. Giles in bed stark naked, so the hearsay story goes Alex did not tell his dad. Alex felt sure his father would think the boy was lying and give him a whipping for telling a lie. Most of us who know the family well think that Mr. Giles came home drunk. Mrs. Giles and Amos plied him with more booze until he passed out. Then in some manner they smothered him, hauled his body to the river, wrapped him with bailing wire, then rolled him down the bank into the water to make it appear as if he committed suicide. Naturally, there was no water in his lungs."

"My, my!" I said. "What a gruesome story."

As we walked back toward the house, I barely heard a word Harry was saying. I began to reminisce. Harry's version of the so-called suicide brought back the memory of Jimmy Shaw's father's case.

The similarities between both cases were great, although in the case of Alex's father the suicide or murder happened in Little Muddy River fourteen miles downstream and fifteen years later.

The only difference between the two cases was motive.

There's an old saying, "Truth is stranger than fiction." I can believe it.

"What's the matter, Charles? You have hardly said a word since we left the car."

"Oh, nothing. I was just thinking."

"By the way, how is Mary Lou Hawkins doing in school?"

"No problem there, Harry. She's a little old for the seventh grade, but she's a go-getter. Never fails to do her homework. She's a polite little lady if I ever saw one."

"Glad to hear it, Charles." Looking at his luminous watch, he said, "Nine forty-five. I'll get my better half and be on our way. I've got a lot of fence to build tomorrow."

Fairy and I said good-bye to Mrs. Giles. Then we went home where I worked the three problems that Yetlo Olivetti brought to my attention. As I suspected, all three answers in the book answer sheets were correct.

The next day Yetlo had the wind let out of his sails when I explained the solutions to him. He didn't say a thing, just hung his head, swallowing his pride.

Chapter 16
Mary Lou Hawkins

As the days rolled on, I was really beginning to feel that I'd be a successful teacher after all. About that same time something else crossed my mind. I couldn't put my finger on it, but I had a premonition that something bizarre was soon to happen.

At four o'clock that Thursday afternoon, the youngsters were leaving school on their way home. On her way out Mary Lou Hawkins stopped by my desk.

"Something on your mind, Mary Lou?" I inquired.

"Oh, no, not really. Ma asked me to see if you needed any eggs. I'm going to deliver Widow Browning two dozen eggs after supper tonight. Since I pass your place, Ma said I could leave some with you if you're running short."

"As it happens, Mary Lou, we bought two dozen eggs at the Woodway Store last Saturday morning. Thanks just the same. By the way, doesn't Widow Browning live across the main highway between Elkville and Royalton?"

"Yes, she does, Teach. Why did you ask?"

"Mary Lou, it doesn't seem safe for a young lady to be walking in that area after dark."

Mary Lou hesitated a moment as she shuffled her feet. Then she said, "Shucks, Teach, I visit Widow Browning twice a week after supper. Nothing's happened to me yet. She is getting old and likes for me to help with the cleaning, washing dishes, and mending clothes. Good-bye, Teach."

Apparently, Mary Lou had her fill of my lecture. She was seventeen years old and in my seventh grade class. She finished the eighth grade last year. She was in the seventh grade not because she was a slow learner. An undiagnosed disease struck her down two days before Christmas when she was in the fifth grade. She lingered in and out of consciousness for three years before she became well enough to return to school. Now she was her old self again, everybody agreed. She was five feet, four inches tall and weighed 106 pounds. Her beautiful smile set off her naturally curly blond hair, and she always wore a pleasant smile.

Before going home for the evening, I swept the floor and put my desk in order. All in all it had been a tough day. In addition to teaching my scheduled number of classes, I stopped two fights and one hair-pulling event.

I hardly entered the door when Fairy put her carpet cleaner inside the storage cabinet. She had been cleaning house. Then she said, "Boy, you sure look beat! Why don't we have an early dinner [supper] and take in a movie this evening? Fern Eskew stopped by today. She said Clark Gable is playing, but she couldn't remember the name of the picture."

I groaned. "Give me a minute to catch my breath," I said as I fell into a kitchen chair.

"You've had your minute, what do you say?"

"The more I think about it, the more it sounds like a good idea, Fairy. It's the middle of the week and the movie will only set us back a quarter each. I've had it today! It would be a blessing for both of us to get out of the boondocks for a couple of hours. By Jove, Fairy, let's do it!" So we did it.

Returning from the movie, we turned off the main highway to continue our way home over a dirt road. We had scarcely made the turn when my wife excitedly shouted as she pointed toward the northeast. "Look! A falling star. Some folks in our community claim that's an evil sign; other say, it's an act of God. How do you explain it, Charles?"

"According to astronomers it's a small solid body, called a meteor, entering the Earth's atmosphere from outer space. The fire is caused by the friction resulting from its rapid motion when it enters the atmosphere.

"Gee. You sound just like a scientist."

"I'll let you in on a little secret. Two weeks ago my seventh grade geography class had a lesson on meteors. So I'm not so smart after all."

By now we were crossing Black Bottom Swamp. It was a quarter of a mile long, lined on both sides of the road with sassafras sprouts and weeds among the oak and hickory trees. Although the road commissioner recently raised the roadbed two feet, it still left much to be desired. Since the swamp was never completely dry, the road was full of potholes caused by moisture working its way upward.

We had almost reached the swamp's end when Fairy said, "Hear that, Charles?"

"Hear what? I don't hear anything."

"Stop the car! Hear it?"

"Yes, I do now. Sounds like someone moaning."

I pressed hard on the Model T Ford reverse pedal. Then I stopped, pressed hard on the clutch pedal, turning the car so the lights would flood the area from where I thought the moaning originated. I stopped the car and both of us jumped out.

"Look, Fairy! See that hand sticking out of that clump of bushes!"

We parted the bushes. There lay a woman, bloody and muddy. Her lips were swollen and one eye was swollen shut. Her dress was torn to shreds and her torn undergarments were lying several feet behind her.

Blood was oozing out from a neck wound. I used my handkerchief to slow the bleeding. Then Fairy brought her handkerchief soaked in a nearby puddle. She began washing some of the blood and mud from the woman's face.

"Charles, it's Mary Lou!"

"My God, Fairy! What fiend did this to her?"

We straightened her torn dress the best we could. Then we gently carried her to the car, easing her ever so carefully onto the backseat.

Slowly I turned the car around and headed straight for Dr. Leo Flemming's office in Royalton since the nearest hospital was twenty-two miles away.

Doc Flemming was no ordinary hick town doctor. He was a skilled surgeon, having had his medical training in the Harvard Medical School where he graduated third in his class. Having done his internship and three years of residency in a New York hospital, he practiced for three years in a Brooklyn, New York, hospital.

Big city life had no appeal either for him or his wife. So when he saw an advertisement for a doctor in Royalton, Illinois, they hurried there as fast as their touring car could take them.

The people of Royalton and nearby communities were so glad to have a doctor of his caliber that they built him a house attached to what he called a clinic. It had a waiting room, an office, an operating room, and two recovery rooms, each with two full-size beds.

Arriving at the clinic, I slammed on the brake pedal and blew the horn. Doc Flemming rushed out immediately. When he saw what I had, he turned on his heel, rushed inside the clinic, returning with a hospital bed on wheels, where we gently placed Mary Lou. Then we wheeled her inside to the examining room where Doc was joined by his wife, a registered nurse. Mary Lou was still unconscious, but Doc had stopped her neck wound from bleeding.

I telephoned the sheriff in Benton. The switchboard operator informed me that he was in Royalton. There were a series of fights in progress in Joe's Poolroom, and the town's one policeman had requested a backup. I telephoned the poolroom. Order had been restored, and the sheriff said he'd meet me at Doc's in a matter of minutes.

When the sheriff came into Doc's waiting room, I briefed him on the situation.

In a few minutes Doc entered the waiting room. He removed his operating gown and wiped the perspiration from his forehead. Then he said, "Gentlemen, I've stopped all the bleeding and she is resting, but she is still unconscious. This bothers me a great deal."

"Doc, can you be more specific with regard to what you found when you examined Mary Lou?" inquired the sheriff. "I want all the evidence I can get to bring this fiend to justice."

"Yes, of course. There were extensive bruises over the whole face and scalp. There were several puncture wounds, the most severe being the one on the right side of the neck. There was a fracture to the skull, probably caused by a blunt instrument such as a tree limb or baseball bat. The nose was partially blocked with caked blood."

"Have the parents been contacted?" the sheriff wanted to know.

"Oh, yes. Mrs. Flemming sent Ron Sheffield to their home. As you know, no one in the rural area has a telephone, and Ron is most reliable. He does odd jobs and runs errands for us."

While Fairy waited in Doc's waiting room, the sheriff and I drove in my Model T Ford out to the scene of the crime. When we arrived, the sheriff opened what he called an evidence bag. In it he put Mary Lou's torn undergarments, her shoes, and scraps of torn dress and slip. Her brassiere was never found. Perhaps the fiend kept it as a prized souvenir. We were getting ready to leave when something caught the sheriff's eye.

"What do we have here?" he said as he stooped to pick up a small key case partially covered with an oak leaf. "This is most interesting."

"What is it, Sheriff?" I anxiously inquired.

"The letters J.B.N. on the lower edge of the key case," he said as he handed it to me.

"Are you thinking what I think you're thinking, Sheriff?"

"I'm afraid I am. J.B.N. could be no other than Joe Bill Nolan. He has the reputation for being a sex maniac but he's never been convicted, although he's been arrested on several occasions and charged with various sex crimes. This time I think he has tied the noose around his neck. Charles, do you know anything about his criminal history?"

"No, Sheriff, I'm afraid I don't. You see, I'm new to this area and haven't had time to catch up on many of the past events."

"OK. I'll fill you in on our way back to town. First of all, Joe Bill's parents are fine upstanding Christian people, as are his two sisters and one brother. If there ever was a black sheep in a family, Joe is it."

"How do you come to that conclusion, Sheriff?"

"When he was fourteen years old, he stabbed a playmate in the back due to an argument over a marble game. Mr. Nolan paid the doctor bill and the boy's parents dropped the charges.

"Shortly after his sixteenth birthday, Joe Bill robbed a candy store and was recognized by the owner. Again Mr. Nolan came to the rescue by returning the money plus a hundred-dollar tip if charges were not made.

"A year later Joe Bill entered the high school girls' locker room, stripped nude, and hid in one of the toilet stalls. When the girls returned following PE, he jumped out of the stall, shouting, 'Look at the big monkey.' The girls' screaming brought the PE instructor on the run from her office. She reported the incident to the principal. Immediately Joe Bill's high school education was terminated.

"Between ages seventeen and twenty-one he was arrested on several rape charges. No convictions were ever made, primarily because his father hired the best defense attorneys in the state. He's about twenty-two now, and I think he's met his Waterloo."

While I was listening to the sheriff talk, I came to one quick conclusion: This was going to be one case not swept under the rug.

When we arrived at Doc's clinic, the sheriff called his office, instructing one of his deputies to put out an APB on Joe Bill Nolan. He was a twenty-two-year-old; he was unmarried. He was a thin sad-looking character with an impish face, wearing a leather jacket and a low-neck sweater, crepe soles on his shoes, and a baseball cap.

The next morning found Joe Bill behind bars. "I'll be out of this joint within the hour," he bragged to his cell mate. "Most likely right now my old man is arranging bail."

"What you in for?" inquired the cell mate.

"Hell, I don't know. This lousy sheriff gets his kicks out of arresting me for no reason at all. What are you in for?"

"I lost my job. A man has to do something to make a buck or two. So I made a little moonshine. I was set up. Soon as I made a sale last night to a man wanting some booze, the revenuers slapped the cuffs on me, and here I am."

The sheriff telephoned Mr. Nolan, informing him that his son was a suspect in a rape case. Mr. Nolan didn't say anything for a moment, then he said, "Sheriff, from now on that boy is going to fight his own battles. I've got him out of one scrape or another for the past eight years. No more. I'm through."

"Mr. Nolan, when the judge sets bail, do you want to post bail for Joe Bill?"

Another hesitation. "No, Sheriff, I do not! I will hire him a local attorney, no more big city expensive lawyers. That is all I'm going to do for him!" With that said, Mr. Nolan hung up the phone.

After a coffee break on Thursday at midmorning, the sheriff ordered a deputy to bring Joe Bill to the office in handcuffs.

Joe Bill stomped into the office in a rage. "When's my old man going to bail me out of this joint?"

"Sit down, Joe Bill! I'll ask the questions. In the meantime keep your trap closed 'til you are spoken to.

"Your father isn't going to bail you out this time."

"That's a lie——"

"Shut up!" the sheriff barked as he interrupted Joe Bill. "I have some questions to ask. Where were you yesterday evening between six and ten o'clock?"

"I happened to be in Elkville."

"Anybody see you?"

"Sure. Lots of people saw me."

"Joe Bill, name just one of them."

"That's impossible! I don't know anyone there."

"If so, all we have is your word that you were in Elkville last evening. Isn't that the truth of the matter?"

"You said it, I didn't," Joe Bill responded in a sarcastic way.

"You were not in Elkville at all. Isn't that true?"

"No, it is not!"

"Joe Bill, are you familiar with Dugan's speakeasy located three miles north of Royalton?"

"Am I familiar with it? Sure thing, but I was not there last night."

"You were seen on the dirt road where it crosses Black Bottom Swamp."

"Sheriff, what the hell does that mean? I don't remember ever being there."

"Joe Bill, let me refresh your memory. We have witnesses that will swear on the witness stand that you were seen at Dugan's speakeasy on at least three different occasions including last night. Not only were you seen there, but you were drunk on several occas——"

"That's a damn lie. Sheriff, you don't have a thing on me. I'm clean and you know it. So let's cut the crap."

"Joe Bill, isn't it true that you were drinking in Dugan's yesterday afternoon and that you left around 5 P.M. and returned later after you raped Mary Lou?"

"No, it isn't."

"Joe Bill, why do you wear crepe soles on your shoes?"

"My feet hurt. Crepe soles are easier on my feet."

"Isn't it true that with crepe soles on your feet, you can sneak up on young girls in the dark, grab them from behind, then rape them?"

"Sheriff, you know that's another one of your damn lies. You know I've been arrested many times for rape but never convicted. Smoke that in your pipe!"

"Joe Bill, what were you doing last evening on the old dirt road where it crosses Black Bottom Swamp?"

"Nothing because I wasn't there, so lay off that question. Don't ask it again."

"Why did you attack Mary Lou Hawkins?"

"I don't know what you are talking about."

"Oh, but I think you do."

At this point the sheriff worked an old police ploy on him. "Mary Lou identified you."

"She couldn't because it was pitch-dark," Joe Bill blurted out before he realized what he was saying.

"Why did you do it, Joe Bill?"

"I'm not answering any more questions 'til I see my lawyer!" he shouted, showing both anger and rage.

The sheriff ordered the deputy to return Joe Bill to his cell where he remained for six weeks until his trial date.

Joe Bill's trial began promptly at 9 A.M. with Judge Harlan Poindexter presiding.

The prosecutor was Tom Jenkins, and he was another in the long line of those who cared very little for Joe Bill.

The defense attorney was Harold Little. He had been practicing in Benton for almost a year. His record was eleven losses and one win.

Joe Bill never took the witness stand in his defense. From time to time, he glanced over at the jury. There he saw no sympathy or understanding.

First, Jenkins paraded four witnesses to the witness stand, one at a time. They verified everything that the sheriff charged against Joe Bill, except, of course, the attack on Mary Lou.

The sheriff was the next witness. This was old hat to him, and he came through with flying colors.

The last witness was Mary Lou. She took the stand, head bent forward with tears in her eyes. Jenkins took time, over the objections of Little, to calm her and to get her in a frame of mind to answer his questions. When her tears were dried, he led her very patiently over the whole episode. She was a brave little lady, giving her answers clearly.

Defense attorney Little did all in his power to discredit statements made by the four witnesses, the sheriff, and Mary Lou, but to no avail. Each witness held steadfast to his or her side of the story.

Little just didn't have what it takes to be a successful defense attorney. One person in the courtroom was heard to say, "Why, Little couldn't put up a good defense for Santa Claus if he were tried for breaking and entering on Christmas Eve."

Judge Poindexter charged the jury, and the bailiff led them to the jury room. They remained there for less than an hour. Then they returned to the courtroom.

"Have you reached a verdict?" Judge Poindexter asked the foreman.

"Yes, we have, Your Honor."

"How find you all? Guilty or not guilty?"

"We find the defendant, Joe Bill Nolan, guilty, Your Honor." With that a wild cheer arose from the spectators.

"Order in the court. I'll have none of that," the judge shouted. When quiet resumed, Judge Poindexter said he would pronounce sentence the following Monday at 9 A.M. "Court adjourned!" he said as he struck the gavel hard on the bench.

Joe Bill was given ten years in the state penitentiary less time served in the county jail.

Although some deep scars remained on Mary Lou's face, she returned to school. After graduating from the Dutch Hill one-room country school, she went on to high school followed by four years of college where she majored in Business Administration.

Chapter 17
Never a Dull Moment

The next few days passed uneventfully. There were no fights or discipline problems to resolve.

On the following Monday morning, I arrived at school early. After putting the fifth grade arithmetic test problems on the blackboard, I pulled down the map of Europe. It was fastened to a roller which, in turn, was fastened to the wall just above the blackboard.

Several classes came to the recitation seat and left. Now it was time for the fifth graders to take their arithmetic test.

"Fifth graders, take out your pencil and paper. I have the questions on the blackboard. When I raise the map you may be——"

"Teacher, I didn't know we were having a test today," broke in Jake Monroe.

"Don't believe him, Teach!" chirped several students in unison.

"He used that trick all last year to get out of taking tests," said Wayne Roberts.

"I did not! You——"

"Enough of that! Jake," I said, "I announced this test two days ago. No more arguments. Case closed!"

"May we use pen and ink instead of a pencil?" Susan Slavins wanted to know.

"Yes, Susan." With that I raised the map.

Any time pupils were tested I supervised them from the rear of the room instead of the front. In this way I could better watch for children copying, while they had a difficult time keeping track of me.

I noticed Irene Singer's head bobbing up and down as if she was looking for something on her lap. *Aha*, I said to myself, as I looked closer. *She's copying from material written on her handkerchief.* I didn't say anything. When the period ended, I collected the papers.

"Irene," I said, "you didn't give me all your work. Let me have the rest of it."

"Why, Teach, everything is on my test papers," she said as if she was guilty of no wrongdoing.

"No, not all. Give me your handkerchief," I demanded. "Thank you, Irene. Your study period is next, so you will have time to do your test over. When it's time for lunch, I want you to bring your test paper to my desk. Then I'll return your handkerchief."

As the children hurried out of the room to eat their lunch, Irene came to give me her test paper. She looked terrified as her eyes met mine.

"Are you going to give me a whipping, Teach?" she inquired with tears in her eyes.

I began awkwardly, "No, of course not! That would not accomplish anything. What is important is why you copied when you always do so well on your tests."

"I don't know," she said as she looked down at her shoes.

"Oh, but I think you do. Why?"

"Well, if you must know, my parents give me a nickel for every A I bring home on my report card. If I have a failing grade, I get a whipping," she whimpered with tears streaming down her face.

"Irene, as you know, I make home visits. Ask your parents if I may visit tomorrow. I give you my word, you will profit by it. So don't worry any longer. I promise to help you. Will you ask them?"

"Yes. I'll give you their answer in the morning," she said as she awkwardly left the room to join her playmates.

Although I told Irene not to worry, she had a sad, worried look on her face all of the next day.

The time was 7:35 P.M. My face flushed as I knocked on the Singers' front door. I wondered in what frame of mind I'd find them.

After the introductions I was asked to sit down in an old-fashioned rocking chair. *So far so good*, I thought.

"Mr. Neal, Irene is upstairs doing her homework. Do you want her to meet with us?" Mrs. Singer inquired.

"Not necessarily," I replied. "I would like her to meet with us a little later, however."

We got right down to the business at hand. After a thirty-minute session, the Singers agreed to discontinue the success/failure rewards. They realized, they said, that their plan was making a nervous wreck out of Irene; but they had declined to stop it for fear her grades would fall.

I assured them they had no reason to worry on that score. "Irene," I said "is an intelligent child and will make good grades without giving her prizes." Then we had Irene join us at which time we talked for another half hour about her Sunday school work and about everything else but school-related subjects.

As I stood, getting ready to leave, Mrs. Singer said, "We would like to invite you and Mrs. Neal over for supper some evening."

"Thank you very much," I replied. "I'll look forward to that with pleasure. Just say when."

While driving along the bumpy dirt road, I thought about the home visit. Mr. Singer struck me as a very interesting person. I liked him. He had a wonderful personality, intelligent, animated, bold, and irrepressible.

Mrs. Singer was gracious, well mannered, and a good conversationalist.

I arrived home at 9:45 P.M. Fairy met me at the door, and I gave her a real big hug.

"What's that for, Charles?" she inquired. "The Singers didn't treat you to moonshine whiskey, did they?"

"Oh, no, nothing like that. I'm happy because I think my home visit this evening was really worthwhile. I predict it will pay big dividends, particularly to Irene."

The following day was a glorious, warm fall day. A few minutes after noon, I sat down with some of my pupils on the open schoolhouse porch. Before eating lunch, I was admiring the beautiful fall colors. The yellow sweet gum leaves, the light red maple leaves, the dark red sumac bushes, intermingled in the forest adjoining the schoolhouse yard, never ceased to fascinate me. How I wished I were an artist so I could capture on canvas that rare beauty right before my eyes. Suddenly, pupils' giggling and guffawing caused me to turn to see what the fuss was all about.

"Look, Teach," Julia Slater remarked, "here comes an old, dirty bum walking this way. A bum came by here last year. Teacher made us all go inside. Then she locked the door. Must we go inside now?" she wanted to know.

"No, Julia. I want all of you to stay put and mind your manners. He is a human being just like all of us."

By now the man was directly opposite us. He was about six feet tall, much underweight, had on a worn pair of blue trousers, a tattered gray shirt, a black slouch hat, and a shaggy beard. He carried a bundle over his shoulder. Because of the bundle, bums like him were known as "bindle stiffs."

Later, I told my pupils that the word *bindle* was a slang word for *bundle*. The bundle held the bum's (hobo's) bedding.

"Good day, sir," I shouted.

The man jolted to a stop, paused for a few seconds, and turned his head, all the while looking at me with dark-circled eyes. Then he rubbed his face thoughtfully. Finally, he said, "Sir, were you speaking to me?"

"Yes, I'm under the weather today," I lied, "and was about to throw away my lunch. Have you had lunch?"

"Sir, I haven't had anything to eat since last evening."

"Would you like to eat my lunch before I throw it away?"

The man stood still, transfixed. Then he replied, "I appreciate it very much if you don't mind having an old bum around."

As I gave him my lunch, I invited him to sit on the porch. He thanked me again before wolfing down his food. He started to leave when Jim Settlemeir offered him an apple, which he gratefully accepted. Then several of the other children gave him some of their lunches: three oranges, two bananas, and one peanut butter sandwich.

He ate the sandwich. Putting the fruit in his bundle, he thanked us again and started to leave.

"Going far?" I asked.

"Well, yes. I guess you could say that. Bound for Florida. Hope to get there before cold weather catches me. I was a typesetter for a large Chicago newspaper until six months ago. Then the paper folded. I tried and tried to find another job, but had no luck. In the meantime my wife died. I couldn't see spending the winter in Chicago, so I hit the road. How far is it to Elkville?"

"Three miles," I answered.

"That's swell. I understand a freight train comes through around four o'clock going to Florida. I'll hop on it. Unless the bulls throw me off, I should arrive in Florida sometime tomorrow afternoon."

As he was leaving, he turned around and said, "Mr. Teacher,

boys and girls, you have been the kindest people I've met since I left Chicago two weeks ago. Thanks again for everything and may God bless all of you."

After he left several of the children spoke up at once. "What are bulls?" they wanted to know.

"Bulls," I answered, "are railroad detectives. Since they treat freeloaders riding freight trains cruelly, they have been nicknamed 'bulls.'"

It was a cloudy Monday late in October as I came out of the schoolhouse to supervise the playground lunch period. Most of the children seemed to expend more energy in playing their games than usual. *Could all this excitement be due to Halloween being just around the corner?* I wondered.

Everyone was enjoying life to the fullest except the Olivetti brothers and Wayne Roberts. They were huddled together in the northeast corner of the playground talking softly and making motions to each other oblivious to the other children. Clearly something was in the making. Perhaps they were only making plans to trick or treat unsuspecting neighbors on Halloween night. I hoped that was all. *Oh, well*, I said to myself. *Everything comes out in the wash.*

Dismissing the three boys from my mind, I started back to the schoolhouse to retrieve my dollar pocket watch, which I had inadvertently left on my desk.

As I stepped into the room, third grader Iva Mae Roberts was sitting in her seat, head bent down over her arms folded on top of her desk. She was crying her little heart out.

Sitting on top of the desk across the aisle from her, I said, as soothingly as I could, "Iva Mae, what is it? Why are you crying?"

Silence.

"Iva Mae, I want to help you. Please tell me what's the matter."

More silence.

"Iva Mae, how can I help you if I don't know what's the matter?"

"No," she blubbered.

"Well then, tell me——"

"I can't. They will kill me if they find out I told."

"Told what, Iva Mae?"

"Promise not to tell?" she said as she wiped the tears from her eyes.

"Promise and hope to die if I do!" I said as I crossed my heart with my right hand.

"I heard Wayne, Yetlo, and Ricardo talking last night. They didn't know I was listening. They are going to whip you first thing after lunch when books take up."

"Don't worry about a thing," I said as I took my handkerchief and finished drying those pretty blue eyes of hers. "You have three minutes 'til bell time. Run outside and join your friends."

So that's what all the huddling and whispering was about among Wayne, Yetlo, and Ricardo. I was to be in for a surprise. *Well, we'll see about that*, I said to myself as I rang the bell, ending the lunch period.

I stood outside the door, letting all the children come in. Then I stepped inside, locked the door, put the key in my pocket, walked to the back of the room, removed the three-foot steel poker from its rack on the potbellied stove, and placed the poker on my desk. Next, I faced the children, looking to the right, then to the left, all the while keeping silent for thirty seconds.

"Before we begin the next class I have an announcement to make," I said as I scowled facetiously.

Looking at my watch I said, "It has come to my attention that it's time to whip the teacher and run him out of the schoolhouse, exactly as it was done last year. Anybody have anything to say?" I glared at Ricardo, Yetlo, and Wayne.

Silence.

"I'm waiting, and my patience is getting mighty slim."

Silence.

"OK. Then I have something to say! If any of you still have a desire to whip the teacher, there are three things I want you to think about: one, I'll take on any of you, one at a time; two, if you try to mob me somebody or bodies will end up in Dr. Flemming's clinic in Royalton. And I can guarantee you mine will not be one of them," I said as I raised the poker from the top of my desk.

Silence.

Returning the poker to the desk, I said, "Number three: All of us can forget this ever happened. Call it a bad dream if you like."

This was a traumatic experience, to say the least, for the little ones. They were crying all through my declaration of war. This made me very sad, because I always believed that a school should provide a happy environment. These last few minutes were a far cry from happy ones. *Oh, well,* I thought, *I'll make it up to them during the rest of the term.*

Since there was no charge from the bullies, I called the next class to the recitation seat. The remaining classes and the recess period passed without incident. However, the atmosphere was heavy. It reminded me of the lull before the storm and the settling of the smoke following a fire.

News in the boondocks travels fast. The following day Director Pirka stopped by the school at morning recess time. He was on his way to Royalton.

"Heard about the trouble you had with three of your pupils," he said. "I'll bet you had some scared moments."

"No, not really. However, this is not for publication. I weigh 175 pounds, did considerable boxing while in high school, and was in several rough-and-tumble fights before I was married."

"Well, you have the backing of the community. Everyone I've talked to is glad you took care of the bullies," he said as he started toward his car.

Several days later when I left the house on my way to school, the weather was chilly but invigorating. The sun was partially hidden behind light gray clouds. It was the kind of day that made one glad to be alive.

Long before I reached the playground that morning, children's voices filled the air. Thinking I was late I looked at my watch: 8:20 A.M., ten minutes before time for the first bell. *What gives?* I wondered. *Is there some kind of surprise in the offing?*

When the children spotted me, they came charging. "Well, well. What's going on here?" I said.

Several of the children stopped in front of me; others clutched my arms. "May we have a Halloween party?" asked Nancy Spinlow.

Apparently she was the spokesperson for the group. "So this is what the fuss is all about, is it, Nancy?"

"We never had a Halloween party last year," moaned Addison Wainright.

I scanned the faces in front of me. It was a happy and jubilant crowd, all waiting for an answer to Nancy's question. "If you all want a Halloween party that much, the answer is yes!"

Whoopies, hurrahs, and laughter came in abundance.

As we came onto the playground, I said, "Later I'll appoint a committee to work out the details, one member from each of the six classes. To get things underway I'm naming Nancy as chairperson [as far back as 1930, I couldn't understand why anyone would insult the feminine sex by calling a girl or a woman a chairman] of the committee. Time for the first bell."

Anyone seeing the happy expressions on their faces would never suspect that only a few days ago some of the pupils and I almost had an altercation.

We spent the remaining days before Halloween making it an educational project. Using books that I borrowed from the Royalton City Library, children from grades four, five, and seven researched the subject of Halloween for theme-writing materials. The little ones told original ghost and goblin stories to older pupils who had volunteered to do their writing. In addition, all the children rehearsed daily a three-act play, *The Ghost Came at Midnight*.

The party was scheduled for 7:30 P.M. so coal miners who were fortunate enough to have jobs and farmers could attend.

The audience and the pupils, dressed in various costumes, began arriving early. I wore a black-and-white striped prisoner's uniform. Fairy wore the traditional witch's costume, including the black dress, hose, shoes, and hat.

"Just look at the jack-o'-lanterns, ghosts, and goblins hanging from the ceiling," said Mrs. Settlemeir to her friend.

"Yes, aren't they spooky? I counted five jack-o'-lanterns, four ghosts, and six goblins," she replied. "I understand the older children made all of them."

"Did you ever see so many hollowed-out pumpkins? All ten of them resemble grotesque faces and they're all fitted with lighted candles," remarked Mrs. Roberts.

Before the party got underway I stepped outside to talk with some of the men sitting on the porch.

"Did you get tricked or treated last night?" Mr. Olivetti asked Mr. Poloski.

"Yes. I'm mad as hell!"

"Why you mad? Can't take joke ha, ha, ha?"

"No joke. Just damn foolishness."

"Why? What dey do?"

"Some bullies dumped my outhouse. That's what they did!"

The author appropriately dressed for the 1930 Halloween party.

"That's funny! Can't you take a joke?"

"Funny, hell! I was in it when they turned it over!"

"Gentlemen, time to start the party," I said as I stood up and walked toward the door.

Since the children were so enthusiastic and had put out so much energy to make the party a success, I paid $4.95 for a five-gallon wooden bucket full of mixed Halloween candy to add to the festivities.

Entering the building I said, "Ladies, gentlemen, and boys and girls," as I started down the aisle, "here's my treat for the party. Take some candy as I walk by."

When I came to Alex Giles, sitting with his mother, he hesitated to take the candy.

"Have some candy, Alex," I said. "Put a few extra pieces in your pocket to eat on your way home."

"Alex, thank Mr. Neal," Mrs. Giles said as he took his candy. It was plain to see that he had not fully recovered from his father's death.

The children were considerate, each one taking only a few pieces of candy. Not so with some of the grown-ups. What they could not get into their mouths, they put into their pockets. Calling them greedy would have been the understatement of the year. I've seen farmers' hogs less greedy at the feed trough.

Next came dunking of apples in a tub of water, which lasted about one-half hour. The three-act play, *The Ghost Came at Midnight*, climaxed the party.

A number of parents stopped to thank me for inviting them and to tell me what a wonderful time they had.

Last but not least, I saw school director Joe Taylor edging his way toward me, a sourpuss if I ever saw one. I was confident that if he and the devil entered a popularity contest, the devil would win head and shoulders above him. To this day, a more despicable man I've never met. I became totally exasperated every time I saw him.

"Did you enjoy the party, Joe?" I said, hoping to start our conversation on a positive note, if that was possible.

"Can't say that I did. By the way the school district won't pay for the candy. There's no———"

"Money in the budget, and besides it would come under unessential expenditures," I said as I interrupted his worn-out speech.

"Well, that's the long and short of it! I still contend that parties have no place in a school. They stifle learning," he said with his cap pulled down over his right eye as he shuffled out the door. *Good riddance*, I said to myself.

"Charles, shall we clean up this mess before we go home?" asked Fairy.

"No, I'm tired. Let's lock the door and go home. I'll come down in the morning for the cleanup job. I don't have to be in the bandstand until 8 P.M."

To supplement my teaching salary I played saxophone and clarinet at dances on Saturday and Sunday night. I was averaging forty-eight dollars a month for eight four-hour sessions.

As we stepped outside the schoolhouse, the Pirkas were waiting for us.

"Since we pass your place we wondered if we might walk you home," said John Pirka.

"We would be delighted to walk with you," I said.

"It's nice of you to ask us," piped up Fairy.

"Hell, there ain't no fun walking by ourselves," said Mrs. Pirka. "John and I raise too much hell arguing."

"Charles, how do you folks like your new home?" inquired Mr. Pirka.

Recently, we had moved out of Joe Taylor's house to one nearer the schoolhouse. Losing the ten dollar a month rental fee caused him to be more venomous toward me than ever.

"John, the nice thing about it is its nearness to the school. I save about twenty-five minutes of walking time between my house and the schoolhouse."

We were nearing our place when Mrs. Pirka gave her assessment of the party.

"Damn good party, Charles. Only thing wrong with it."

"What's that, Mrs. Pirka?" I asked as if I couldn't make a good guess.

"Some good old moonshine would have put some life in the party. They sure were a bunch of dead asses if I ever saw any."

"Now, Maude," said Mr. Pirka, "this was a school party not a roadhouse blow out. What——"

"Mrs. Pirka," I interrupted, "moonshine is illegal. If we had

The author plays clarinet for the birds prior to his playing that evening in the county fair band. Playing clarinet and saxophone in county fair bands, at dances, and giving private music lessons supplemented his 1930–31 $95-a-month teaching salary.

served alcoholic drinks, the good church people by now would have had us driven out of the community."

"To hell with the damn holier-than-thou people. They are not so pious by a long shot," responded Mrs. Pirka.

"Now, Maude, don't be too critical of our neighbors."

By now it was time to bid the Pirkas good night. As we entered our house, they could be heard still arguing the pros and cons of moonshine whiskey.

November came in like a lion. An early snow dotted the landscape, making the first two weeks extremely cold. Several nights the temperature dropped to zero, unusually cold for southern Illinois.

Then it happened. The flu bug invaded southern Illinois during the middle of the first week in November. It came in with a vengeance! Then it spread like wildfire from family to family, except one—the Greentree clan. That's what everyone called them. It was an odd family to say the least.

There was Joshua Greentree, the father, coal hauler in the winter and ice deliveryman in the summer. Few people in Royalton had refrigerators.

Joshua, known as "Honest Abe" to his buddies, was a tall, skinny, wiry man with soft brown eyes and a shock of wavy brown hair. He never owned a suit of clothes, wearing a pair of blue overalls, blue work shirt, a slouch hat, and a pair of ankle-length work shoes. It was rumored that he never removed his clothes, day or night, until they wore out. He also never ran out of telling interesting stories, and most people liked him.

The mother's name was Mary. She was a plain woman, not real ugly, not pretty either—five feet, three inches tall; hawkish, acquiline nose; wide-set brown eyes; long brown hair; no makeup. She always wore a blue gingham dress down to her ankles. Rumor also had it that she never removed her clothes, day or night, until they were worn out. Be that as it may, she raised the best flowers for miles around, always taking blue-ribbon prizes at the county fair. She was known far and wide as "the flower lady."

Then there was Gabriel, the twenty-eight-year-old son. He was a hard-working man, helping Joshua in the ice delivery business, who was about to have his first date. "That alone didn't make him a queer or an oddball," remarked one of the neighbors. "But then again, something must be wrong with him to wait that long before taking a shine to the girls."

Gabriel was six feet tall, weighed 160 pounds. Like his father he had soft brown eyes and a heavy crop of brown hair. Unlike his father and his mother, he was meticulously clean, owning a brown suit, a couple of white shirts, an assortment of ties, and a pair of brown dress shoes. During working hours he dressed exactly like his father with one difference: He put on a clean set of work clothes each day. Also at the end of each day, his father drove his team to the Royalton Coal Mine. Here Gabriel would dismount, go into the company washhouse, and take a warm shower. The mine superintendent allocated locker number 145 to him for his own personal use to store his clothes, towel, washcloth, and soap. After showering, he walked the quarter mile to his home.

Home—if you can call it that. The house was a building sixty-two feet long, sixteen feet wide, covered with unpainted eight-inch car siding. There were no windows and only one outside door. Fifty feet from the rear of the house was the family outhouse.

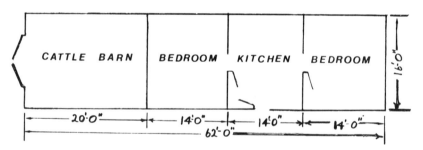

Floor plan of the Greentree clan's combination house and cattle barn. The building was without windows and had only one door leading to the outside of the house.

Let's go through the house, starting with the parents' bedroom, fourteen feet by sixteen feet, on the west side, then through a door to the fourteen-foot by sixteen-foot kitchen, where a heating stove is used for cooking and heating during the winter. Also, the room has a table, three chairs, and a china cabinet. The only outside door to the house is located on the north wall of the kitchen. From the kitchen, go through the door to Gabriel's bedroom, fourteen feet by sixteen feet. Here he built a three-foot by six-foot dust-proof clothes closet. In addition to a bed and dresser, there is a washstand, a washbasin, and a two-gallon galvanized water bucket. Since there was no running water, he carried it from a well next to a burned-out house about one hundred yards away. The east wall is solid, no door. Now return to the kitchen, then out the door to the east wall of the building. Enter through a seven-foot by eight-foot door. Now we are in a sixteen-foot by twenty-foot barn. Here two workhorses, Gabriel's buggy horse, and a milk cow are housed.

The entire house had no floor as such. Instead, Joshua and Gabriel hauled black cinders, removed from the coal mine furnaces, and packed them firmly on the ground as a floor substitute.

It was in this house the flu bug refused to enter. Likewise, it refused to infiltrate the Greentrees themselves. Some said if Joshua or Mary took off their clothes, they were so dirty they would stand erect by themselves. No one had an answer as to why Gabriel didn't catch the flu. He kept his body as clean as anyone in Dutch Hill. The good people just couldn't understand it. However a few did claim that it had to be the work of the Lord.

Attendance kept dropping. More and more pupils were down with the flu. By Friday, the end of the first week in November, only four pupils showed up for school. All the rest had the flu. Fairy had been in bed since Wednesday with it. I was feeling a bit on the weak side, with a headache, and was perspiring profusely. However, I decided to teach as long as pupils were able to attend. Then Dr. Flemming put a stop to that. He ordered me to bed, placing the following notice on the schoolhouse door: "School closed until further notice." Every family in Dutch Hill, except the Greentrees, had one or more family members down with the flu. Dr. Flemming and his wife, the nurse, worked twelve to fifteen hours daily making house calls. Mrs. Flemming not only helped the doctor with his patients, but she was also an angel in disguise. She rounded up the church women in Royalton not sick with the flu to help during the epidemic. Food was prepared and delivered by these good women to the needy in both Dutch Hill and Royalton. This act of mercy was truly meals on wheels.

There was another kindhearted soul in Dutch Hill: none other than Mary Greentree. Every morning she milked Bossy the cow. Then she made deliveries to the sick until her supply of milk ran out.

Since the cow, as well as the horses, were fed mostly on what they could salvage from wild grass, the milk had a light blue color. Naturally, none of the sick would drink it. They didn't want to hurt Mary's feelings so they accepted it with a "thank you." Then as soon as she was out of sight, those who were able, threw it out the backdoor. Actually, the milk was so bad the cats refused to drink it.

Dr. Flemming had some most welcome help from one of the Royalton barbers, Bill Eskew. He had an MD after his name but preferred barbering to practicing medicine. Some thought his preference strange until they learned how he acquired his credentials.

He attended the St. Louis Medical School for two years, all the time that was required then for an MD degree. He told me how the school located students. It would send salesmen out into an area some three hundred miles around St. Louis. A salesman would come into a community and obtain the names of the boys from the high school principal who were seniors. Next, the salesman would call on the parents of each boy, telling them that for a fee their son could become a bona fide medical doctor. Of course, the salesman received a hefty fee for each student enrolled. There were no entrance requirements, other than a fee and a graduation from any high school. The idea of having an MD in the family thrilled most parents to the point of literally forcing their sons to become medical doctors. Bill Eskew was one such son.

After two weeks the flu ran its course. At that time there were no antibiotics, but most of the patients fully recovered. However, several of them, running high fevers, suffered permanent brain damage, causing some to refer to them as "queers."

Weather seems to have a way of becoming tricky. Suddenly, the weather made an abrupt change. The sun remained out all day. The temperatures were averaging a high of 72° F with a low of 49° F. Perhaps this sudden change, for the better, had more to do with eradicating the flu than anything else.

Having the flu wasn't bad enough for me. On the first day of opening the school after the epidemic, I saw Joe Taylor approaching me on the playground during morning recess. The devil himself would have been more welcome.

"Good morning, Joe," I said with tongue in cheek.

"Well, I don't know what's good about it, but one thing for sure, you can't play sick any longer. Now you'll have to earn your money.

You were out nine school days. You'll have to make them up at the end of the term, you know, if you want to draw your last month's pay."

"Yes, Joe, I'm fully aware of that. Now what other bad news can you come up with?" I no longer cared what Joe said or what I said to him. I had leads on three excellent jobs for next year in city schools. One was just waiting for me to sign a contract. I later signed it.

"Charles, were you really sick or were you playing possum?"

"Joe, I resent that remark. I'll just forget you ever said it. Did you have the flu?"

"No, can't say that I did. Never been sick a day in my life. I don't know, but I guess a person can be bad off with it. At least——"

I rudely interrupted him. "How do you account for the fact that twenty-three people died in Dutch Hill and Royalton. To say nothing of the fourteen deaths in Benton. According to Dr. Flemming all of them died from the flu. Of course, you call Dr. Flemming a quack. You know, don't you, Joe, that you're the only one in Dutch Hill and Royalton who feels that way. But then again, Joe Taylor is always right! It's everyone else who's wrong!"

Joe didn't say a word. He just stood there like a barbershop Indian.

Having said my piece, I turned on my heel and said sneeringly, "Joe, it's time to ring the bell to take up books. I wouldn't want to hold up recess, thereby cheating the school district out of a few pennies." I started toward the schoolhouse, leaving him standing in his tracks. As I walked back to the schoolhouse I began evaluating my experiences thus far as a teacher. Most of them were enjoyable. However, the few that were not—especially the likes of Joe Taylor—took all of the joy out of teaching.

Most of the residents of Dutch Hill held me, the teacher, to almost a life of celibacy. It was their desire I not drink alcoholic beverages, smoke tobacco, or gamble. Furthermore, they expected me to attend church regularly.

Living such a dull, drab life took all the joy out of teaching. Worse, it caused me to look upon the school district as a spider's web. Since Joe Taylor was constantly spitting venom at me, figuratively speaking, he was the perfect specimen for portraying the spider.

Since I had to dance to the tune played by the residents, I saw myself as a fly caught up in the spider's web for the second time—once when I was a pupil and now when I was the teacher.

Chapter 18
Teacher Learns a Thing or Two

Every since I left Joe Taylor standing in the schoolyard, I was down in the dumps. Teaching, which I loved so well, took a backseat in my life. I'm convinced that if it had not been for Fairy's encouragement, I would have resigned my teaching position that very day.

It was the Friday before Thanksgiving. The day was beautiful in more ways than one. At noon the temperature was 70° F on the thermometer located just outside the schoolhouse door. The sun was shining, and there wasn't a cloud in the sky.

Perhaps it was the delightful change in the weather that brought me out of the doldrums. I really couldn't account for it, but I took a new lease on life. I vowed to forget Joe Taylor and everything he stood for. For the remainder of the school term, I would treat him like an inanimate object.

As I was eating lunch at my desk, I looked out the window at the forest beyond the schoolhouse yard. What a beautiful sight to behold! If there ever was an artist's paradise, I was looking right at it. Fall rains had been good to us. They brought out nature's beautiful colors in all their splendor. The colorful oak, maple, hickory, and persimmon leaves, the red sumac and evergreen cedars created one of nature's wonders seldom equaled but never excelled.

As I took my last bite of food, the door literally flew open. In came a man six feet tall, weighing around 180 pounds. He was intelligent looking, around thirty, wearing eyeglasses, and had his hair slicked back, pompadour-style. He wore a white shirt, blue tie, gray pair of slacks, and his feet looked most comfortable in a pair of black loafers.

"Mr. Neal, I believe?" he said as he shook my hand vigorously.

"That's right," I replied.

"My names's Harry Turner. I represent the Pickwick Publishing

Company of New York. We publish nothing but the best sixteen-volume set of encyclopedias in the world."

"Mr. Turner, you're wasting your time. Our school district is practically broke, and I'm not authorized to buy anything. The secretary of the board does the purchasing."

"No, no, no, my good fellow! I'm not here to sell you anything. All I want is a favor."

"What kind of favor?" I said, wondering what was coming next.

"Well, you see, Mr. Neal, we don't advertise in newspapers or magazines. People like me go out to various communities, leaving some literature and order blanks with a few select families."

"How do you arrive at the select families?"

"Well, that's where I need your help," he said.

"How can I help?" Like a greenhorn poor country schoolteacher, I was playing his game exactly as he wanted.

"If you will give me the names of six families with children in school, I'd appreciate it."

"How are you going to use the names?" I asked.

"I'll call on them this evening. There won't be any sales pitch. I'll simply leave some literature along with five order blanks with each family. As they visit with their neighbors, they can give them the literature along with order blanks. It's as simple as that."

"OK. I'll give the names of six people as well as draw a map, showing how to find them." Until this day I still wonder how I could have been such a dunce to fall for a city slicker's game.

"Oh, this is swell!" he said as he looked at the names on the map. "Mighty nice of you to do this. I thank you from the bottom of my heart."

That said, he shook my hand until I thought my knuckles would crack. I walked him to the door and watched him climb into a new Dodge coupe. Then he drove down the road toward Royalton.

The following day Tom Meeker came to the schoolhouse and told me exactly how Harry Turner really operated. Essentially, this is what took place.

That evening the Meeker family, Tom, his wife Mary, and their eleven-year-old son, Jerry, had finished eating supper (dinner, to them, was eaten at noon). They had just settled comfortably in the living room waiting for their six o'clock favorite radio program to hit the airwaves when there was a knocking at the front door.

"Who could that be?" inquired Tom.

"I have no idea," replied his wife as she stood, stretched her arthritic legs, and walked to the door.

When she opened the door, she saw a tall man, heavyset, with eyeglasses. He was wearing a lightweight, three-piece blue suit, a gray hat, and a pair of shiny black shoes, so glossy you could see a reflection of yourself in them.

"Hello. Miss Meeker, I take it," he said, as he grinned from ear to ear and removed his hat.

"Yes, I'm Mary Meeker."

"Oh, you must be the daughter of Mrs. Meeker, the elder?"

"No, I'm the only Mrs. Meeker in this house."

"Since Jerry is your son, I was expecting to see a much older lady. Mrs. Meeker, I have a surprise for you and Mr. Meeker. May I come in and explain it?"

"Certainly. Around here we never let our guests stand outside regardless how nice the weather."

"You folks certainly have a beautiful home," he said as he walked into the living room.

"I heard you tell the wife that you had a surprise for us. Suppose you begin by telling us who you are and what it is you want," stated Mr. Meeker.

"Gladly, gladly. My name is Harry Turner, and I represent the Pickwick Publishing Company of New York. We publish the best set of sixteen-volume encyclopedias in the good old USA. We never h——"

"Hold it right there!" broke in Mr. Meeker, showing anger in his voice. "We're not buying any books and that's final."

"Of course not. Remember, I have a surprise. We never high-pressure anyone to make a purchase."

"Then why are you here?" said Mr. Meeker calming down a bit.

"Pickwick Publishers don't spend money advertising in newspapers and magazines. Instead, they select one special family in a community. Then representatives like me call on these special people, just like I'm doing right now."

"You're not kidding me a damn bit, Mr. Turner. You've got something up your sleeve, and I want to kn——"

"Now, Pa, don't get riled up," broke in Mrs. Meeker. "Give Mr. Turner a chance to explain himself."

"OK. Your turn, Mr. Turner."

"The surprise is here in these three volumes for your inspection. Also, I want to leave six pieces of literature, along with order blanks. I would appreciate you handing them out to your friends," he said as he gave Mr. and Mrs. Meeker and son Jerry each a book.

"If you please, look through the books. Then tell me what you think of them," he said as he placed the literature and order blanks on the end table next to Mr. Meeker.

"What good is that going to do?" asked Mr. Meeker as he squirmed in his chair.

"It will do a lot of good, Mr. Meeker. The publisher is interested in knowing what people like yourselves like and what they dislike about the volumes. You see, Mr. Meeker, when reprinting time rolls around, certain items will be rewritten or eliminated, depending on how readers react."

"Look, Ma, here's an article about President Hoover. We studied about him last week in our history class," said Jerry excitedly.

"And here's an article about the Spanish-American War. My father was in that war. Do you have time for me to read the whole article, Mr. Turner?" inquired Mrs. Meeker.

"Sure thing. There's more in——"

"Look here, Ma," said Mr. Meeker excitedly. "Here's a story about the Civil War. Grandfather Meeker served four years in that war and came home without a scratch."

"Now, folks, I see you like what you see. The sixteen volumes sell for $15.95 in any bookstore in America. However, since you are a special family, you can have the new set I happen to have in my car for the very low price of ten dollars. What do you say?"

"What do you think, Ma? Think we can afford it?"

"Pa, they're mighty nice, and they would certainly broaden Jerry's education."

"I think we can spare ten dollars, Ma. Why don't you get it out of the butter and egg money?"

"I'll go out with Mr. Turner and help him bring them in," volunteered Jerry as he jumped with joy.

Mr. Turner completed the transaction, thanked Mr. and Mrs. Meeker profusely, walked out the door, got into his Dodge car, and drove away.

It wasn't hard to imagine the feelings of the Meekers when,

several days later, they discovered there were five more special families in our little community. And three of them bought their encyclopedias at the special price of ten dollars. Of course, Mr. Turner was nowhere to be found.

Lucky for me, the good people never found out about the role I played in the scam. In my opinion the encyclopedias were the worst set in the world, not the best as Mr. Meeker claimed.

It was four o'clock, the school day was finally over, and I was disgusted.

I was hot, I was hungry, and my feet hurt as I walked from the schoolhouse to my home. Still, it was some comfort to realize it was TGF (Thank God for Friday).

Fairy met me at the door. From the expression on her face, I knew a surprise was in the offing. What it was I didn't know; yet I knew it would be something good.

"Guess what?" she said as she gave me a peck on the right cheek.

"Look," I said, "I'm just not good at guessing games right now, maybe later."

"Have a rough day?"

"Oh, no worse than usual. It's disgusting though."

"What's disgusting? Tell me about it."

"It's Joe Taylor again."

"What did the mean old school director gripe about this time?"

"He visited school this afternoon. He claims our recess periods of fifteen minutes are much too long. Furthermore, he told me children can't learn anything running around shouting like a bunch of wild Indians. And he said that the game of baseball is a complete waste of time!"

"Forget about old man Taylor, the old codger! He's just hateful because we moved out of his house. Guess what? Your folks sent an invitation for us to visit them over the weekend. Isn't that nice?"

"Sure is. It will give us a break to get away for a few days. I don't know if old Liz [the name we gave our old Model T Ford sedan] will hang together that long."

"It's only twenty-three miles. I'm game to give it a shot if you are."

"Oh, what the heck! You only live once. Let's pack up and get going."

The weather had turned cold. No matter how hard I tried, I couldn't crank the old engine fast enough for it to start. The cylinder oil had congealed, making it almost impossible to move the pistons up and down.

I did what every Ford owner did under such conditions—built a fire on the ground directly below the oil pan. In less than fifteen minutes the cylinder oil thinned. On the first crank, the engine sputtered a few times, backfired several times, then ran like a threshing machine. Soon we were on our way.

Old Liz was hitting on all four cylinders for about twelve miles (With no speedometer, this was only a ballpark figure). Then the engine coughed several times. Finally, it decided to run, but was hitting on only three of its four cylinders.

Just as we pulled up in front of my folks' house, old Liz had another coughing fit, sputtered a couple of times, then died.

"I think Old Liz has had it," I said to Fairy. I was convinced it would never again run. And I was right, so I thought. Later I sold it to Tom Pulley, a shade-tree mechanic, for fifty dollars. He, in turn, rebuilt the car, selling it for $125.

The folks were glad to see us. They even held up supper for us. Fried chicken, mashed potatoes and gravy, homemade biscuits, and Arbuckle coffee were a most welcome treat after a trying day.

After supper we gravitated to the living room where Dad spoke up. "See you're having a heap of car trouble. Think you can make it home Sunday evening?"

"No, I really don't. It's not some small problem this time that has old Liz down. The main bearings are noisy as are the rod bearings. The crankshaft seems out of line, the radiator leaks, and the foot brake, reverse, and clutch bands are shot. The old wreck isn't worth the money it would require to put it in good running order." There is where I was wrong.

"Son, as I passed the bulletin board on the outside wall of Miners Hall, I saw a for sale sign. Dave Childers wants to sell his 1930 Model A coupe."

"What's he asking for it, about five hundred?"

"No. Davie's in financial trouble. His asking price is $275, and the speedometer shows only 3,400 miles."

"Price seems reasonable enough, but we have only two hundred in the bank between us and the poorhouse. You say he's having money problems?"

"Yes, that's right. He may lower the price a few dollars for cash."

"Nothing tried, nothing gained. I'll see old Dave tomorrow, offering him a two-hundred-dollar check for the car. He can damn well take it or leave it."

"I'm afraid he'll leave it. Want to hear my suggestion?"

"Sure, Dad," I said. "An old worn-out cliché can best describe my feelings. I'm between a rock and a hard place. Shoot! I'm all ears."

"Go to the bank. Have the teller count out two hundred one-dollar bills. Put them in a paper bag. Then when you and Dave begin negotiating price, dump the two hundred greenbacks on the table. That green stuff has a psychological effect on most buyers. For some reason they just can't keep their hands from picking up the money."

I tried the plan. It worked like a charm. Dave and I went to notary public's office to make the transaction. Dave left with the sack of two hundred one-dollar bills; I left with the Model A Ford and a clear title for its possession.

The following Monday was uneventful in school—no major problems. Best of all, Joe Taylor didn't show up with his line of garbage.

That evening, I glanced at the clock at 6:55 P.M. I had just finished checking the fifth grade arithmetic papers and was about to check the seventh grade themes when my wife yelled from the kitchen, "Seen the current issue of the *Illinois Farmer* magazine yet?"

"No," I said sadly, "I'm knee-deep in checking papers."

"How's Wayne Roberts coming along? Is he stupid as the teacher put on his report card last year?"

"I may have thought so last September, but not anymore. In fact, an amazing thing happened to Wayne. With the little added help I've given him after school, he is making more progress than any other pupil."

"Then he'll get promoted?"

"Without a doubt."

Finished washing dishes, my wife brought up the *Illinois Farmer* again as she walked into the living room. "Look at the advertisement on page 92."

"OK. I'll check the rest of the papers tomorrow morning."

She giggled as she said, "I see. Putting off for tomorrow what you don't want to do today. Good idea. I'll try that with housework sometime."

"No, not exactly," I replied as I yawned, stretched my arms, and opened the magazine to page 92. What I saw was amazing.

A sure way to kill potato bugs. Send one dollar for materials and instructions. To order send check or money order to Potato Jim, P.O. Box 422, Springfield, Illinois. Allow two weeks for delivery.

Our garden was overrun with potato bugs. On several occasions, I had picked enough bugs to fill a quart can. The ad seemed like a dream from heaven. I wrote out the order that very evening. Then I placed it in the rural mail box to be picked up by the mail carrier the following morning.

One week later a package came in the mail. I was amazed at the quick response. Opening it I found two small blocks of wood labeled A and B. The instructions read: "Place potato bug on block A. Place block B on top of block A. Strike block B a hard blow with a hammer. A sure way to kill potato bugs."

The country schoolteacher again bit the bait, swallowing it hook, line and sinker.

The time was 10:35 A.M. that Thursday morning. Recess had been underway for about five minutes when I caught a long high fly in left field.

Since I had played baseball ever since I was old enough to hold a bat, playing left field for both sides was the sporting thing to do.

I was getting ready to watch the next pitch when school director Pirka stopped his 1928 Ford touring car in front of the schoolhouse, blew his horn, and waved for me to come over. (He finally, due to the nagging of his wife, gave up the horse and buggy for a used car.)

As I walked toward his car, I wondered what he wanted. There was one thing I knew for certain: John was not about to tell me how to teach school. He just wasn't that kind of person. He was just the opposite of director Joe Taylor. John was most personable. He never gave anyone a hard time, though he always stood up for what he thought was right. No one could push him around.

As I approached the car, John stuck out his large, skinny hand and said, "Shake, Teach! How's the world treating you?"

"Very well, John. No complaints."

"Has Joe Taylor been pestering you lately?"

"No, now that you mention it, is he sick? I haven't seen Joe in, let me think, in more than three weeks, and that's a blessing in disguise."

"No, the old coot isn't sick. Pay no attention to him. There isn't a farmer for miles around that hasn't had good old Joe tell him what's wrong with his farming methods. You won't believe this, but he actually hates his wife. Says she doesn't know how to cook. He even hated his own mother. Said he was glad when she died."

"I'm not surprised, John."

"In my book he's a pain in the —— and I don't mean nose. I didn't invite you over to give a lecture on Joe Taylor. Want to go to Royalton with me tonight?"

"Why? What's up?"

"A man from Tulsa, Oklahoma, is giving a big feed in the high school gym followed by a lecture on oil wells in that state. I understand he is closing the meeting by offering a few oil well shares for sale."

"Oh, I don't know. However, it would give us a chance to socialize a bit. Sure, why not?"

"OK. I'll pick you up at 6:30. The meeting starts at 7:30."

He pushed in the low-speed pedal on his car, waved his hand, and gave me a big smile as he drove away.

The rest of the school day was full of routine activity.

John showed promptly at 6:30. Soon we were traveling down the road toward Royalton.

Getting out of the car, we walked down a wide sidewalk until we came to the high school entrance. Since we were about fifteen minutes early, we sat down on one of the wide banisters to wait. John whiled away the time by smoking a cigarette.

He had been sick for three weeks early in the spring, but he was looking much better tonight. There was a healthy color in his face, and his eyes sparkled.

As we entered the gym, John said, "Look! There's Mayor Banister on the speaker's platform."

"Must be a pretty important meeting for the mayor to participate," I replied.

"I see Senator Orthwein sitting at the table close to the speaker's platform."

"John, I wonder why he came. He must have driven at least two hundred miles."

"There's only one answer: votes. He's on the ticket for reelection this coming November."

At 7:30 sharp Mayor Banister introduced the speaker, Sam Hunt. He was wearing leather boots, khaki work clothes, and his face was suntanned.

"Ladies and gentlemen," he said. "I represent the Tulsa Oil and Gas Corporation. See this—— I see the girls are bringing in the food. We'll have a short meeting following the dinner. Everyone is invited to stay. Enjoy your meal!"

"John," I said, "I thought we were to hear a lecture on oil wells. I suppose that was the bait for bringing in the suckers."

"Charles, let's not count our chickens before they hatch. Maybe a short lecture is included as part of the meeting."

Following the dinner of fried chicken, mashed potatoes, string beans, coffee, and ice cream for dessert, Mr. Hunt struck the speaker's lectern with the gavel, bringing the meeting to order.

"See this large map of Casper County, Oklahoma," he said as he pointed to it. "The three red pins show locations of oil wells now in the drilling stage. The fourteen blue pins indicate future sites where we already hold leases for drilling."

"You haven't hit oil yet, have you?" chided a coal miner sitting at the table next to the door.

"No, but I can tell you this: We have a Mr. Amos Summers on our payroll. He is considered the foremost geologist in the country. He located the seventeen sites on the map. Over the past ten years his batting average for locating oil is 90 percent."

The miner was a bit pushy. "If there isn't any oil at these locations shown on your map, his batting average could be zero. Isn't that a fact?"

Mayor Banister stood up, coming to the rescue. "David, we could spend the entire evening second guessing Geologist Summers, but this is not the purpose of this meeting. So let's get on with it. Please, ladies and gentlemen, let's hold our questions until Mr. Hunt calls for them." A happy thought, but Mr. Hunt never called for questions.

The mayor sat down and Mr. Hunt again took the floor. He explained how Mr. Drake drilled the first oil well in 1859, in Titusville, Pennsylvania. This, according to Hunt, touched off a real oil boom. He said that practically all the oil produced in the nineteenth century was used to meet the demands for kerosene, wax, and lubricants. Gasoline was considered useless, and it was drained into the rivers.

He pointed out that Geologist Summers batted 90 percent because he used the gravimeter, the magnetometer, and the seismograph. Even after the use of each of these instruments was explained, I was completely in the dark about them, and I think everyone else in the audience was as dumbfounded as I was.

Next, Mr. Hunt opened his briefcase. Then he brought out one of his oil shares, holding it up so that everyone could see it. It was a work of art, twelve inches by fourteen inches printed in English script, ending with a gold seal placed near the lower right-hand corner.

"These sell for twelve dollars a share. Each share gives you a part ownership in all seventeen wells. I predict in less than a year these shares will double in value. In addition, royalties will start coming in on the drilled wells. Also, ladies and gentlemen, buying your shares tonight is a once-in-a-lifetime proposition. I assure you they will never be offered at this low price again."

"I guess I'm the devil's advocate," shouted another miner as he stood up. "What guarantee can you give us on what you have just said?"

"Well, I can only say this: I have so much confidence in these wells that I took out 132 shares for my mother, her entire life savings. The floor is now open for buying shares."

"What do you think, John? Want to buy a few shares?"

"I don't know," he said hesitantly. "Let me mull it over in my mind for a few minutes."

The meeting concluded with Mr. Hunt selling 193 shares; four of these were bought by John and me, two shares each.

With each purchase we received a small sheet of literature, part of which said the shareholders would receive a monthly progress report. The Tulsa Oil and Gas Corporation's address was included right below Mr. Hunt's home address.

After three months passed and no reports were received, I wrote the mayor of Tulsa for help. His reply was to the point: "No Tulsa Oil and Gas Corporation exists in Tulsa, and there is no one by the name of Hunt living at the address you indicate. Sorry, mister, you folks have been had!"

Chapter 19
Surprise and More Surprises

As the days rolled on I forgot about being taken in on the oil scam. I was really beginning to feel that I'd be a successful teacher after all.

It was Friday. I walked home slowly and unsteadily after school, chuckling to myself at the thought of how easily I got rid of the good women representing the Women's Christian Temperance Union. Either I would never hear from them again, or they would arrange for a time to talk to the pupils at our convenience. Either way I was calling the shots, and I liked that. I made my way up the steps leading to my house. Upon entering, I found Fairy ironing my white shirt.

"Fairy, I'm getting surprises from every corner today. I didn't know this was wash day," I said as I smiled.

"It isn't."

"Then why the ironing?" I asked.

"Well, you are playing clarinet at the Polish dance tonight. Remember?"

"Of course, I remember!" I said rather sarcastically. "What does that have to do with it?"

"Silly, you own only one white shirt. It was dirty, and I washed it so you would look respectable on the bandstand tonight. That's what the ironing is all about."

"Oh, well, I'll buy a couple when we go to Royalton next Monday."

"At $1.25 each? I should say not! One new one will do until one of the stores runs a sale. Then, I'll bet they will sell for a dollar each or maybe as low as six for five dollars.

"Charles, you mentioned surprises a while ago. What gives? What else surprised you today?"

I told her about the WCTU's visit. Then I went into the living room to catnap until suppertime. Since I wouldn't hit the sack before 1:30 A.M., I needed all the rest I could get.

I was reflecting on an article I had recently published and was gloating over the fact that most of the letters received were favorable. But one man from Oak Ridge, a small town near Chicago, took exception to my statement, "You can't make a bird dog out of a cur." He sent me a nasty letter. I thought probably he was some nut, and once he got his anger expressed in a letter would forget it. Was I in for a surprise! "Talk about the devil and he will appear," was about to come true. I was moving into never-never land when I almost jumped out of my chair. Somebody was banging on the door. I stood up, rubbed my eyes, and staggered toward the door. Opening it, I saw a stoop-shouldered slim man dressed in corduroys, with a partial head of gray hair. Deep lines crossed his forehead. His brown eyes were like ice. Because of his atypical features, I guessed his age anywhere between forty and sixty.

"Mr. Neal, my name is Roscoe Hampton, and I live in Oak Ridge, Illinois. We——"

Heaven forbid, I thought. *This nut has traveled more than three hundred miles to further vent his anger about my article.* "What can I do for you?" I said as I interrupted him.

"We must have a talk!" he said coldly as he projected his chin. Projecting his chin led me to think he might be getting ready for a fight. I hoped I was wrong.

"I feel you have maligned the dog species when you wrote, 'You can't make a bird dog out of a cur.' I want you to——"

"I'm sorry, Mr. Hampton," I told him as I interrupted what I thought was the making of an idiotic speech. "I am very busy." I slammed the door in his face.

I should have known crackpots are not gotten rid of that easily. A couple of minutes later my wife came to the living room. "Charles, that man is at the back door now. I wouldn't open the door. He shouted that he absolutely will not leave until he had a word with you."

It wasn't long before he was again at the front door raving like a madman.

"What are we going to do, Charles?" Fairy said as tears came to her eyes.

"If he breaks into the house, I'll use this ball bat on his noggin,"

I told her as I picked up the bat from the side of my chair and placed it on my lap. I always kept a ball bat handy in case some person broke into the house. "Otherwise, I'll let him stand out there and rant and rave until he wears out. Perhaps then he'll leave, I hope."

It was starting to get dark as I cracked the window shade to study his reaction. Just then a car stopped in front of the house. Two men jumped out and hurried toward the front door. When I saw it was John Pirka and Fred Armstrong, I went out the back door and ran around to greet them.

"What's going on here?" Mr. Pirka wanted to know.

"Mr. Neal maligned the dog species, and I'm here to make him apologize," said Mr. Hampton sneeringly.

"The best thing you can do, mister, is to get going pronto!" threatened Mr. Armstrong.

"I'm standing firm. I'll leave when he apologizes, not one minute sooner!"

Then Mr. Pirka and Mr. Armstrong began whispering to each other. This was followed by Mr. Armstrong rushing to the car and returning with a long piece of rope clothesline.

"I'll give you five seconds to get moving," warned Mr. Pirka. Still the man kept his ground. Then the counting began: five, four, three, two, and one.

I saw what was in the making and joined my two friends as we wrestled him to the ground.

"Don't take all evening, Fred," John shouted as he locked a forearm around the man's throat. John and I held him fast while Mr. Armstrong tied his arms and legs firmly, using sailor's knots like he used when he was in the navy.

"Hey, what do you think you're doing?" the man screamed.

"Sir, for your information," Mr. Pirka said, "I am making a citizen's arrest."

The three of us picked up the fanatic bodily and threw him onto the backseat of the car. I went back into the house while my two friends delivered him to the Royalton police station.

It was a cold morning in mid-December. As I approached the schoolhouse I saw little Dennis Ragsdale, one of my fourth grade pupils, coming to meet me.

"Good morning, Dennis," I said. "What brings you to school so bright and early?"

"I don't know. I guess I just got up too early," he replied as he turned his gaze away from me.

"Come on now, Dennis. There's something on your mind. What is it?"

"Mama wants to know if you can come to our house this evening for a home visit. She want you to watch me do my homework."

What a strange request, I thought. I wondered if another surprise was in the offing if I obliged. "Well, Dennis, this is a very——"

"Please, Teach. Please say you'll come. Please," Dennis interrupted.

"OK," I said against my better judgement. "Tell your mother I'll be there around seven o'clock."

"Oh, goody, goody," he replied as he ran to play with other early arrivals.

With a strange feeling of displeasure and anticipation, I arrived at the Ragsdales' house promptly at seven o'clock. Mrs. Ragsdale greeted me warmly. Then she smiled as I was invited into the living room.

It was a cold evening, but there were no cold spots in the living room. The Ragsdales had the only modern hot-air heating system in the community. With a warm handshake, Mr. Ragsdale invited me to sit down. I had met him at the Halloween party. When I was seated, he called Dennis from his room upstairs to begin his homework.

"Mr. Neal, we are not sure that we are doing the right thing with Dennis when he does his homework. We would like to have you observe. Then give us your honest opinion of what it is we are doing right and what it is we need to improve. Is this satisfactory with you?"

"I'll do what I can," I said as I wondered if they expected me to agree with them or if they actually wanted an honest evaluation.

"Good evening, Teach," Dennis said as he entered the living room carrying a tablet, a pencil, and an arithmetic book. Sitting at a small desk next to his father's chair, Dennis began his homework.

As Dennis started to work, his father watched every movement of the pencil. Dennis worked diligently for a few minutes. Then he was interrupted.

"That's the wrong answer, Dennis," Mr. Ragsdale said. "A

dummy can do better than that. Six times seven is forty-two, not forty-nine!"

Five more reprimands and fifteen minutes later, Dennis had tears in his eyes. Finally, his homework was completed. Many of the answers were his father's. Dennis was excused. He waved good night as he rushed out of the room on his way upstairs. To say that I was surprised would be putting it mildly. Why a parent would treat his own child in such a manner was more than I could comprehend.

"Is this the way to conduct homework?" Mrs. Ragsdale asked me.

"What's wrong with it?" Mr. Ragsdale interrupted, showing a bit of arrogance in his voice.

"Rather than criticize Dennis's homework, let me talk about it in general. First of all, nothing succeeds like success. Conversely, nothing fails like failure. As an example, Dennis failed to multiply six times seven. Rather than tell him the answer, let him discover it for himself. And here is where you come in, Mr. Ragsdale, by providing a positive approach. When Dennis give forty-nine as the answer, tell him to prove it. I am certain he will add six, seven times to discover the answer. His class does that all the time during the arithmetic period. Here you, Mr. Ragsdale, act as a guide rather than a provider of information.

"The right kind of homework has many other values besides getting the lesson. Pupils learn good study habits; it fosters initiative and develops self-direction and self-discipline.

"It is much to your credit that Dennis does his homework here in a homey setting rather than be isolated in his room. Also, the fact that both of you are interested in improving the conditions under which he works is a plus in your favor.

"Some parents I know show that everyone has a job to do. They use the homework study period for paying bills, writing letters, ordering merchandise from mail order catalogs, and reading."

I couldn't believe it. I wasn't interrupted a single time. Even Mr. Ragsdale was sporting a smile.

"Well," said Mrs. Ragsdale, "I see that we have a lot of improvements to make. Wouldn't you say so, Dad?"

"Gee, I don't know what to say. I had no idea that homework could be so organized the way you put it, Mr. Neal. I certainly learned my lesson. There'll be some changes made. I can assure you of that."

"Mr. Neal, I don't know when I have learned so much in such a short time. It's no wonder I hear so many reports that you are an excellent teacher," said Mrs. Ragsdale.

After thanking the Ragsdales for letting me come into their home, I said good night. Then I fired up the Model A and headed for home.

With Christmas just around the corner, the children grew restless and agitated. The little ones had visions of Santa Claus bringing them presents. The older children were more realistic. They suffered hard times alongside their parents, so most of them realized the new air rifles, store-bought sleds, and lifelike dolls could be had only in their dreams. Yet they were looking forward to Christmas if for no other reason than the midyear vacation. With no crops to plant or tend, they could spend the week leisurely, doing only what comes naturally.

There was a scraping of feet outside the door. When it opened, a chill surged through my body. In walked the county superintendent, C. M. Stonecipher. With the stride of an army general, he marched to the center of the room, stopping between my desk and the recitation seat.

"Children," I said. "This is your county superintendent of schools, Mr. C. M. Stonecipher."

Silence.

"Boys and girls! What do we say when we have a guest?" I said, rather irritated at the unannounced visit.

"Good afternoon, Mr. Stonecipher," the pupils resounded in unison.

"Good afternoon, boys and girls," Mr. Stonecipher replied as he looked over the top of his ill-fitted spectacles.

"Gee willikers," spoke up Jake Monroe, "I remember you from last year."

The rest of the children were silent with the exception of some mumbling and stifled laughter here and there.

"Mr. Stonecipher, would you like to hear a class recitation?" I inquired.

The school day had only fifteen minutes to run until time for dismissal. I hoped against hope that he would get on with it. But the superintendent didn't seem to be in any hurry.

Looking around like a lost soul searching for daylight, he plunked his fat behind on top of my desk. "The beginners—how are they getting along? As the twig is bent so grows the tree. Most important to start them on the right track early."

What a stupid jerk, I thought. He answered his own question.

"Judge for yourself," I said as I called the first graders to the recitation seat for an arithmetic demonstration.

"Stephen Yardlow, how much is five plus three plus four? Use your pencil and paper if you must find the answer."

Silence.

"Twelve. I think."

"Don't you know?"

"Yes, sir. The answer is twelve!"

"Two times four."

Silence.

"Not sure."

"Not sure? You knew it last Monday."

"Yeah. That was last Monday. Don't know it now."

To my dismay, Stephen let me down. Not to be outdone, I called on Hazel Beckmeyer. "How much is four plus six plus eight plus two?"

"Twenty."

"And four times six?"

"Twenty-four."

"And twenty-eight divided by three."

After a few moments of scribbling on her tablet, she said, "Nine with one left over."

So on and on I quizzed one pupil, then the next. There were far more right answers than wrong ones. I swelled with pride as I dismissed the class.

"Well, I see it's time to dismiss school," said Mr. Stonecipher as he stood up, yawned, then walked toward the door. When the last child walked out of the room, he said, "Hope you don't mind my visiting unannounced."

Heck no, I thought. *What good would it do to tell him I resented having the school schedule disrupted this way.*

"No, of course not," I lied.

"How many boys and girls have you paddled so far?"

"Very few. I've had little reason to use corporal punishment."

"Spare the rod and spoil the child, you know."

By this time I was a bit irritated, to say the least. "As long as these children are orderly and cause no trouble, I have no intention of whipping them. I'm not one to believe education can be pounded into children."

"Well, I must be running along," he said as he tromped out the door on his way to his gray Dodge sedan.

Figuratively speaking, a black cloud hung low over Dutch Hill that Thursday morning as I made my way toward the schoolhouse. Walking along, I became irritated as I thought of school director Taylor's bellyaching to the other directors at their last meeting for voting to dismiss school one week for Christmas. "You can't learn nothin' gallivantin' around the countryside," he argued. Well, I had one consolation: A city school offered me a contract for next year at an increase of thirty dollars per month for a nine-month term, instead of my present one of eight months. And I accepted it.

Topping the hill I saw Ricardo Olivetti sitting on the schoolhouse front porch. Trouble this morning was all that I needed to finish ruining my day. *Oh, well, things can't get much worse than they are*, I said to myself. Starting up the steps, I said, "Good morning, Ricardo. What brings you to school so early?"

"Got a proposition to talk to you about," he replied.

Ricardo with a proposition! *What could it possibly be?* I wondered. Backing down the steps and sitting close to him, I said, "What is your proposition, Ricardo?"

"We've never had a pie supper in this school, although other country schools have one each year. So, my proposition is this: Can we have a pie supper?"

"Want to rephrase the question?"

"Oh, hell, Teach. I didn't mean to say 'hell.' It just slipped out. May we have a pie supper?"

"That sounds much better. Ricardo, I haven't the slightest idea of how to sponsor a pie supper. I've never even been to one, let alone been in charge."

"Well, you can learn tomorrow night."

"How come?"

"Six-Mile School is having one. It begins at seven o'clock. It's a good way for a school to make some extra money."

"Extra money," I mused. "Do you happen to know how much profit they made last year?"

"Teach, it's all profit. The older girls and single women each bake a cake or a pie that they place on a table in front of the room. The auctioneer holds up each package for all to see. Then he calls for bids. The highest bidder gets the package and has the privilege of eating its contents with the girl or lady who baked it."

"Mmm. And they make extra money this way, you say?"

"They sure do. I was told they made $21.25 last year."

"That kind of money gives me an idea. We could replace those pre-World War maps and purchase five or six books to start a school library. What do you think of that, Ricardo?" Little did I know that a big surprise would be waiting for me when we gave a pie supper. I hadn't reckoned with school directors Taylor and Pirka.

"I think that would be great! Are you going tomorrow night?"

"My wife and I most certainly are going."

"May I go with you? I hate to drive Dad's old beat-up truck."

"Sure thing. Glad to have you as our guest."

"May Yetlo go, too?"

"Yes, if you don't mind riding in the rumble seat. We'll pick you up here at the schoolhouse, 6:30 sharp." The rumble seat was an open seat located to the rear of the front seat. A padded lid served as a backrest when raised. When not occupied, the lid was lowered to protect the seat from the elements of the weather.

When Fairy and I arrived at the schoolhouse, we were greeted by eight children, not two. When I told them the car was not powerful enough to haul eight extra people, Wayne Roberts and six of his friends decided to walk.

While the bidding was in progress, the Six-Mile schoolteacher explained the ins and outs of running a pie supper. She was elated when the money was counted. "Twenty-four dollars and fifty cents will buy several books for the library," she told us.

The next night when I told my fellow band members about our pie supper scheduled for the following Friday evening, they were elated. They all promised to come and bring along two fiddlers and a guitar player, "to give the country folks some real hoedown music before the bidding begins," said the bass player.

"I'll get old Joe Atkins to do the auctioning," added the tenor saxophonist.

"All free for the good of the cause," said the drummer as he played a big roll on the snare drum, ending with a loud crash of cymbals.

The children were excited about the pie supper. They made posters. The older ones drew outlines of people eating pies and cakes. Then the primary grade children used crayons to color in between the outlines. Next Ricardo and his peers tacked the posters onto trees and fence posts within a radius of four miles of the schoolhouse.

The week passed without incident. Friday night was cold for December. The sky was clear. The moon shone brightly. Frost was in the air. It was a delightful night for a pie supper.

My fellow band members, the auctioneer, and the three string players arrived early. The single girls and ladies had already placed their pies and cakes on top of my desk. People began flocking in as if pie suppers were going out of style. Soon the three string players were knocking out "Turkey in the Straw" as they kept time by stomping their feet.

The band members didn't bring along their instruments. They were there to enjoy the entertainment and to bid on the pies and cakes.

"Just listen to that technique," said our tenor saxophonist, Jim Williams.

"Maybe we should have them join our band on occasion," suggested drummer, John McClain.

"No way," laughed trumpet player Pete Sandoval. "Those boys can't read a note, but they sure do a good job playing by ear."

"Until the bidding starts," shouted Mrs. Roberts, "let's all go outside and make up a set. We can't let that pretty music go without having a square dance." So out the crowd went to dance to the tunes of the string trio.

At seven o'clock sharp, bang went the hammer as the auctioneer made ready to start the bidding.

"My name is Joe Atkins," announced the auctioneer. "Just look at these beautiful boxes," he said as he held up a pretty blue box that could hold either a cake or a pie. "What am I bid?"

"Twenty-five cents," shouted a man standing next to the windows.

"Twenty-five cents. Do I hear thirty?"

"Thirty," shouted a man from the rear.

"I have thirty. Do I hear forty?"

"Fifty," came a bid from just outside the door.

Heads turned to get a good look at the high bidder.

"Shut the door, Tom," shouted someone from the rear.

"Won't help any. The outside door to the vestibule is closed," he shot back.

"On with the bidding," demanded auctioneer Atkins. "Do I hear seventy-five?"

"Seventy-five," shouted a little pip-squeak standing by the potbellied stove.

"I have seventy-five. Do I hear one dollar?"

Silence.

"Seventy-five. Seventy-five once! Seventy——"

"One dollar," shouted our trumpet player.

"I have one dollar. Do I hear $1.25?"

"One dollar and a quarter," shouted a little old gray-headed man.

There was silence in the room. The place was so quiet one could have heard a dollar bill hit the floor.

"One dollar twenty-five cents once. One dollar twenty-five cents twice. Do I hear $1.50?"

Silence.

"One dollar twenty-five cents three times. Sold to the gentleman in the green shirt!"

"Imagine," a lady sitting in the center row of seats remarked, "men working on the farm for seventy-five cents and, at best, one dollar a day. They're bidding money as if it is going out of style."

The bidding continued until every box was sold. Some of the men were happy with their girls. Others were frowning when theirs didn't measure up to their expectations. Finally, everyone finished eating and all but the musicians began leaving. They came up front, and we began counting the money.

"Charles, from that pile of money it looks as if you really cleaned up," said John McClain.

"I'll bet the kids will be happy when you tell them what you are going to buy for the school," remarked Pete Sandoval. "Charles, it didn't take me long to see there was considerable rivalry among the young men."

"Well, did you do anything about it?" inquired John McClain.

"You're darn tootin' I did," answered Pete with an impish grin.

"Pete, for heaven's sake don't keep us in suspense. Tell us what you did," said John, sounding irritated.

"John, I played the devil's advocate. That's what I did," Peter said as if he knew a secret no one else knew.

"Pete, let's have the whole ball of yarn," said John.

"Well, I kept bids moving along by topping those men I thought had money. When I figured they about reached their limit, I'd stop bidding and let them buy."

"Pete, you're a sly old devil," I said. "I didn't know you had it in you, but I really like what you did."

As the fellows were talking, I noticed John Pirka hadn't left with the other people. He was standing near the rear of the room by the potbellied stove. Finally, I noticed him inching his way to the front of the room.

"Charles, how much did you take in?" John Pirka wanted to know.

"Thirty-two dollars and twenty-five cents," I said gleefully.

"I'll take it," he said.

"What did you say, John?"

"Charles, I said I'd take it! Hand it over!"

"Are you going to buy school equipment with it?" I asked.

"No, of course not. I'll put it in the bank with the education fund," he said as he scooped up the money and put it in his coat pockets.

I was more than surprised. I was thunderstruck. My mind was spinning. I just stood there petrified, not able to say another word. I just couldn't believe what I just heard. After everyone worked so hard to make the pie supper a success, then to have an old skinflint confiscate the money to deposit in the education fund was unbelievable. But it was true, no doubt about it.

Jim folded his arms and said nothing for a moment. Then he blasted out, backed by his 220-pound body fully conditioned from when he was in the marines. "You," he said to John Pirka, "are the lowest form of human scum I've ever seen. I truly hope you rot in hell!"

John Pirka didn't even open his mouth. He just rushed out of the room in nothing flat. Outside he was joined by his wife who was giving him hell for what he did, and she was just the person to do it.

I apologized to the musicians, bid them good night, and turned out the four portable kerosene lamps. Then Fairy and I started for home, not saying a word to each other until we were inside our house. Both of us had all the air sucked out of our sails. All that was left was one big vacuum.

Chapter 20
Christmas

Several days following the pie supper fiasco, I began to realize there was a lot to test one's capabilities, even one's sanity, while teaching in a one-room country school. However, there always was one bright spot. The children's pleasantries made null and void all of Joe Taylor's insults and snide remarks, as well as Joe Pirka's confiscation of the pie supper profits.

On the Monday morning just before Christmas, as I finished ringing the second bell at nine o'clock, second grader Ada Salinque pulled on my coattails. Turning around I said, "You seem awful happy this morning. What's on your mind?" Some of the other children stopped in their tracks to see what she wanted.

"Are we going to draw names like we did last year?" she eagerly inquired.

"Well, Ada, if I told you that it would be letting the cat out of the bag, now wouldn't it?"

"I guess so. But are we, are we?"

"If you'll take your seat, Ada, I'll give all of you some good news."

A few minutes later I made an announcement. "We'll begin today by drawing names to see who buys whom a present. Dennis Ragsdale, want to be the monitor?"

"Yeah, boy," replied Dennis cheerfully.

He gave each pupil a slip of paper on which to write his or her name. Collecting the papers, he put them in a small box and shuffled them thoroughly. Then he walked up and down the aisles as each pupil took a name from the box.

Looking at the name he drew, Robert Dean inquired eagerly, "May we trade names?"

"I think that's customary," I said, "but do it during recess or noon."

Realizing the parents were going through trying times, I set a limit of twenty-five cents for each present. Since the coal mine was idle and the farmers had no field work, we scheduled the Christmas party for one o'clock Christmas Eve. Now all was needed was to round out the two-act play, *Give Thanks for Christmas.*

As I looked at the children, I was suddenly overwhelmed as I thought about Christmas when I was a child. It always brought a warm, joyful gathering of family and friends. My heart sank, knowing that the school party would be the only Christmas some of these children would have.

That evening after supper, while we were in the living room, Fairy had a question. "Charles, are you not feeling well?"

"Oh, I'm okay I suppose."

"Well you don't act like it. I've never seen you with such a downcast look. What gives?" she said as she sat up straight and looked me in the eye.

"If you must know, I'll tell you. It's a shame. The children were so cheerful today. Some of them will have the wind knocked out of their sails come Christmas Day. It's a pity. That's what it is!"

"Charles, don't take it too hard. There's nothing you can do about it."

"Oh, yes, there is!" I replied.

"What do you have in mind?"

"Whether school keeps or not, I'm going to buy a Christmas tree for the room, also I'll buy some boy and girl presents for those who can't afford them. And, as you most likely are thinking, I'll buy a five-gallon bucket of Christmas candy. I hope some of the oldsters have learned some manners between Halloween and Christmas. Then I'm going to have the children put their presents under the tree the day before the party. That evening you and I will check the presents against the enrollment record. Then we'll put our own presents where names are missing. That way every child will have a treat."

Wednesday came quickly. That evening Fairy and I checked the presents under the decorated tree. Only eight names were missing; we corrected this with our own presents.

Looking around, Fairy said, "Charles, there's something missing."

"If there is, you figure it out. I've just about had Christmas up to my neck!"

"Oh, don't be an old scrooge. I have it," she said with a twinkle in her eye.

"Have what?" I asked as I wondered what she was up to.

"Here, I'll show you." With that said, she took colored chalk and drew on the blackboard a huge Santa Claus with a pack on his back going down the chimney.

That drawing brought back memories of when Miss Musgraves drew a similar picture on the blackboard during Christmastime when I was a pupil in a one-room country school.

"Now that everything is set for the party, let's call it a day," she remarked as she drew a big sigh of relief.

"Maybe I'm developing a certain stoicism about Christmas, but to that I say 'amen'!"

The following morning as I called the fifth grade reading class to the recitation seat, there was a knocking at the door. Ambling over to see who it was, I was greeted by a little old man dressed in a fur coat and hat and wearing high leather boots.

"Good morning," I said. "What can I do for you?"

"My name is Ted Wiggins," he replied as we shook hands. "I'm a retired professional accordion player."

"Pardon me a moment." I said as I turned around and called, "Ricardo, take charge of the fifth grade class."

Facing the old man again, I said, "What's on your mind, Mr. Wiggins?"

"Recently, I bough a little farm to tinker around with during my reclining years. Since my wife and I are new to this community, may we attend the Christmas party tomorrow?"

"Yes, sir, Mr. Wiggins," I responded. "It will be our pleasure to have you."

"May I bring my accordion?"

"Certainly," I said, wondering what I was letting myself in for.

"See you tomorrow," he said as he went on his way down the steps and into his car. I returned to my class.

The remainder of the day passed uneventfully. In spite of the big party the following afternoon, the children were unusually calm and collected. Perhaps the newness had worn off, and now everything pertaining to the party was routine. At least I hoped so.

That night was a night of terror for me. One bad dream followed another. I couldn't shake school director Taylor from my mind. In one dream, I died. Taylor kept shouting with a forked tongue, "Send him to hell! Send him to hell!" Finally I awoke with a start. Perspiration was running down my face, and I was shaking from head to foot. Looking at the alarm clock, I saw it was only 3:30 in the morning. From then on, I rolled and tossed until I awoke to the sound of a squalling cat.

Half-asleep, I crawled out of bed, put on my bathrobe, and threw open the back door. With a scramble of clawed feet on the bare kitchen floor, Thomas, our pretty yellow cat, darted between my legs as he made a beeline to his food dish under the kitchen sink.

"Yowooooow," squalled the cat.

"What's wrong with Thomas?" Fairy shouted from the bedroom.

"Oh, nothing much," I replied. "I inadvertently stepped on his big fat tail."

By the time I fed Thomas, I was wide awake. So I made myself a cup of coffee on the kerosene stove and tried to put the horrible night behind me.

I arrived at the schoolhouse at 8:15. Stopping at the open vestibule door, I admired the Christmas scene. Hanging from the ceiling was a large banner with ten-inch letters spelling, "Have a Merry Christmas and a Happy New Year." Silver and gold tinsel hung neatly in concave arches from the tops of the six windows making up the west wall. Below stood three candles, evenly spaced, on each windowsill. The Christmas tree, with all the presents lying below, was decorated with twenty candles all fixed in their holders, strings of popcorn, fifteen glass ornaments, and the Star of David securely fastened to the very top. All of these decorations and Fairy's drawing of Santa going down the chimney provided all the festivities of Christmas that any Christian could desire.

I stood there transfixed. Soon the children began coming into the building.

"Teach, want me to ring the first bell?" chided Addison Wainright.

Looking at my watch I saw it was five minutes past time. "Go ahead, Addison. Give it everything you have," I said as I wondered if I hadn't momentarily fallen asleep.

I scheduled classes for half-time. That way no one would miss a complete class.

Trying to hold attention was an exercise in futility. Although everyone was in a cheerful mood, there were no behavior problems. Even at recess time, there was no arguing or fighting.

Parents and visitors began coming in shortly after noon. Mr. and Mrs. Wiggins were among the first arrivals. He immediately removed his fur coat and hat, sat down, and took his accordion out of the case. After striking a few chords, he played, "Stars and Strips Forever," which put the people in a happy mood. This was followed by numerous Christmas carols, each one followed by one of his own variations to the themes. To say he was good would have been the understatement of the year. He was an expert on the accordion. His tempos were perfect. His crescendos and diminuendos had a gradual rise and fall that was not often achieved by the average musician. His staccatos were sharp. His legatos were smooth flowing, reminding me of a small brook gradually flowing toward the sea.

Now it was almost one o'clock. The visitors came by to congratulate him and to shake his hand. He was about to put his accordion in the case when I edged through the crowd to congratulate him. Then I said, "Mr. Wiggins, would you be kind enough to play an accompaniment as I lead the singing of a few Christmas carols?"

"It would be my pleasure," he replied with the air of a professional musician.

Following the group singing, I announced, "It's time to pass the candy." Before I could reach it, school director Joe Taylor picked up the bucket without asking permission.

"Everyone take some candy," he said as he walked up and down the aisles.

"I'll fix his wagon!" I heard Wayne Roberts say to one of his friends as he rushed to the front of the room. "Ladies and gentlemen," he shouted, showing anger in his voice. "None of the school directors bought the candy! It's a present from Mr. Neal! He's the one that deserves the credit!" Then he sat down.

Taylor's face suddenly turned barn red. Everyone turned and glared daggers at him. Sheepishly, he finished his self-appointed job.

Then he grabbed his coat and hat and fled through the door. "Good riddance!" I heard someone say. Someone else said, "I second the motion."

Agnes Harper, opening the program with a violin solo, "Hark, the Herald Angels Sing," captivated the crowd.

"She is destined to become a virtuoso, no doubt about it," commented Ted Wiggins.

Fourth grader Harley Blair gave a recitation, "Why We Celebrate Christmas." The audience gave him a big hand as they always honored one of their own.

The final number, *Give Thanks for Christmas*, a two-act play, with every pupil participating at one time or another, came off without a hitch.

As the final curtain call was acknowledged, a thundering, "Ho-Ho-Ho. A Merry, Merry Christmas to one and to all!" came from the vestibule. Then the door opened. In came Santa Claus portrayed by Hiram Stein. He was decked out in the traditional red suit and cap, black boots, white whiskers, and he carried a sack on his back. He had the perfect build: five feet, ten inches tall, and a typical roly-poly stomach measuring sixty-two inches around.

He wobbled over to the Christmas tree with a twinkle in his eye. Then he shouted again, "Ho-Ho-Ho. A Merry, Merry Christmas to one and to all!"

Picking up a package wrapped in pretty red paper and tied with gold-colored string, he called out, "Alex Giles!"

Alex came forward on the double.

"Been a good boy all year?" Santa wanted to know.

"Yes, I guess so," Alex said as he looked down at his shoes.

"Mind your mother and do what the teacher asks you to do?"

"I, I try," Alex stammered.

"Then here's your pretty red present and a stick of peppermint candy," Santa said as he took the candy from the sack.

As Alex turned to leave, Jim Settlemeir blurted out from his seat, "Santa, where's your reindeers and sleigh?"

"So sorry to say this, son, but Rudy, the red-nosed reindeer, has a very bad cold and Mrs. Claus is doctoring him at the North Pole. Had to come by airplane this year," he said before he called the next name.

Soon every pupil had a present. With the party over, most of the audience stayed on to visit as farmers in a small community are prone to do.

My wife and I were mingling with the crowd. Talking with the parents and visitors, we gained a good perception of where their interests and desires lay. As I scanned their faces, I was struck by the worried look on most of the men. Many, I am sure, were wrinkled and gray-headed long before their time. Their conversations were centered mainly around the farm. The didn't seem the least bit interested in state or national problems except what President Hoover could do to raise the price of corn.

By this time an old bald-headed codger began telling me all about his wonderful grandchild. Since I couldn't get a word in edgewise, I let my ears stray to the conversation of two men talking about a corn problem.

"Al, can you imagine corn selling at ten cents a bushel?" a man in front of me said to the man next to him.

"Must be a mistake," the other man replied. "I never knew corn to sell that cheap."

"Hell no! There's no mistake, Al. I held on to my corn, hoping the price would come up by Christmas."

"What are you going to do, Harry?"

In a flat toneless voice Harry said, "Don't really know, Al. I can't hold on to it much longer. My bank balance is fast approaching zero."

Al yawned, looked Harry in the eye, then he said, "Tell you what I'd do if I was you, Harry."

Forlornly he asked, "What's that, Al?"

Al folded his arms. Then he gave his words of wisdom. "Why, I'd hold that corn 'til spring, come hell or high water. Then I'd buy me some piglets. Get 'em cheap then. Feed 'em the corn. Have 'em fat as butter balls come fall. The market'll be right for a big profit."

"Yes, Al," Harry said gloomily. "But what will I use for money in the meantime?"

"No problem. The Royalton bank'll loan you enough money to get by on. Your corn and your livestock will be all of the collateral required."

I'd had enough corn for one afternoon. Excusing myself from the old codger who was now wanting to show me twenty-three pictures of his grandchild, I strolled to the back of the room to visit with school board president Harry Rone, who was standing by the potbellied stove warming his hands.

"Congratulations, Charles!" he said beaming. "This was the best Christmas party we ever had."

I laughed. "Harry, I doubt if Joe Taylor would agree with you. But thanks for the compliment. I really appreciate it."

"Charles," he said, hesitating a moment, "I've been meaning to talk to you about him."

"Harry, if it will make you feel any better, give me the whole lowdown. In my book he's a pain in the neck."

Taking a deep breath, Harry began. "When Joe and his wife moved to these parts about fifteen years ago, you couldn't ask for a better couple. They were really an asset to the community."

"Wow!" I said. "Harry, if anyone but you would have revealed this to me, I would have dubbed him a liar."

"Now just a darned minute, Charles!" he said as he squared his shoulders. "Joe is a strange man today. This is for sure, but he hasn't always been this way. What I told you a moment ago is absolutely true!"

"Oh, I don't doubt it for a moment, Harry. I was totally surprised, that's all. In my opinion, he is a strange man indeed. Hard to understand, hard to really know what makes him tick. I've felt all along that trying to figure him out would be an exercise in futility," I remarked authoritatively.

"Five years ago on a hot day in August, Joe received the shock of his life. You've noticed his gray hair, haven't you, Charles?"

"Well, yes, I have. Seems a little premature for a man of his age," I said.

"Right. And for good reason, too."

"What's that, Harry?" I inquired.

"That particular day, Joe had business to transact in Royalton. It took most of his day. Tired and exhausted he returned home around five o'clock to find a note propped up on the dining room table. In the note his wife told him that she had it up to her neck with him and that she was leaving for good with their three-year-old boy and the hired man. Joe searched everywhere, not leaving out his in-laws. He even hired a private detective to no avail. If his hair didn't turn white overnight, it did shortly thereafter. Now, can you tolerate him a little better, Charles?"

"I don't know," I said hesitatingly. "I'll think about it. One more thing, Harry. Why is it that he always votes the same way as John Pirka on every issue that comes before the school directors?"

"That's simple enough, Charles," he replied. "John gives Joe's lowdown good-for-nothing brother a few days of farmwork each month."

"So essentially, he's buying Joe's vote and getting some cheap labor to boot," I said.

"That's the long and short of it, Charles." Glancing at his watch Harry remarked, "Time to be ambling along."

Soon the stragglers were on their way out. Fairy and I followed them, for we decided to come back during the vacation to clean up.

Since John Pirka didn't bring my paycheck to the Christmas party, I called at his home the following morning, arriving there at 9:15.

Mrs. Pirka met me at the front door. Looking over the top of her glasses, she said, "Saw you drive in. Shucks, I haven't seen you in a coon's age. How's the missus? Have you had any more bad teeth? Got rid of the headache you had last week? Bet those old teeth caused it." She rattled from one question to another, sounding like the quacking of a mechanical duck.

"I'm fine. The missus is fine. No more toothache. I came to get my check," I said as I stood shivering in my shoes.

"Don't know what 'n hell is the matter with me, letting you stand there in the cold. Do come in and sit a spell," she said as she pointed to a comfortable rocking chair in the living room.

"I need some Christmas money. That's why I came to get my check," I demanded impatiently.

"Well, that's too bad. John isn't——"

"John isn't what?" I shouted.

"John is on his way to deliver country butter to his customers. He took the school checkbook with him."

"Why? Just why would he do that," I said getting more irritated all the time.

"Some damn fool notion of his, that's why! Every day school money stays in the bank, it draws 3 percent interest. He was hoping you wouldn't pick up your check until after the new year," she said matter-of-factly.

Getting up I said, "He's in his buggy. I can catch up to him in a few minutes."

"Can't tell you which way he went, but I can tell you where to catch him in Royalton."

"Where? Where? For heaven's sake, woman, get on with it," I said getting more impatient by the minute.

"He stops at the Blue Front Cafe at 10:30 to have a piece of Myrt's cherry pie and a cup of coffee. Might as well wait here a little bit. The cafe is not the warmest place in the world. Come out in the kitchen while I make up more butter for him to deliver this afternoon."

I watched her mix equal amounts of butter and oleo in a small tub. Then she used a hand-operated butter mold to produce one pound chunks of butter-oleo.

"I'm curious," I said. "Why mix your country butter with oleo?"

"For one thing we buy oleo at ten cents a pound. By selling the butter-oleo at twenty-five cents a pound, we make a nice profit. For another thing, oleo gives the finished product a better flavor," she replied as she wiped her greasy hands on her dress.

I nodded. Then laughed. I thought about what she just said. *Aren't there any honest people left in the world?* I asked myself. *The scam is no different from the slick salesman selling gold bricks or the Brooklyn Bridge, only less money is involved here.*

"By the by, Charles, what do you know about the Blue Front Cafe?" she said, more as an afterthought.

"Well, Maude, nothing, nothing at all. Fairy and I stop by once in a while for a quick snack. That's about it."

"It's a mom-and-pop operation. However, Myrt, that's mom, does most all of the work. Her good-for-nothing husband, Bart, does everything he can to get out of work. He's a diabolical manipulator! That's what he is. He lets Myrt do all the cooking, dish washing, and cleaning. Once in a blue moon he'll carry the dirty dishes from the dining room back to the kitchen. Claims he can't do much work because of a back injury caused by picking up horseshoes at a horseshoe pitching match. That poor slob of a man can come up with more excuses for sitting on his rear end than a dog has fleas. He's just no damn good!

"Perhaps you've noticed that skinny, gray-headed, wrinkled, poor excuse for a man sitting around talking to some of the patrons, laughing boisterously most of the time?"

"Come to think of it, I have. Always chewing on a matchstick that makes it almost impossible to understand what he's saying. Is that Bart?"

"That's the old SOB! If I were his wife, I'd shoot him and put him out of his misery. But then again, he isn't worth the powder needed to blow out his brains."

I laughed.

"You think that's funny! It's not! It's pathetic. That's what it is. Oh, yes, the old damn fool does one other thing. He says he's the manager, so he hires all the waitresses. Unless the applicants are female, blond, skinny as a rail, and good-looking, they're not employed. You see, Charles, he thinks he's God's gift to women.

"Oh, yes, there's one other thing you should know. He informs the waitresses that they are not to carry dirty dishes back to the kitchen or do cleanup work in the cafe. Can you imagine that?"

"No, I can't, Maude." Looking at my watch, I saw it was 9:55. "Maude, it was nice talking with you, but it's getting late so I'll be on my way." With that said, I jumped out of the chair and headed for the door. I had enough loony talk for one morning.

For living with that Bart, Myrt deserves a reserved seat in heaven, I thought as I started my car.

A moment later I was on my way to the Blue Front Cafe. Arriving there, I picked up my school paycheck from Joe Pirka. Then I headed for home to get Fairy and we were both on our way out of the boondocks for a much-needed Christmas vacation.

Chapter 21
Tobacco Invades the School Premises

Following a delightful Christmas vacation, I took on a new lease on life. Now I was more than ever determined to show the world that I was an excellent teacher.

One Thursday afternoon in January, during recess, I heard shouting from behind the boys' outhouse. *Something's wrong*, I said to myself. *If a competitive game was in progress, the boys and girls would not be hiding behind the outhouse.*

Peeping around the edge of the building, I spied Joyce Murray and Rachel Reed standing side by side, each taking a turn to see who could spit tobacco juice the farthest. Each one was backed by a audience of several pupils.

Just as I was about to say something, both girls made an about-face and let fly with amber spittle against the back wall of the outhouse.

Coming from around the building, I shouted, "Joyce! Rachel! Of all things, girls chewing tobacco! What do you have to say for yourselves?" The pupils watching the spitting match stood back awestricken.

"Nothing," said Rachel.

"What about you, Joyce?" I demanded.

"Nothing at all. Nothing at all, Teach. Just having a little fun. That's all. Nothing wrong with that, is there?" she said in a flat toneless voice.

"Nothing wrong that a little scrubbing won't cure!" I said as I ordered them to get a bucket, some soap, and a mop from the storage closet. "Fill the bucket half-full of water, mix in the soap, and get back here on the double!" Looking at my watch I said, "Hurry it up! You have seven minutes of recess time left. When I ring the bell, I'll expect this wall to be spic-and-span. Then you two girls will remain in your seats at dismissal time.

"The rest of you get on with your playing someplace else on the playground. Rachel and Joyce can get along very nicely without your supervision."

The pupils were tense the rest of the afternoon, wondering what I was going to do to Rachel and Joyce. The few remaining classes came to the recitation seat, recited in subdued voices, returned to their seats, and were glad when class was over.

At dismissal time I waited until the school yard was cleared. Then I said, "Girls, come to the recitation seat. I want to have a word with you."

Joyce came stiff-legged and giggling. Rachel, with head down, came laughing.

"Girls!" I said. "This is no laughing matter! Sit down and wipe that laughter off your faces this very instant!"

"Teach, are you going to give us a whipping?" Joyce wanted to know.

"Do you think you deserve one?" I shot back.

"I certainly do not!" responded Joyce.

"What about you, Rachel?" I asked.

"Please don't whip us, Teach," she begged.

"OK, for the time being," I answered. "Let's talk about it. Then I'll decide the punishment," I said as tears came to Rachel's eyes.

"Where did you get the tobacco?" I inquired.

"I gave it to Rachel!" Joyce boasted. "My daddy grows it in his garden. So what's wrong with that, I'd like to know!"

"Two things that I think of offhand," I said. "First, I will not have my pupils using tobacco in any form on the playground or in the schoolhouse. Second, we are too far north to raise good crops of tobacco. Although I don't use it myself, I'm told homegrown tobacco is terribly strong and hardly any man will touch it, let alone a woman."

"Are you going to whip us?" Joyce blubbered.

"Don't you think you deserve a whipping?" I said as I looked both girls in the eyes.

"No!" they both bellowed out together.

"OK. This time I'll let you be the judge, and I'll abide by your decision. However, let a word to the wise be sufficient. If I catch either one of you chewing tobacco again in or about the school premises, you'll get a genuine paddling. This is not a threat," I said. "It is a matter of fact. You're both excused. So be on your way."

With the girls out of my hair, I had another problem to consider. My fourth grade class was having more than their usual difficulty with their multiplication problems. For some unknown reason, some of them had developed a fixation on wrong answers. For instance, one pupil memorized six times nine equals sixty-six. Another one insisted that five times seven equals forty-two. Still another one said repeatedly, seven times eight equals fifty-five. *What to do?* I asked myself. Time was of the essence. During the six-hour day, I was scheduled to bring twenty-five classes to the recitation seat. To give more time to certain classes, I had to design a system contrary to rural school-teaching practices, so I reverted back to the old process of using monitors for problem classes.

That evening I prepared 144 four-inch-square pieces of white cardboard. On one side I printed the multiplier and multiplicand in large block numbers, with the answer on the reverse side. *I'll lick these teaching problems, or I'll know the reason why,* I said to myself.

The next day I called on school director John Pirka. He was in the backyard breaking up large pieces of coal for his living room heating stove. My visit was short. I explained how my monitoring system would work. Then I asked him if the directors would purchase an extra recitation seat along with two small chairs for the monitor's use.

His face suddenly turned red. His Adam's apple kept jumping up and down in his throat. He pulled his trousers higher up on his stomach. Then he said, "Charles, you can come up with some of the craziest ideas about teaching school that I have heard of! Our school has got along this far with only one recitation seat, and it's going to get along from now on with one recitation seat! The answer is no! We would consider it an unessential expense."

"I'm not surprised, John," I replied. "I expected to be turned down. Just thought I'd ask anyway."

"Listen, Charles, Maude just brought some chocolate cookies out of the oven. Come in and sample some with a cup of coffee."

This is my time to act bullheaded, I thought. "No, thank you, John," I answered. "Eating now would spoil my appetite for supper." I turned on ny heels and walked away.

That weekend I brought eight wooden boxes into the schoolhouse, placing six in a row side by side in the rear of the room away from the potbellied stove. Next, I placed two boxes in front of the improvised recitation seat for the monitors to sit on.

When school began the following Monday morning, I explained the purpose of the boxes as well as how the monitor system worked.

"Yes, Robert. What is it?"

"Teach, I didn't know you wanted some boxes. Heck, we've got a whole slew of 'em. Need any more, just say the word."

"Thanks, Robert. That is very kind of you."

With the fourth grade class seated on the boxes, one monitor used the flash cards to drill the pupils individually. While that monitor handled the cards, the second monitor took notes on the names of the pupils and the kinds of mistakes they made. Later they could use the cards individually to learn the answers to the combinations missed. The monitor system was a blessing in disguise. While the monitors drilled the pupils, I was free to teach the next class.

Tuesday morning, during recess, Robert Dean and Melvin Swartz approached me on the playground.

"Well boys, what's on your mind this bright January day?"

"We've been wanting to talk to you since the girls squirted spittle on the back wall of the boys' privy."

"Glad to talk anytime. You know I have an open-door policy with my pupils. What say we sit down on the schoolhouse porch?"

"Did the girls tell you really why they did that?" Robert wanted to know.

"No. I had a feeling they were not telling me everything," I replied.

"With good reason," spoke up Melvin. "Had they told you everything they might have stirred up a hornet's nest."

"Really?" I said, more interested now than ever to hear what the boys had to say. "How's that?"

"Look at the schoolhouse," said Melvin, looking very proud. "It looks nice painted white. Look at the dingy-looking, unpainted outhouses. Last year one of the boys threatened to come here some dark night and set fire to both of them."

"Oh, my," I broke in. "That's called arson. Never, never do that! There isn't a statue of limitation on arson crimes."

"What's statue of limitations mean?" spoke up Robert.

"Not statue, boys, but statute. A statute of limitations is a statute that sets time limits upon the right to sue in certain cases, such as a specified time the victim in a horse-and-buggy accident can sue to collect damages following the accident. For example, a person may commit arson and get away with the crime for a number of years before being caught, tried, convicted, and sent to prison.

"I know a man who was finally tracked down twenty years after burning a neighbor's house. He was caught, tried, convicted, and is now spending his last days in prison. You see, boys, there is no time limit set for arson."

"Gee," Melvin responded, "I didn't know it was that serious."

"Neither did I," said Robert. "You'll never catch me burning someone else's property!"

"Melvin, you gave me an idea a few minutes ago when you said, 'painted white.' Can you boys paint?"

"Oh, sure, Teach. All us farm boys learn how to paint," answered Robert.

"Would you boys help me a couple of Saturday mornings to paint the outhouses white?" Both boys nodded their heads up and down.

"OK. I'll see what I can do to come up with necessary paint and turpentine." Glancing at my watch, I saw it was time to ring the bell.

While going home after school, I asked myself a question: *Will Joe Pirka have a heart attack when I ask him this evening to okay paint for the outhouses?* I laughed at the answer I expected. "Can't do it. Paint for the privies is not in the budget. Besides it comes under unessential expenditures."

After supper I called on the Pirkas, arriving there around 6:30.

"Good evening, Mrs. Pirka," I greeted her as she opened the front door.

"It's cold enough for hell to freeze over. Come in. Come in and sit by the heating stove. And by the way, Charles, I'm getting damn tired of hearing you call me Mrs. Pirka."

"Well," I inquired, "what would you have me call you?"

"We've known each other long enough to eliminate that damn formal stuff. Call me 'Maude.' Sounds more friendly-like."

"OK, Maude, where's John?"

"Oh, he's out feeding the chickens and milking the cows. While we're waiting for him, let's you and I talk."

"Sounds good to me," I said. "What do you want to talk about?"

"Charles, I have a question to ask you. Will you answer it?"

I decided to borrow some of her language to see if we couldn't become more informal with each other. "Shoot," I said. "I'll do my damn best to answer it."

"Now that's the way I like to hear a man talk. Sounds a hell of a lot more friendly that way.

"Charles, do you really like living out here in the boondocks with no electricity, gas, or running water?"

"Well," I answered with a laugh, "it does take some getting conditioned to. Some people out here claim I have running water just because of the hand-operated pitcher pump that brings water to the kitchen from the cistern."

Chuckling, I went on, "Call it running water if you will, but to our dismay, we must take our baths in a number two washtub."

"Hell, Charles, you folks have only lived out here for about three months. What——"

"Five months tomorrow," I corrected.

"Well, I'm damn sick and tired of it. Day in and day out, week in and week out, month in and month out, year in and year out. After much jawin' and cussin' him out, he finally broke down and brought a used Model T Ford car. Now you know what, Charles?"

"No, Maude, I don't know what. Why don't you tell me what?"

"He still insists on getting about in that damn old horse and buggy! Says gasoline is too high at eighteen and twenty cents a gallon. Do you know that I haven't seen a pitcher show in five years? What'n hell do you think of that, Charles?"

"How would you and John like to see one tomorrow night? Fairy and I plan to have supper at the Blue Front Cafe, then take in a picture show."

"John won't go! Says pitcher shows are the work of the devil. Hell, yes!" she said as she pushed her glasses up on her nose. "I'll go!"

"Splendid," I said. "We'll pick you up around 6:30, eat supper at the Blue Front Cafe, then take in the show."

"What's playing?" she asked eagerly.

"It's a cowboy-Indian picture."

"Goody, goody," she cackled. "I love those cowboy pitchers," she said as we heard John coming through the back door.

"Well, well, Charles," he greeted me as he came into the living room, "what bring you out on a cold winter night like this?"

"I have a favor to ask," I replied, wondering why I would waste my time asking him anything for the betterment of the schoolhouse.

"Shoot," he said. "I have an open mind tonight. Guess it's the cold weather. Makes one feel frisky."

I explained the problem with the unsightly outhouses, informed him of the tobacco problem, told him of the boys' volunteering to help me paint the privies.

"How can I help?" he inquired as his facial expression showed interest.

"John," I said, "I don't mind doing a little extra work beyond my teaching contract, but I am getting a little sick and tired of putting out my own money to improve the schoolhouse and its premises."

"John," interrupted Maude, "why in hell can't you directors jar loose once in a while and give Charles a little financial——"

"Enough of that, Maude. You run the house and we'll run the school. So just shut up!" he said as he excused himself to check on one of his milk cows.

"Maude, I notice you never talk back when he orders you to keep quiet. What hold does he have over you?" I wanted to know.

"It's real serious. Someday when I know you better, I'll spill the whole jar of beans," she replied as we heard John reentering the house.

When John returned to the house, he said, "Charles, I've been thinking. How much paint do you need?" he said with a gleam in his eyes.

"Three gallons of white paint, one quart of turpentine, and three four-inch paintbrushes."

"Well," he said, "I think the budget will stand the expenditures. I'll write you an order to the Royalton Hardware Store. When will you do the painting?"

"We should have a break in the weather any day now," I said, overjoyed with his generosity. "We'll put on the priming coat the first Saturday when the temperature is above 50° F. Then, when the next good Saturday comes along, we'll put on the finish coat."

"Good enough, Charles," he said as he handed me the order.

After saying good night to both of them, I left for home in a far more jovial mood than I had when I entered the Pirka home.

The following Monday after recess, I was giving special attention at my desk to two third graders who needed help with their reading lesson. I had some time free from classes because the fourth graders were seated on the recitation box seats in the back of the room. This time the monitor was drilling them in spelling from a list of words I had prepared.

I noticed Joyce Murray ducking her head every now and then. *Very unusual*, I thought. *Could she be chewing tobacco?*

I arose from my seat, tiptoed around the west wall. Then I quietly moved toward the rear. Standing behind her seat for a moment, I saw it. She was chewing tobacco and spitting the juice into her inkwell.

"Joyce," I said, "what are you doing?"

"Studying my history lesson."

The pupils turned in their seats to see what was taking place. Even the pupils on the recitation box seats looked around to see what was going on.

"Yes, I can see that. I can also see that you are chewing tobacco. Don't swallow the quid! Remove your inkwell from the desk. Then take it outside. Draw some water from the well and wash out the inkwell. While you're outside, spit the quid from your mouth. When finished, you may return to your seat. At dismissal time, I want you to remain," I said as she picked up the inkwell and started toward the door.

That afternoon when I dismissed school, Joyce remained transfixed in her seat. I waited until I thought all of the children were off the playground, then I said, "Joyce, come to my desk."

"What for?"

"You know what for!"

"Are you going to paddle me?"

"I'm going to do what I promised you and Rachel I'd do if I ever caught either one of you chewing tobacco again. Get up here pronto and stop wasting time," I said as I took "the Board of Education" from the top desk drawer. Using an eight-inch piece of broom handle, I had cut a two-inch slit into one end. Then I slipped a man's composition shoe sole into the slit, fastening it securely with two one-inch finish nails. I rebelled against using a wooden paddle or a hickory switch. The first could cause physical damage, while the latter left red welts on the body. "The Board of Education," dubbed by the boys after I used it on two of them for stealing "stung like hell," as one of them said after getting a taste of it.

She came up reluctantly.

"Bend over the desk," I said.

I gave her eight stinging spanks to her buttocks, just enough to make tears come to her eyes. She was a tough little girl. The spanking didn't really hurt, but it did wound her pride.

"You may go," I said.

She stood up, turned around, and glared at me before she walked out through the door. Then she turned around and stuck her head inside the door.

"When I get home, I'll tell my daddy on you!" she shouted with anger showing in every word. "He'll give you a taste of our own medicine! He thinks you're an upstart, not even dry behind the ears." Then she wheeled around, heading for home.

I grabbed my coat and hat, locked the door, and ran to catch up to her. When she heard me approaching, she began to run. I ran along with her. She turned her head sideways to keep from looking at me. Soon she was getting out of breath.

"Joyce," I said, "take it easy. You can't outrun me as I was out for track the four years I was in high school."

She slowed her pace, looked away from me, and was as quiet as an Egyptian sphinx. Soon we entered the Murray property.

Edward, her father, was coming from the barn.

"My, my," he said jokingly, "it's a fine kettle of fish when my little girl needs a chaperone to bring her home from school."

"Mr. Murray," I said, "Joyce has something to tell you. Then if she happens to forget something I'll be glad to complete the story."

With several half-truths, she told her side of the story. I filled in the voids.

"Joyce," her father asked, "is what Mr. Neal says true?"

"Yes," she muttered, looking down at the ground.

"Go into the house, Joyce.

"My little girl chewing tobacco! It's hard to believe!" he said as if talking more to himself than to me. "Thanks for coming, Mr. Neal. I appreciate it very much."

As he offered his hand, I shook it vigorously. Then I started for home.

Another day, another dollar. *And a not-too-perfect day to boot*, I said to myself.

Chapter 22
Motivation

While coming to school that Thursday morning, I realized the end of February was fast approaching. Also, I realized something else, too. I couldn't put my finger on it exactly, but most of my pupils, especially those between grades three and seven inclusive, showed very little interest in arithmetic. Oh, they worked their assignments, but lacked incentive to go that extra mile.

Their attitude brought back memories of a young man I once knew who despised farming. He would walk behind the plow as his father ordered, but his interest in plowing had much to be desired. He didn't care whether the furrows were straight or crooked. Nothing mattered to him except quitting time. How much he was like my pupils. He lacked motivation as they did.

Entering the schoolhouse, I said to myself, *Neal, you're a failure!* I couldn't take that. So while teaching my classes that morning, I tossed around several ideas in my head on just how I could best motivate the boys and girls most effectively, especially in Arithmetic. I wouldn't tolerate being a failure. I had to succeed! By one o'clock I had formulated a plan.

I didn't begin my afternoon class. Instead, I said, "Boys and girls, I want to take a few minutes to discuss a problem with you.

"It's no secret," I said. "Arithmetic and spelling aren't your most popular subjects. Our cipher matches and spelling bees fall flatter than a lead nickel.

"What gives? Why?" I wanted to know.

"It all has to do with last year," volunteered Melvin Swartz.

"It was teacher's fault," said Nancy Spinlow.

"Yup!" said Jerry Meeker. "She would appoint two captains, then let them choose their team members. Mary Lou was always selected to call the problems. Same thing with spelling bees. Mary Lou called the words."

To my dismay I said, "How did the teacher spend her time?"

"She sat up there and read a book," giggled Agnes Harper as she pointed a finger toward my desk.

I couldn't believe my ears. For some reason I laughed.

"You think that's funny?" spoke up Robert Dean. "We were so bored we did our best to make fun and games out of both the cipher matches and the spelling bees.

"Here's one thing Wayne and I did to liven up one spelling bee. We asked Mary Lou to call out woodpecker when it was Wayne's turn to spell. 'Woodpecker,' she said.'Woodpecker,' he repeated stifling a laugh. 'Vould wood. Sock-edle-de-peck-X O-R, woodpecker.' Of course, the room was in an uproar. Then an amazing thing happened. Teacher darned near jumped out of her chair. Either she had been asleep or was so interested in her reading that she hadn't heard a word we were saying."

"Let's forget about last year and talk about this year. How many of you remember seeing a large want ad last week in the Royalton newspaper?"

Several hands went up. "I know every word of it!" shouted Addison Wainright. " 'Fifty dollar reward for information leading to the arrest and conviction of the person or persons responsible for stealing lumber from the Southern Illinois Sawmill. Contact Roger Green, manager.' I know it by heart because I want that fifty dollars!"

"Good! Very good, Addison! If the reward had not been offered, would you still report the guilty party if you knew who did the stealing?"

"Gee willikers, heck no!" he was quick to reply.

Then I explained my plan. "The day following either a cipher match or a spelling bee each winning team will get a reward of two gallons of ice cream, two bottles of soda pop, and two pieces of cake. The losing team will also be rewarded, getting one gallon and a half of ice cream, one bottle of soda pop, and a small piece of cake."

"Teach, you really mean it?" asked Yetlo Olivetti as if he didn't believe his ears.

"We'll have a cipher match a week from today. Then you'll see for yourself, Yetlo. How many will study hard in the meantime, hoping to be on the winning team?" Every hand shot high into the air.

Begrudgingly, I called on the Pirkas that evening, arriving at seven o'clock. John invited me in. Then he sat down in his favorite rocker.

Maude was sitting on the sofa opposite him knitting a pair of men's dress gloves. I sat down on a straight-back chair.

I explained my motivation plan to John and projected what I thought would be the outcome in increased interest and accomplishments. He just sat there, stone-faced, reminding me of a store window dummy.

Finally, I said, "Well, John, what do you think of it?"

"Might do what you say it will do," he replied gloomily. "Then again it might not.

"Charles, your refreshments come under entertainment. There's simply no money listed in the budget under that category. Sorry."

Maude put down her knitting. Then she said, "Sounds like a damn good idea, Charles. If we had something like that when I went to school, I wouldn't have dropped out in the sixth grade. Mind if I visit?"

"Absolutely not! On the contrary, I'd be happy to have you."

"You know, I bake a mean angel food cake. Would four cakes be enough?"

"Sure would. If you'll cut the cakes, Mary Lou Hawkins will hand out the soda pop, and I'll dish up the ice cream. How does that sound, Maude?"

"Sounds fine! We'll sure make one hell of a team, you and me."

As I went out the door, I turned around and said, "We will start serving around half past two, a week from tomorrow. Better be a little early."

"I'll be there promptly a little before half past two," she said with a gleam in her eyes.

After the morning recess the following Thursday, the pupils elected two captains. Melvin Swartz received the largest number of votes, automatically becoming captain number one. Robert Dean, the runner-up, became the second captain.

Next, the teams were chosen, starting with the beginners, then moving up through the grades. As captain number one, Melvin had the honor of calling the first beginner. Next, Robert called. Then they called back and forth until both teams were formed. We were now ready to begin the cipher match promptly at one o'clock, right after lunch.

Following lunch the teams took their places with team number one lined up against the east wall and team number two against the opposite wall.

"Before we begin," I said, "the challenged pupil has the option to figure against the one still standing in addition, subtraction, long division, multiplication, decimal or common fractions."

Melvin named one of his team members, Hazel Beckmeyer, to start the ball rolling. She challenged Stephen Yardlow from the opposite team. She turned him down. The she turned down three more pupils before being turned down herself by Ada Salinque. Ada cleaned out the primary children by turning down five. Then she called Rachel Reed, turning her down in long division. She was careless in her next choice when she called Harley Blair. He was excellent in any category in arithmetic. He called for addition.

This boy could add two columns of figures at one time. Hardly had they written their problems on the board, when Harley had the answer. Ada hung her head as she took her seat. She realized too late that she made a wrong choice. Then he turned down three pupils, calling Alex Giles next. Alex was good in decimal fractions. I gave out the problem. Harley finished slightly ahead of Alex, but the decimal point was in the wrong place. Alex had the correct answer. He turned down six pupils. Next, he called captain Melvin Swartz who went down easily in defeat. It was obvious he was elected on a popularity basis, rather than for his ability in arithmetic.

Now Alex called Mary Lou Hawkins. Because of her age she asked to abstain.

"No," I said. "You are a team member. You were selected by your peers, and I can't allow you to fail their trust." She turned down the two remaining pupils on the second team.

A big cheer went up from the victorious team. Then captain Robert Dean thanked his fellow team members. Next, he walked over to Melvin's seat and congratulated him and his team for putting up a good fight. Then I thanked Robert for his sportsmanship as I thought how many of us oldsters could profit by following his example.

I cut classes five minutes less than half-time Friday morning so that all were covered. The children were orderly. They were bubbling over with enthusiasm, hardly able to wait for the party.

The Olivetti boys brought two one-inch by twelve-inch by eight-feet boards in their father's beat-up truck. These were placed across the desktops on which Mary Lou Hawkins placed a red-checkered tablecloth.

"Harley Blair and Dennis Ragsdale," I called, "bring in the orange and strawberry soda pop and put them on the table.

"Wayne Roberts and Robert Dean, bring in the ice cream. Put it next to the soda pop."

It was exactly 2:30 when I saw Maude Pirka bringing in the cakes.

"Glad to see you, Maude. How are tricks?" I said, hoping she would clean up her speech.

"Never felt better, Charles, and had less," she said, happy as a lark.

"Let's go! Let's go!" I shouted. The pupils didn't have to be asked a second time. "Get in line. Team one to the right of the table. Team two to the left."

Maude served the cake. Mary Lou handed out the soda pop. I dished up the ice cream.

After everyone was served, Maude and I sat back and listened to the chatter.

"I like this treat better than the whole Christmas party," said Jake Monroe.

"Teach is not such a stick-in-the-mud as I thought," confided Nancy Spinlow to Rachel Reed.

The Olivetti brothers and Maude Pirka had a surprise for us.

Ricardo played "Turkey in the Straw" on his harmonica. She and Yetlo did an imitation of a square dance to the delight of us all. My pupils kept time with their feet. I knew Ricardo played the harmonica, but I didn't know that Yetlo and Maude knew how to dance. My pupils got a big bang out of watching those two perform.

"Congratulations, Mrs. Pirka," I shouted. "Didn't know you could dance!"

"You ain't seen nothing yet!" she shouted back. "If you think this is good, you should have seen me dance when I was younger. I shook a mean leg then!" So far she had cleaned up her speech as well as acted like a real lady.

Finally the party came to an end.

"Now for the cleanup," I shouted. "Put your empty soda pop bottles in the cardboard box as Wayne passes it up and down the aisles."

Yetlo carried his table boards out to the truck. Mary Lou folded her checkered tablecloth. Ricardo swept the floor. After everyone was out of the building, I thanked Mrs. Pirka for her cooperation and praised her for her entertaining dance with Yetlo. Then I locked the door, and we all started for home.

The following Monday morning Irene Mason was absent, as she had been on Friday. "This is unusual for Irene to be absent two days in a row. Anyone know the reason?" I inquired.

"She's sick," said Joyce Murray.

"What's wrong with her, Joyce?"

"Don't know."

"Does anyone know whether she has seen a doctor?" I asked.

"No," volunteered Jake Monroe. "I was over there last evening. She was lying on a pallet behind the living room heating stove. She's really sick. Her ma was putting cold, wet towels on her forehead."

"Her old man won't take her to a doctor," spoke up Melvin Swartz. "He wouldn't spend five cents to see Jesus Christ ride a bicycle around the square in Benton. He's tighter than bark on a tree." This caused my pupils to break out in laughter.

"That's enough!" I said. Right then I knew I had to make a home visit that evening.

A full moon was rising that evening when I donned more warm clothes and drove my Model A Ford to the Masons' home.

I was admitted by Tom Mason, Irene's father. He was a tall gangling man with a lean face and stooped shoulders.

"Jake stopped here on his way home from school. Said you was a comin'. Glad you could make it. Irene's real sick! But I believe in the Good Book. The Lord will take care of her," he said matter-of-factly.

"That may be so, Tom," I said. All the time I was wondering how I was ever going to motivate this man to do something constructive for his daughter. "I, too, believe in the Good Book. However, it also says, 'The Lord helps those who help themselves.' Maybe he needs a little help with Irene?

"By helping the Lord a farmer I once knew raised an excellent corn crop. Parson Rutherford was driving along a country road when he noticed a farmer looking over the fence admiring his corn crop.

"Stopping his car he said, 'Brother Simpkins, you and the Lord certainly have raised a fine crop of corn.'

" 'Yes, sir, Parson. But you should have seen this field when the Lord had it by himself.' " I doubt if Tom got the message. But it gave me some time to think how I might help Irene.

While we were talking, I was observing Irene's condition. She was hallucinating. "Bring my breakfast. I don't want to be late for the cipher match," she said over and over and over again.

"Tom, mind if I check her pulse?" I asked.

"No. Can't say that I do," he said in a flat, toneless voice.

Her pulse was rapid. She was burning up with fever.

"Do you have a fever thermometer?" I asked Tom.

"No. 'Tended to get one, but never got 'round to doin' it."

Nodding my head to the left I walked with Tom into the kitchen. I didn't want the little ones to hear what I had to say.

I was surprised to see two of the three exposed walls bare of one-inch by four-inch ceiling boards. I didn't say anything about them at the time, because I had more important things to discuss.

How can I motivate this man to do something constructive for his daughter? I asked myself a second time.

"Tom, the Lord gave you and Mrs. Mason a pretty, intelligent daughter. Now, what can you do to help the Lord cure her?"

"Wall," he sighed, "don't rightly know. Have any suggestions?"

"We can start by taking her to Dr. Flemming in Royalton."

"Kain't do that! Don't have no money to spare!"

"Now look, Tom! We're talking about your daughter's life, for God's sake! Doc is an understanding man. There is something you can do or give him besides money," I said as I shook my head in disgust. "Put a couple of blankets and a pillow on the backseat of my car. Then you and I will carry her out of the house and into the car. Do I have your okay?"

"Wall, I guess so if you think it's best. I'll wrap her up real good," he replied.

On the way to Royalton I asked him about his kitchen destruction. Being the lazy, shiftless person that he was, he said he had pried boards from the walls over the past several years to use for kindling in starting morning fires in his coal stoves.

Before I could carry on the discussion any further, we arrived at Dr. Flemming's clinic. Tom and I carried Irene inside where the doctor directed us to the examining room.

Twenty minutes later he said, "Tom, your little girl has pneumonia. I wish I had seen her a couple of days sooner. If I can break her fever tonight, she'll pull through. If not, well, you know the answer."

"Kain't do it. Kain't do it. I don't have no money to keep her here!"

"Look, Mr. Mason, you don't have any choice! She stays! There's something you can give me besides money. I don't want any more chickens, eggs, or home-killed meat! I have enough of those things now to start a store. Does your wife sew?"

"Wall, yes, she do a little if I kin get her a goin'."

I interrupted. "Doctor," I said, "she makes all of Irene's clothes. My wife and I have always admired them. They look as if they were store-bought, and her stitches are letter perfect."

"OK. That settles it then," said the doctor. "I need six hospital gowns. I'll furnish the material and the patterns if your wife will make them. That will satisfy the bill, even if your little girl stays here for a week or more. What do you say, Mr. Mason?"

"Wall, that sounds copesetic to me," he drawled.

"What kind of an answer is that?" the doctor wanted to know.

"Doctor, that means yes," I interpreted as I grinned.

"Now that's settled, I have another proposition for you, Mr. Mason."

"What's that, Doc? Want the wife to do more sewin'?"

"No, this time I want you to do something for me. Do you have oak trees on your farm?" the doctor wanted to know.

"Shucks, Doc, we've got oodles and gobs of oak. What you want it fur, Doc?"

"I want it cut into eighteen-inch pieces for my fireplace. I'll pay three dollars a cord delivered, and I'll need six cords. Think you can handle it?"

"Wall, if you-uns 'ill give me 'bout three weeks, I kin do it."

"Fair enough, Mr. Mason," Dr. Flemming said as he walked us to the door.

On the way back, Tom was unusually quiet for the first mile.

"Cat got your tongue, Tom? You haven't said a word since we left Dr. Flemming's clinic."

"Bin a thinkin'. Would my wagon heaped full make a cord?"

"Tom, that depends on the size of your wagon. A cord of wood is eight feet by three feet by three feet, or any pile of wood where the length times the width time the height equals seventy-two cubic feet."

"Don't know nothin' 'bout cubid feets. Kin you——"

"Then forget everything I told you," I interrupted. "Here's a simple way to do it, Tom. Drive two stakes into the ground eight feet apart with three feet sticking above the ground. Then fill the space with two rows of eighteen-inch pieces of wood three feet high between them."

"That's a cord?" he shouted in disbelief.

"Yes, it is, Tom. Why do you ask?"

"Man, I been cheated! My wagon piled high was 'posed to be a cord, said the baker who buys wood from me. Why heck, Mr. Neal, I could almost get two stacks like you say in my wagon. Know what he pay?" he inquired.

"No, Tom, I have no idea."

"Two dollars fifty cents for that big load of wood! I've been cheated all 'round by that old skinflint! He'll not take me for a ride anymore—the old devil!" he said as he slapped his right leg hard.

By now we reached Tom's home.

As he got out of the car, I said, "Tom, I'll check on Irene tomorrow during my lunch hour." Then I revved up the engine and started for home.

Fortunately, Irene recovered nicely. She returned to school the following week. After a bit of nudging by Dr. Flemming, Tom came through with his part of the bargain. So did Mrs. Mason. The doctor praised her work to every patient who ever used her gowns.

Since the cipher match, my pupils showed more and more interest in their schoolwork. So their interest wouldn't wane, I announced a spelling match a week from the following Thursday afternoon.

There came a cheerful look on their faces. Dennis Ragsdale stifled a shout.

"What about a party, Teach? Are we going to have another party?" Susan Slavins wanted to know.

"Do you think we should?" I asked as if I didn't know.

"Yeah, yeah!" came the reply loud and clear from all my cheerful pupils, shouting as of one.

"OK," I said. "I'll take care of the details. Also, I'll have the soda and ice cream here in time for the party."

Classes continued uneventfully for the following week except for two things: My pupils were showing more and more enthusiasm day by day. They were more orderly and studious than when I took over the previous August. Also, during daily dismissal I noticed that every fourth, fifth, and seventh grade pupil took their blueback speller home.

Thursday morning came none too soon for the boys and girls. At eleven o'clock they elected captains. It was no surprise that Melvin Swartz and Robert Dean were chosen. Then they chose their teams, and I dismissed them for lunch.

Mary Lou Hawkins begged off being a team member. She didn't think it fair for her to always win. This time I agreed by giving her the task of calling the words. I would serve as referee.

The teams were in line, one on the west wall, the other on the east when Jake Monroe had a question.

"Teach, can you spell saloon?" he said with a gleam in his eyes.

"Saloons are illegal, but I think I can spell it. Correct me if I'm wrong; a hess-an-a-one hell-two hoes-and a hen," I said as I laughed.

"Aw, shucks! Someone told you," Jake said forlornly.

"Yes, Jake. When I was a first grader in a country school one of the older pupils pulled that gag on my teacher," I said.

"Captains," I said, "we will start with the beginners and work upward through the grades."

The match began with Hazel Beckmeyer and Ada Salinque. Ada won with the word *Mississippi*. Hazel omitted one *p*.

Ada turned down five pupils. Then she was turned down by Rachel Reed. She challenged Harley Blair, turning him down on the word *coffee*. Harley omitted one *e*. Team one turned down and team two turned down until only Robert Dean, team number one, and Irene Mason, team number two, remained. Irene won on the word *entomology*. Then a big cheer went up from the second team. Irene complimented Dean and his team for putting up a real challenge.

Since it was three o'clock, I dismissed school for the day.

I again cut classes five minutes less than half-time Friday morning. The children were orderly but full of enthusiasm. Alex Giles told me that waiting for the party to begin was like waiting for Christmas.

The Olivetti brothers set up the table as before. Then Mary Lou covered it with a checkered tablecloth. Just then Mrs. Pirka came into the schoolhouse with four angel food cakes. Since she had been the life of the previous party, I had again given her an invitation to attend. I told a couple of boys to bring in the soda pop and ice cream from my car.

"We're ready to go," said Mrs. Pirka as she finished cutting the cakes.

"Ready with the soda pop, Mary Lou?"

"Ready as I'll ever be," she answered.

I was ready to dish up the ice cream. Then I yelled, "Come and get it. Get in line! Team one to the right of the table. Team two to the left."

Everyone was served and enjoying himself. I never heard such chattering. It reminded me of a flock of geese eating wheat shoots in Farmer Elwad's field.

Halfway through the party Harry Rone came in and motioned for me to come over.

"Harry, let's get away from all this chatter," I said as we stepped into the vestibule. "If I had known you were coming, I'd have saved some refreshments."

"Think nothing of it. I was on my way to Royalton. Just stopped by for a moment to give you some good news."

"Well, Harry, I'm always open for good news. What is it?" I said, anxiously waiting.

"As president of the school board I thought I should be the one to tell you."

"Tell me what, Harry?" I piped.

"Joe Taylor won't be bothering you anymore."

"That's good news!" I said as I felt happier than I had in several months.

"There's more. Two nights ago two of our neighbors called on

Joe. Essentially, they told him not to hassle you anymore, starting at that very instant, unless——"

"Unless what, Harry?" I said, anxious to hear more.

" 'Unless you want to wake up in the hospital with a couple of broken limbs,' they told Joe."

"Harry, do you think he'll take their advice?"

"I can't give you their names, Charles. But if you knew their reputations, you'd never ask that question."

"Harry, that's remarkable," I said as we parted company.

When everyone finished eating cake and ice cream and drinking soda pop, Ricardo played "Pop Goes the Weasel" on his harmonica, and Maude and Yetlo danced.

The party was a big success. It was now three o'clock.

When the cleanup was finished, I dismissed school. Another day, another $4.75 for a full day of teaching, I reminded myself.

Chapter 23
Community Service

A few unremarkable days passed by following the school party. Suddenly I was beset with requests for help of one kind or another. At first I couldn't understand why I was besieged. Then it dawned on me. News traveled fast in Dutch Hill. Tom Mason had spread the word to almost every person in the community about my showing him an easy way to figure a cord of wood.

Men came to me to figure truckloads of coal and sand taken from the Mississippi River, bushels of grain in their bins, and even a trick problem in *Lady's Friend* magazine.

At 8:30 that cool March morning, I arrived at the schoolhouse to find a man sitting on the steps. He had a strong angular face, with high cheekbones and hollows beneath them.

"I'm Burt Aiken," he said as he stood up, removed his cap, and introduced himself. "Are you Mr. Neal?"

"Yes, sir, I am," I replied as I shook his hand, wondering how long this would take. Books were only ten minutes away.

"My wife, Edna, heared how you heped Tom Mason with his problem. She wondered if you could hep her solve her problem. Her magazine give five dollars to the first twenty-five winners. Could you he'p her?" he asked eagerly.

"Well, I don't know, I said. "May I see the problem?"

"Here it is," he said as he handed me a wrinkled, dirty page from the magazine.

Glancing at the problem, I chuckled to myself. My Uncle Bill tutored me through *Ray's Arithmetic*. It contained dozens of problems more difficult than this one.

"Burt," I said, "I'm pressed for time just now. Come back anytime tomorrow. I think I'll have a solution for you then."

"OK. Thanks a million, Mr. Neal. My wife 'll be tickled pink," he said as he donned his cap and walked to his truck.

Classes went on as usual for the rest of the day. No problems. Everyone had their lessons.

At 8:30 the following morning, Burt Aiken met me at the schoolhouse steps.

"Did you work it? Did you work it?" he said, excited as a child seeing his first circus.

"Oh, yes, Burt," I said as I gave him the solution written on a sheet of notebook paper.

"Thank you! Thank you! Edna will be tickled pink," he said as he nervously folded it and put it into a large envelope. "I'm putting it and the application on the morning train in Royalton. By the way, did you know Tom Mason was stupid, just like his daughter, Irene?"

"No, I didn't," I lied. "One thing for certain, Burt. Irene is far from being dumb. She is intelligent as well as a conscientious pupil."

"If that's so, she takes after her ma. That's why," he said. "Have you heard about Tom's trip the barbershop?"

"No," I said hoping Burt would soon be on his way.

"Wall, he never had a barbershop haircut. His ma cut it while he was home. Then his wife picked up where his ma left off. Last fall he said he was goin' to Royalton to get a real haircut. You know where Jake's Barbershop is located, don't you?" he wanted to know.

"No, I don't," I said, wondering what was coming next.

"It's on the side street next to Crawford's Garage. 'U. R. Next' is printed in capital letters about eight inches high. Tom walked into the barbershop. This is the way the scuttlebutt goes.

" 'Is Mr. Next in? I wants him to cut my hair,' said Tom.

" 'Mr. Next stepped out for a while. Either one of us will be glad to cut your hair,' said the barber nearest the door.

" 'Mr. Next has gone for the day,' said the second barber as he interrupted and turned away to laugh.

"'Wall, I don't wants no one but Mr. Next to cuts my hair,' Tom said as he left the shop in a huff."

By now I had heard variations to this story several times. I couldn't believe there were that many stupid people in our community.

"Then there was the time he was sent to the plumbing shop to borrow a left-handed pipe wrench.

"Now that's what I calls stupid. Don't you agree, Mr. Neal?"

"Look, Burt, if you have everything you need, please pardon me as I must put test questions on the blackboard for my first class," I said, evading his ignorant question. Apparently he got the message and was soon on his way to Royalton.

Wednesday, the second week in March, was a murky day. Low, dark clouds hung over the landscape. The temperature was 61° F. The air was still, like the lull before the storm. Arriving home at 4:15, I was bushed. After supper Fairy and I decided to get relief from our doldrums by taking in a movie. Shortly we were under way. Rain began pouring down as if it were going out of style.

As we parked across the street from the Royalton Theater, I saw several people, gathered under the protective cover of a store awning, watching a man lying on the sidewalk. Both of the man's feet rested in the gutter as rainwater rushed over them.

"I wonder if he's hurt," Fairy said as we got out of the car.

"I don't know," I said. Then we walked over to the outstretched figure.

"He ain't hurt, mister," shouted someone under the awning. "Just old Dobbin drunker than a hooty owl."

"How can you tell?" I yelled back. "How do you know? He could have had a stroke or be in a diabetic coma."

"I know," the man shouted back. "He's the town drunk. He was thrown out of the speakeasy down the street. When he got this far he collapsed in a drunken stupor."

"Someone give me a hand so we can move him under the awning," I pleaded.

"No need for that," the spokesman for the group shouted back. "The town marshal is out of town. Someone called the sheriff in Benton about forty-five minutes ago. He should be here at any moment. He'll take care of the old drunk."

Upon receiving my teaching certificate last summer, I had promised myself to do a certain amount of community service. By no stretch of the imagination did I think it would include the likes of this.

The rain was coming down harder by the minute. Fairy said she would wait for me in the theater lobby.

I bent over the man on the sidewalk.

"Young man, can you hear me?" I said as I shook his shoulders.

Silence.

"Wake up! Wake up!" I shouted in his left ear. More silence.

I guessed his age at forty-five or fifty. He was far from being pretty. His eyes reminded me of two holes in a blanket, his lips were swollen, his cheeks puffy, and he had a large growth on the left side of his nose. His trousers, topcoat, and shoes were soaking wet from the rain.

"Wake up! Wake up!" I shouted as I bent closer and shook him again.

"Get the hell out of here!" the man shouted as he suddenly came alive. I stood up as the stench of the mixture of feces, vomit, and urine reached my nose.

"Up we go, young man," I said as I turned my head and attempted to raise him to a standing position.

"Damn you. Leave me be," he said in a semidrunken stupor. Kicking me in the shin, he broke my grip, sliding back to the sidewalk.

At that moment the sheriff arrived. He and his deputy grabbed the man by his arms and jerked him to his feet. "Dobbin, you stinking bastard, we're hauling you to jail where you can sleep it off and return to your family tomorrow."

"What you doin'? Turn me loose!" the man shouted drunkenly.

The police officers literally pitched the drunk into the backseat of the patrol car. Then they headed back to Benton.

I took off my soaked shoes and put on a pair of work shoes that I kept on the backseat of my car. Pulling the collar of my raincoat up tight around my neck, I headed for the theater.

The following Tuesday, another visitor came to get help. It was during the lunch hour when a kindly man of perhaps forty-five, about six feet tall with an aquiline nose, light blue eyes, and a slight limp came over to where I was standing on the playground.

"Glad to see you again, John," I said as we shook hands. I met John (Three-Finger Jack) Boswell shortly after coming to Dutch Hill. At that time I'll never forget what he said, "I cut off my thumb and index finger while working in a sawmill." Of course, there was no company insurance to pay the doctor's bill.

"You remember me! That makes me feel real good, Mr. Neal."

"John, I always remember nice people," I said, smiling from ear to ear. "How can I help you?"

"Well, my wife said not to bother you, that you had enough to do teaching some of these brats we have around here."

"Hogwash, John. I help the people in Dutch Hill with their problems by bringing in my pupils who volunteer to help. The older ones help solve the problems, while the young ones look on. We call such experiences the application of arithmetic to community problems.

"Last Saturday Amos Spillard wanted to know the size of a coal house that would hold fifty tons of coal. First, my pupils and I figured the dimensions of the required lumber. Then, we gave him a list of other materials, including size of nails, a hasp, and a lock. John, we never refuse a request as long as my pupils are permitted to help.

"Ricardo Olivetti came up with a name for such services: Practical Arithmetic."

"I don't know whether you can help me or not," he said as he handed me two crude drawings of a hog house. "I want to build six of them, but can't figure how much lumber to buy. Can you and your pupils help me?"

I examined the drawings carefully. Then I replied, "I have two suggestions. The perspective drawing shows three feet six inches for the width. Here you will have no waste, providing you use boards fourteen feet long. Not so with the sides. With a length of five feet six inches, you'll waste one foot on every board, even by using boards twelve feet long. I suggest changing the length to either five feet or six feet. What do you say?"

"Sounds good, Mr. Neal. Let's make the length six feet. I don't want no waste."

"Good decision, John. Using boards twelve feet long, you'll have no waste. Using fourteen-foot boards for the roof, you'll have six-inch overhang on both the front and back. Although they are not dimensioned on the drawing, they appear to be approximately six inches each.

"The framing drawing shows two-by-twos for the floor joists. I recommend two-by-fours. With the knotty lumber we buy today, two-by-twos will soon break. What do you say?"

"Sounds okay to me," he said cheerfully.

"Then it's settled. My pupils and I will work out the details after school today. Then I'll have Agnes Harper bring you a list of materials required for the job. As you know, she passes your house on her way to and from school."

"I sure appreciate what you and your pupils are doing to help me out. I'll never forget it as long as I live," he said as we shook hands and he started for home.

On Thursday morning of the third week in March something unexpected happened. As I approached the schoolhouse, Sadie Jenkins, a third grader, came to meet me.

"I've been sitting on the steps waiting to give you $2.50," she said cheerfully.

"Two dollars fifty cents," I repeated. "What on earth for? Christmas is long gone."

"Mrs. Aiken won the magazine prize. Isn't that wonderful, Teach?"

"Yes, of course, but what is this money for?"

"She said you worked the problem, and she wants to share the prize," she replied as she handed me the money and started to join her friends.

What should I do? I asked myself. If I return the money, Mrs. Aiken will be highly insulted. Then I had an idea. "Come back, Sadie, I want to talk with you."

"What do you want, Teach?" she asked.

"You read fairy stories, don't you?"

"Sure do. Sometimes I act like a fairy," she said.

"Sadie, let's suppose a fairy is here waving her wand and she says, 'Sadie, what would you buy if you had $2.50?' "

"Gee, that's easy!" she said jumping up and down. "I'd buy the red pair of slippers with gold buckles that I saw last Saturday at the Royalton Mercantile Store. They cost $1.95." Then a pause. "I'd buy my mother a dozen handkerchiefs for fifty cents. Then I'd buy myself a Baby Ruth candy bar for the remaining nickel. Boy, I wish it were true!"

"Sadie, when is your birthday?" I asked.

"The twenty-fourth of July. Why?"

"Well, I won't be here then. So I'm giving you a birthday present now. Here's $2.50. Now run along and play with your friends."

"Holy cow! Thanks, Teach. Thanks a million," she said as she skipped joyfully to join her peers.

That very day during the morning recess a short, stout man with a shock of salt-and-pepper hair on his head walked over to where I was talking to one of my pupils. He was about six feet tall. I guessed his weight at approximately 185 pounds.

"Mr. Neal, I'm John Olivetti," he said as he stuck out a large callused right hand.

"I remember you, John. We met briefly at the school's Halloween party. It's good to see you again," I said as we shook hands.

"My boys give you no trouble, no?" he inquired as he looked at me uneasily.

"Absolutely not, John. You have two fine boys."

"Da better stay dat way!" he said in a firm voice.

"I've been looking forward to meeting you again, John. How can I help you?" I inquired.

"I'm in concrete business. Can you help figure job?"

"I don't know, John. I spent two summer vacations working for a concrete contractor. What's your problem?" I asked.

"I lose money on jobs. Bring too much materials on job sometimes. Sometimes not 'nuf materials. Either way I go in hole."

"Well, John, don't you figure the amount of materials required for each job?"

"No can do. That's what I wants you to learn me."

"Do you have a particular job in mind?"

"Sure do. I wants to bid on church concrete job for foundation, floor, and walls. This big job. Can't guess how much materials buy."

"Do you have the specifications?"

"The what?"

"Specs?

"Sure thing. Right here in pocket is specs."

Looking at my watch, I said, "John, it's time for me to end recess. Tell you what. Can you come here tomorrow at four o'clock?"

"Sure thing. Anytime you say," he said with a big smile on his face.

"Then it's settled, John. Most of my pupils will want to help. So we'll make your problem a school project. See you tomorrow at four," I said as I went into the vestibule to ring the bell.

The following afternoon John Olivetti came into the schoolhouse promptly at four o'clock. He beamed admiringly as we shook hands.

"Boys and girls," I announced, "school's out. Those of you who want to remain, gather up front, facing the blackboard. Fifth and seventh grade pupils, bring along your tablets and pencils." Then an amazing thing took place. Not a pupil went home, not even the little ones.

Later, I was to learn everyone admired and liked John Olivetti and his wife. In time of sickness it was John and his wife who first came forward to help.

"Now," I said, "let's get down to business."

John looked agitated as he sat on the recitation seat working his feet up and down.

"John, do you have a question?" I inquired.

"Sure do. I think nobody has de answer. On two sidewalk jobs, concrete break to pieces. Had do dem over for free. Too much clay in sand. Do you know how help, Mr. Neal?" he asked pitifully. "I go in hole too much."

"Yes, John, I can help you so that you'll never have to worry about having too much clay in your sand.

"Ricardo and Yetlo," I said, "be sure to copy exactly what I am about to say.

"Place four inches of sand into a one-quart glass Mason jar. Then fill it to one inch of the top with water. Screw on the lid. Shake well and allow it to stand for two hours. If more than one-fourth inch of clay is on top, don't use the sand."

"I'll be dam——" John shouted excitedly. "I 'pologize, Mr. Neal. Shouldn't cuss in school. Please forgive?"

"We forgive you, don't we, boys and girls?"

"Yeah!" they all shouted as one.

"John, today my pupils and I spent arithmetic time and the afternoon recess working out the material lists, one each for the foundation, floor, and walks," I said as I handed the lists to him.

Putting on his glasses he said, "You no guess how much materials needed?"

"No, John. First, we figured the number of cubic yards for each of the material lists. Then we figured the amounts of materials required. From what your boys told me, your mixtures are close to a standard mix. This is known in the trade as a 1 (cement)—2 (sand)—4 (gravel). However, by using a shovel as a measuring device, your mixtures are not uniform.

"Ricardo, give your father the drawing we made during today's noon hour. It shows how to make a measuring box. You'll notice it's four feet long, two feet, four inches wide; and ten inches deep. Using two bags of cement (a bag of cement contains one cubic foot), a half-box of sand, and one box of gravel mixed with the right amount of water makes nine cubic feet of concrete, or one-third of a cubic yard."

"Now looks easy and all years I make big job trying to guess mix," he said, as excited as was one of my first graders when he learned how to spell his dog's name. "How much I owe, Mr. Neal?"

"John, you don't owe me anything. This was part of my teaching day. From now on your boys can figure your jobs, and you can be assured of turning out quality work. John, before you leave, I do have a question. Why don't you use Redi Mix concrete and save yourself a lot of work?"

"No can do. With depression, contractors cut each other's throats. No can make good profit that way."

John thanked me profusely. We shook hands. Then all of us started for home.

My pupils were seeing arithmetic in an entirely different light. No longer were they seeing numbers in abstractions. Now they were seeing the practical application of arithmetic to everyday problems. Arithmetic came alive, so much so that they yearned for more education to follow the eighth grade. For example, Ricardo and Yetlo had only two things in mind when I came to Dutch Hill: 1) Run the teacher out of the school. 2) Quit school the day they reached their sixteenth birthdays. Now a metamorphosis was emerging. Instead of doing everything destructive and mean, they were loyal and well-behaved boys, looking forward to attending high school next term, then on to college. I'd like to think I had a small part in helping to shape their new attitude.

Chapter 24
Finis

A few days later my pupils, their parents, and I took on a happy mood. Perhaps the change in the weather had something to do with it.

Snow came to an end. The rains were few and far between. The bright sun and the mild breezes turned the rural muddy clay roads into usable streets.

No longer was it necessary to attach chains to our automobiles' rear wheels so as to be able to travel from one place to another.

It was the last Friday in March. The English assignment for my fifth grade pupils was to write short themes about subjects of their own choosing. They were to name a subject and define it, limiting the theme's length to one-half to one page.

My pupils were always full of insights. One of the more significant examples was brought out in Susan Slavins's theme, titled "Frugal."

"Frugal means to save," she told the class. "Once upon a time a blond-headed damsel was picking violets along a riverbank. She came too close to the edge and tumbled into the water. 'Frugal me. Frugal me!' she shouted.

"A handsome young man happened to be horseback riding nearby. Hearing the damsel in distress, he rode hard to the riverbank. Dismounting he shouted, as he jumped into the water, 'Have no fear. I'll frugal you.' He frugaled her. Later they were married and lived happily ever after."

On the first Monday in April, one of my pupils brought me a note, telling me school director John Pirka wanted to see me at 7 P.M. "I want your input" was the surprising part of the note. *What does he have in mind?* I wondered. I knew he was buttering me up. But why? I had no idea.

Mrs. Pirka answered my knock. Opening the door, she said, "Come in, Charles! Come in!"

I smiled as I returned her greeting. "Where's John?" I inquired. "Am I too early?"

Putting down her knitting and offering me a seat, she said, "John had to go to Royalton for a new horse collar. He'll loaf a spell at the Royalton Cafe, probably buying some floozy a cup of coffee right now."

"I didn't know John was a ladies' man," I said as I chuckled.

"He isn't. It's in his head. You know, Charles, he reminds me of an old tomcat I knew when we lived in St. Louis."

"How's that, Maude?" I said as I gave out with a big belly laugh. "How does he remind you of the tomcat?"

"Well, this old cat, named George, was neutered. Just as night follows day you could see him walking back and forth on top of a wooden picket fence. For some reason that yard was a gathering place for all the cats in the neighborhood. When——"

"But, Maude," I interrupted, "how can you compare John to a neutered tomcat? That's really a laugh!"

"First let me finish what I started to say. When I asked George's owner why the cat walked back and forth on top of the fence, she replied, 'He does that because he is now a consultant.' John hasn't been good in bed for the past ten years, so, not to his face, I call him a consultant. Actually, the girls at the restaurant couldn't care less about him, but they do like his free coffee."

"Maude, you've given me a side of John I didn't know existed."

"There's another side you don't know about. Remember some time back, I told you I would explain why John has such control over me?"

"Why, yes, I remember. You said when you knew me better you'd tell me all about it."

"Charles, my mother died in St. Louis of pneumonia fever on February 2, 1924. John claims, falsely, that I placed an electric fan in an open window, directing the breeze over Mother's face, causing her death prematurely."

"Maude, what a horrible thing for him to say! It's hard for me to believe any man would say such a dastardly thing about his wife, especially you."

"There's more, Charles."

"What's that, Maude?" I asked eagerly.

"He says that if I don't obey him to the letter, he will report me to the authorities."

"Oh, I wouldn't worry about that, Maude. It would be his word against yours."

"Charles, it's not that simple."

"You mean there's more?"

"Yes. When John was in the world war, his buddy, Amos Gilmore, from St. Louis was in enemy territory where he was shot and bleeding severely. John came out of his trench, rushed across the enemy's line, dodging bullets as he ran, and dragged Amos back to a first-aid shelter where he was patched up. Then he was sent to an army hospital where he fully recovered.

"Amos said he would do anything for John, even lie for him. That's exactly what John would ask him to do if I was ever brought to trial.

"So you see, Charles, it would be two words against mine. As long as Amos is alive, I have no choice but to dance to John's tune. Charles, I know you'll keep this under your hat."

"Maude, you can bet on it. I wouldn't hurt you for any amount of money."

Maude picked up her knitting when she heard John slam the back door. "End of story," she said.

"Charles, I apologize for being late. Got hung up a little longer than I expected," said John as he entered the room.

Maude gave me a wink as if to say she fully understood why he was "hung up."

John authorized me to dismiss school the following Tuesday so the election could take place inside the schoolhouse. Although the polls didn't open 'til seven, he wanted the building opened at six. I was to help him bring in the three voting booths. Then he said, "That takes care of election preparation."

John never did ask for my input, but I wasn't surprised, actually, I expected as much.

We made a small talk of the next fifteen minutes. Then I excused myself. Maude saw me out. As I stepped out into the night, she whispered in my ear, "Keep your eyes open for the double ballot box. Don't say I didn't warn you."

As I said good night, I wondered what she meant by a double ballot box.

Although it was the last month of school, my attendance was almost perfect. This was exceptionally gratifying since there was no attendance officer to investigate truancy cases.

If a pupil wanted to come to school, he did. If he would rather stay home, he did. He and his parents had a freedom of choice of either his staying home and working on the farm or going to school. Since all of the work in Dutch Hill was either done by animal or human power, there was plenty of hard work year-round for the entire family.

Early in the term my pupils and I decided to make the school beautiful and attractive. Cleaning the windows and attaching attractive drapes to them was only one of many things we did to give the room a homey atmosphere.

Since the boys and girls had a hand in making their school their home during school days, woe to the one who should desecrate any part of it.

I found out early in the term that pupil justice was much more severe than teacher justice. For example, their favorite punishment was "running the gauntlet." The offender was made to crawl between the legs of six or eight of the older boys standing in line. As he came through, each boy gave him a whack or two on the buttocks with a switch, a belt, or a paddle. And some of these boys would really lay it on.

It wasn't uncommon at all for some boys to squeeze their legs tightly, holding the offender long enough to give him several hard licks before releasing him. If I had administered half the punishment to one of my pupils as they did, I would have been brought into court for child abuse.

Only a few of Dutch Hill's children went beyond the one-room school. For most, it was work, dating, marriage, children, death, and burial in the Dutch Hill Cemetery.

I was under the impression that every child in our school district was in attendance, but I had a surprise coming right after I rang the nine o'clock bell to begin books that Wednesday morning.

Following the children was an unusually tall woman, every bit of six feet, six inches, wearing a blue housedress and a pair of men's work shoes. She was at least thirty-five years old, with straight black hair, high cheekbones, and a pair of sad brown eyes.

"My name is Mrs. Gardner," she said. "This is my ten-year-old son, Grover. He's never been to school. Can he begin this late in the term?"

"Why, I——"

Interrupting me, throwing his chest out, and looking me straight in the eyes Grover shouted at the top of his lungs, "I'm going to be in the first grade if you will have me."

That struck my boys and girls as funny. They did their best to stifle their giggling and laughter but just couldn't hold them back.

"Hold it right there!" I demanded. "This is no way to greet a new pupil! Apologize to Grover!"

"We apologize, Grover. Welcome to our school," they said in unison.

"Thank you, boys and girls. That was real nice of you."

"To answer your question, Mrs. Gardner, he can begin as of now. Frankly, I didn't know we had any more school-age pupils in Dutch Hill. Why did you wait so long before entering him?"

"Well, Mr. Neal, we live on the other side of the Black Water Swamp. When there's high water we must take a rowboat to get out of the place. Most folks don't even know that anyone lives over there. We just didn't think an education would do him any good. Dad and I thought he could make a good living, after we're gone, hunting, fishing, and trapping in the swamp. Then last week he became deathly sick. Dad took him by horseback to Dr. Flemming in Royalton. You know the doctor, don't you, Mr. Neal?"

"I certainly do, Mrs. Gardner. He is a mighty fine doctor as well as a perfect gentleman."

"After the doctor examined Grover and packaged some medicine, he had a long talk with him, pointing out what he was missing by not going to school. Ever since then he's been driving us almost insane wanting to know when he can start school."

"Well, Mrs. Gardner, his worries are over." After seeing her to the door I assigned Grover a seat with the first graders. Then I told the children there would be no school tomorrow because of the school directors election.

Promptly at six o'clock on the Tuesday morning of the school directors election, the door opened. In walked director John Pirka carrying a ballot box. Following him came incumbent Joe Taylor carrying something similar in size to the ballot box. It was covered with a red-checkered tablecloth. Placing the covered box in the cloakroom, he said, "Charles, lock this door. I don't want some voter meddling in something that is of no concern of his."

I was suddenly overwhelmed. Could that be another ballot box? I asked myself. None of the present board of directors had been defeated during the past ten years. This was most remarkable since neither John nor Joe would ever have won a popularity contest in Dutch Hill. Most of the people in Dutch Hill couldn't care less about either of them.

"Charles," called Harry Rone, "will you give me a hand in carrying in the three voting booths? John and Joe are busy giving the judges their instructions as well as getting everything else set up so the election process can begin on time."

"Sure thing, Harry. I see that Harry Sizemore is running against Joe Taylor."

"Yes, Charles, that's right. You see, we are elected on staggered terms. This means that one of us goes out of office each year."

Big deal! I thought. *He must think I'm awful stupid, explaining simple school election laws to me.*

As we walked out the door I said, "Harry, who do you think will be elected this time, Joe or Henry?"

"Well, Charles, that's a good question. However, if I were a betting man I'd put my money on Joe. School board elections don't pull in many voters. I'll be surprised if fifty people come in today."

State law required posting of the school budget on election day for public inspection. As Harry and I were placing one of the booths in position, I saw Joe tacking the budget on the back side of the vestibule door, which remained open against the wall for the entire day. Hardly a convenient place to post a budget for public inspection.

The election process began promptly at seven o'clock. It moved along uneventfully until closing time. Then John Pirka invited the judges to step outside, saying he had a personal matter to discuss with them. As soon as they exited the outside door, incumbent Joe Taylor had me unlock the cloakroom door. Then he pulled a fast switch, exchanging the legal ballot box with the illegal one kept in the cloakroom. Of course, he removed the cover.

When the judges and John returned, John unlocked the bogus

box and the counting of votes began. The final tally gave the lead to Joe Taylor with fifty-seven votes to six for Henry Sizemore. I had heard of many devious ways politicians had in fixing elections, but I had never heard of anything as brazen as the one I had just witnessed in Dutch Hill.

My school was not all work and no fun, even if some fun was a bit off-color. One of the most humorous things to happen was in mid-April, when I had my three first graders at the blackboard for their spelling lesson. I also taught phonics to all my pupils.

Grover Gardner had been in school about two weeks. Although he was eager to make up for lost time, he hadn't mastered all of the classroom amenities. Because he was only a beginner in the first grade I gave him easier words to spell than his peers.

"Grover, spell *cat*," I said.

"C-a-t," answered Grover as he sounded each letter of the word.

"Now spell it, Grover."

"I-t," he shouted loud and clearly.

Although my pupils were getting acclimated to his antics, I could hear some giggling.

"Not *it*, Grover. *Cat* is the word to spell."

"Well, Teacher, why don't you say what you mean. You said *it*, and I spelled *it*."

"OK. Grover, calm down and spell *cat*. Then write it on the blackboard."

"C-a-t." Then he wrote *kat*. "How's that, Teacher?" he wanted to know.

"All correct but the first letter. Grover, last week we learned that another letter in the alphabet sometimes has the sound of *k*. Do you remember the letter?"

"I remember. It is *c*."

"Now spell *cat* and write it again."

"C-a-t," he said. Then he wrote *cat*. "How's that?"

"Perfect, Grover."

Turning away from the blackboard, he blurted out, "I'll be damned and go to hell, I spelled *cat*!"

"Grover, I know you are proud of yourself, but we don't allow swearing inside the schoolroom or outside on the playground."

"I'm sorry, Teacher. I just can't get the hang of school. It'll never happen again."

And it never did.

That very day another unusual event happened. It was during the afternoon recess that school director Joe Taylor called on me. When I saw him get out of his car, I wondered what gems of wisdom or condemnation he would offer. But I was in for a surprise.

"Good morning, Charles," he said as he offered me his long, bony hand.

While shaking hands, I still wondered what he had in mind. His attitude was much too kind for Joe Taylor. *Has he lost his mind*, I wondered, or *had his conference with two of his peers really changed his attitude toward me?*

"What can I do for you, Joe?" I inquired.

"Oh, nothing really. I just wanted you to know how pleased I am with the way you painted the two outhouses. Makes a world of difference. The white schoolhouse, the white privies, and the green grass just coming up really makes a postcard picture."

"Thank you, Joe. I had some excellent help. Two of my pupils, Melvin Swartz and Robert Dean, were a real help. Then, too, we had two successive Saturdays when the weather was ideal for painting."

"Well, Charles, at any rate, I compliment you on a job well done. Oh, yes, there's another thing. We directors are meeting to organize tomorrow night at seven o'clock at the Pirka home. Can you meet with us?"

"Why, yes, I don't have anything planned for tomorrow evening," I replied as I couldn't help but wonder what came over him. He was much too kind for Joe Taylor, but, then again, I supposed his conference with two of his peers changed his opinion, especially about me.

"Organization won't take over three minutes. Then we would like to discuss a new contract with you for next year."

"OK, Joe. See you then," I said as he started to walk toward his car.

On the following evening I met with the three directors at John Pirka's house. They seemed to be in a jovial mood. They laughed at Joe Taylor's jokes and gorged themselves on Maude's coffee and homemade rolls.

"I call the meeting to order," said Harry Rone, as he sat sober-faced in his chair.

"I nominate Harry Rone as president and John Pirka as secretary," said Joe Taylor.

"Other nominations?" inquired Harry. Pause. "There being no other nominations I am the president and John is the secretary."

For me, this was a lesson in futility. I doubt if any of the directors ever heard of *Robert's Rules of Order* or cared less about them.

"The chair is open for new business," announced Harry.

"Members of the board," Harry said, "I move we renew Charles's contract for next year for a hundred dollars per month. Do I hear a second?"

"That's entirely too much money to pay him," John said, shaking his head, showing a fit of anger.

"Now, let's keep our cool," spoke Joe. "It's time to negotiate. Taxes haven't been coming in as well as expected. Gentlemen, whether we like it or not, we are between the rock and the hard place."

"Without a second, the motion dies," said Harry.

In a toneless voice Joe said, "I move we offer Charles a new contract at eighty dollars per month. That's all we can afford!"

I sat there feeling frustration build up inside me.

"I second the motion," said John.

"Any objections?" Harry wanted to know.

"Since there are no objections, we offer you a new contract at eighty dollars per month for an eight-month school term," said Harry. "What say you, Charles?"

I looked at them with a sense of loathing, stood up, and walked to the door. "Gentlemen, and I use the word loosely," I said, "I have had a contract since March 14 for the next school year paying $125 per month for a nine-month school term. So it's with a great deal of pleasure that I reject your offer. Thanks for nothing!"

Before I went out the door I paused so my words would sink in. "Gentlemen, as far as I'm concerned, you can take this job and stick it up, and I don't mean your noses!" Then I turned on my heel and stepped out into the night.

I blew my top, and I wasn't at all ashamed of it. In fact, I got a real thrill out of it.

The children and their parents were wonderful to work with.

No teacher could ask for more. But those cheap skinflint directors were something else. Everything was fine just as long as I spent my own money purchasing materials to make for a better school environment. There's one thing I found gratifying about leaving Dutch Hill. I no longer would have to listen to director Joe Taylor's stupid, idiotic remarks. *Thank God for that!* I said to myself on my way home.

My wife and I remained in Dutch Hill the weekend before school terminated. By late Saturday night almost everything was packed, ready for the moving truck scheduled for one o'clock the following Monday.

Shortly after breakfast on Sunday morning, I heard shotgun blasts coming from the north. Putting on my jacket, I proceeded to find out what was taking place. I soon found out. Several of the young men in Dutch Hill, just to have some fun, took to shooting Widow Spindler's chickens while she was attending Sunday school and church in Royalton. They were using wheat instead of lead pellets in their shotgun shells. When shot, the poor birds would squawk, jump high into the air, land, and run away cackling. To these misguided souls this was fun.

Since some of my male pupils were watching, I sat down on the grass, passing the time talking to them. Everything was going along according to plan until one of my pupils, Wayne Roberts, a seventh grader, got the bright idea that he wanted to shoot the Rhode Island Red rooster of the flock.

The temptation was too much for some of the men. Someone put a regular shell into a twelve-gauge shotgun and handed it to him. He braced the gun stock tightly against his shoulder, took aim. Then he pulled the trigger. He had braced himself well so the recoil didn't knock him off his feet. His aim was perfect. But instead of doing what Wayne expected, leaping high, the rooster fell over dead.

Quickly dropping the gun Wayne ran over to the fallen rooster, held him up on his legs, and attempting to bring him back to life. Of course, it was no use. The poor victim was deader than a doornail.

I jumped up and ran to Wayne.

"It's no use, Wayne," I said. "That was a cruel trick to play on you. I want you to tell your father how it happened. I'm sure he'll want to pay Widow Spindler for the rooster."

With tears in his eyes, Wayne went straight home.

That evening I went to the Royalton Drugstore for a box of

aspirin tablets. As I entered the store I saw a familiar face sitting at a table drinking a malted milk. I recognized him as the young man who gave Wayne the shotgun that morning.

In the meantime someone had altered his face. He sported two black eyes, a puffy left cheek, and a two-inch cut across his chin. I had a strong feeling that he had met up with Wayne's father.

On the last day of school we went on a hayride to Silver Creek. Addison Wainright's father placed a large wooden frame on his wagon. Then he spread several bales of straw on the frame. This made for comfortable sitting.

School being almost a thing of the past, we let down our hair, told jokes, riddles, and stories until we arrived at the creek bank.

The weather was chilly but the boys and girls insisted on going for a swim. Since no one had a bathing suit, I ordered the girls to take the deep hole north of us and the boys the deep hole to the south.

Following the swim we had an early lunch. Then I gave each one his or her report card. Everyone was promoted. Although Grover Gardner had been in school less than a month, I promoted him conditionally to the second grade because of his progress coupled with his mother's promise to teach him during the summer months.

Finally I shook hands with each of my pupils and wished them well for the following school year. Some of the girls had tears in their eyes. Then we hopped on the wagon and Mr. Wainright headed for the schoolhouse, dropping off some of the boys and girls as we passed their homes.

When Fairy and I arrived home, the trucker had our furniture loaded and ready to roll.

At 12:58 P.M. I whipped the Model A Ford out of our driveway onto the dirt road for the last time, the truck moving right behind us.

While driving through Dutch Hill I said, "Fairy, when I die I want to go to heaven."

Startled, Fairy replied, "Wow! Gee willikers! Charles, what on earth brought that up at a time like this?"

"Well, the way I see it, when school director Joy Taylor dies I am confident that St. Peter will give him a one-way ticket to hell."

"Charles! I'm surprised at you. What a terrible thing to say. Is he the only person in Dutch Hill who gave you a lot of trouble?"

"Absolutely! The other two school directors were skinflints when it came to spending tax dollars for school improvements.

Otherwise, they were pretty good joes. In fact, with the exception of Joe Taylor, I could not have asked for better cooperation from the people in Dutch Hill."

"Charles, you know if Grandpa were still living, he would give forth with that old cliché; There's always at least one bad apple in every barrel of apples."

"I'd agree with Grandpa, and Joe is that bad apple! I say he is bound for hell just as sure as I am certain that God makes little green apples. I've had him up to my neck, and I don't want his company for an eternity," I said as we continued on our way toward our new home.

Epilogue

While relaxing under a pin oak shade tree in my backyard, just prior to my manuscript going to press, I began to doze. Then, for no sound, logical reason at all, I began reflecting on my one year of teaching in a one-room country school.

Even though I made many mistakes, frequently I was complimented by the parents as being a good teacher. That didn't inflate my ego too much, because the people of Dutch Hill claimed, to a person, they never did have a good teacher.

The school directors' policy was to hire the cheapest teachers they could find. One director said, "We've always paid the lowest salaries in the county. This practice keeps the tax rate at the lowest possible level." Of course, he could have also said, "That is why we have had the poorest teachers in the county."

So I suppose my salary of ninety-five dollars per month, the second highest in the county, set off a wave of optimism. Most likely parents put their trust in the old saw, "A new broom sweeps clean." I was new. I was paid a high salary. So I had to be a good teacher; or so they reasoned.

On the credit side of the ledger, I never used or condoned the use of three types of punishment practiced in most schools during the 1930s:

1. Have a pupil stand on tiptoes as he touches the blackboard with his nose. Next the teacher draws a circle around the damp spot left by the nose on the blackboard. Then the pupil is forced to stand, for a specified length of time, on tiptoes with nose inside the ring.
2. Have a pupil sit in a corner facing the wall while wearing a dunce cap.
3. Punish disobedient pupils by beating them with a length of rope or a piece of stranded one-half-inch wire cable.

On the debit side of the ledger my means of punishment had much to be desired. I did use the method of taking away privileges for certain offenses. And I'm not proud of the fact that I used the paddle on a few occasions for more severe infractions. However, more humane punishments other than paddling would have produced better results, without alienating the offenders, had I known about such methods at the time.

To be sure, I made some home visits, and some of them produced positive results between the parents and me. However, I failed to make enough of them. Because of lack of experience, I found myself floundering, wondering exactly what to say when I entered many of the homes.

Having no college training, much of my teaching was done by trial and error. I should have spent time visiting and talking with other teachers when my school was not in session. (Instead, I spent the time either hunting or fishing). By so doing I'm confident I would have been better able to impart knowledge to my charges, as well as have been better able to develop in them a desire to want to learn by seeing a positive reason for so doing.

Because I failed to develop a balance among teaching, relaxation, exercise, and sheer pleasure, teaching at times seemed so routine. Yes, at times it also seemed boring.

Get up 6 A.M. Dress, eat breakfast. Then head for the one-room country school. Here it was listen to the pupils recite their lessons; give new assignments for the following day; settle a few discipline cases, some moderate others severe. Then as sure as winter follows fall, school director Joe Taylor would come into the picture. His attitude and snide remarks alone would have driven most teachers to drink.

Doing such menial tasks day after day, week after week, month after month, if one isn't careful, tears at one's moral fibers. Some of my peers in neighboring schools couldn't take it. They were exasperated. Some sought counseling. Others simply left the teaching profession. None of them seemed to realize that every job presents problems and that running away from them solves nothing, whether it be in the teaching or any other profession.

As the school term moved along, I began to realize that an understanding spouse makes all the difference in a teacher's life.

And I was fortunate enough to have just such a spouse, my wife, Fairy.

I leaned more and more on Fairy for moral support whenever I became disgusted with the daily routine of teaching. Often I would bring up some of the more pertinent problems and propose solutions with her. She would listen, think on them a moment. Then she would praise what she thought made good common sense and criticize what she thought was unrealistic or impractical.

Her judgment was good, and I knew it. I always complimented her on her suggestions that later proved to be better than mine. When I did, she would reply with an impish grin, "You know, Charles, two heads are better than one, even if one is a blockhead."

Early in the term, had I peered into a crystal ball, undoubtedly there would have appeared three characteristics common to *all* successful teachers:

1. Where some teachers see hopeless, unteachable children, a good teacher sees youngsters with potential dreams. Then his or her job is to unlock those dreams.
2. When others give up on children, a good teacher strives to give them the two best things a teacher can bestow on any youngster: hope and belief in himself or herself.
3. Always in the back of a good teacher's mind is the self-evident truth: Nothing succeeds like success.

Nineteen thirty to 1931 was the only year I ever taught in a one-room country school. After that I moved up the educational ladder, serving as an elementary school supervisor, a high school principal, a laboratory elementary school principal, and concluding my career as a director of student teaching with the rank of professor of administration at Southern Illinois University, Carbondale.

One final word: There never was anything wrong with a one-room country school that a good teacher couldn't cure.

The author and Fairy on their way to a 1931 parent meeting.

List of Selected Publications

Heimler, Charles H. Charles D. Neal, Consultant. *Principles of Science*, Book I. (Columbus: Charles E. Merrill Books, Inc., 1966)

———. *Principles of Science*, Book II. (Columbus: Charles E. Merrill Books, Inc., 1966)

Neal, Charles D. *The Student Teacher at Work*. (Minneapolis, MN: Burgess Publishing Co., 1959)

———. *What Is a Bee*. (Chicago: Benefic Press, 1961)

———. *What Is an Insect*. (Chicago: Benefic Press, 1961)

———. *Sound*. (Chicago: Follett Publishing Co., 1962)

———. *Adventures in Science*. (Racine, WI: Whitman Publishing Co., 1963)

———. *Exploring Light and Color*. (Chicago: Children's Press, 1964)

———. *Safe and Simple Projects with Electricity*. (Chicago: Children's Press, 1962)

———. *Do-It-Yourself Housebuilding: Step-by-Step*. (New York: Macmillan Publishing Co., 1973)

———. *Build Your Own Greenhouse*. (Radnor, PA: Chilton Book Co., 1975)

———. *Build Your Own Tennis Court*. (Radnor, PA: Chilton Book Co., 1977)

———. *Do-It-Yourself Housebuilding: Step-by-Step*. (Briarcliff, NY: Stein and Day Publishers, 1977)

Neal, Charles D.; Butts, Gordon K., and Clemmons, J. D. *The Beginning Teacher at Work*. (Minneapolis, MN: Burgess Publishing Co., 1971)

Neal, Charles, D.; Cummins, James N.; and Heinz, Charles R. *Exploring and Understanding Chemistry* (Sixth Grade). (Westchester, IL: Benefic Press, 1970)

Neal, Charles, D., and Perkins, Otho E. *Science Skilltext*, Book IV. (Columbus: Charles E. Merrill Books, Inc., 1965)

———. *Science Skilltext*, Book V. (Columbus: Charles E. Merrill Books, Inc., 1966)

———. *Science Skilltext*, Book VI. (Columbus: Charles E. Merrill Books, Inc., 1966)

West Frankfort Public Library
402 East Poplar Street
West Frankfort, IL 62896